Communications
Programming
for Windows 95

Charles A. Mirho
Andre Terrisse

Microsoft Press

PUBLISHED BY
Microsoft Press
A Division of Microsoft Corporation
One Microsoft Way
Redmond, Washington 98052-6399

Library of Congress Cataloging-in-Publication Data
Mirho, Charles A.
     Communications programming for Windows 95 / Charles A. Mirho,
  Andre Terrisse.
          p.   cm.
     Includes index.
     ISBN 1-55615-668-5
     1. Communications software. 2. Digital communications.
  3. Microsoft Windows (Computer file)   I. Terrisse, Andre.
  II. Title.
  TK5105.9.M57   1996
  005.7'1265--dc20   96-14927
                                                                CIP

Printed and bound in the United States of America.

1 2 3 4 5 6 7 8 9 QMQM 0 9 8 7 6

Distributed to the book trade in Canada by Macmillan of Canada, a division of Canada Publishing Corporation.

A CIP catalogue record for this book is available from the British Library.

Microsoft Press books are available through booksellers and distributors worldwide. For further information about international editions, contact your local Microsoft Corporation office. Or contact Microsoft Press International directly at fax (206) 936-7329.

Acquisitions Editor: David Clark
Project Editor: Ina Chang
Technical Editor: Jean Ross

TABLE OF CONTENTS

ACKNOWLEDGMENTS

I would like to acknowledge my wife, Erika, for her patience; my mother, because mothers should always be acknowledged; and finally Hermann D'Hooge at Intel and Toby Nixon at Microsoft, for their hard work and dedication.

Charles Mirho

INTRODUCTION

The personal computer is a very useful communications platform. Not only is it relatively inexpensive, but it is good at moving, storing, and manipulating the kind of data that people use to communicate with one another. A personal computer can serve as fax machine, copy machine (by way of scanners), e-mail center, Internet interface, and video entertainment center. A central element of all these types of PC communications is the telephone line.

Support for fax technology and modems is a standard part of Windows 95, which is already on tens of millions of desktops (and laptops) across the world. What's more, fax/modem hardware is now a standard part of many PC motherboards. Large offices might still require an industrial-strength fax machine, at least for a while, but the market for stand-alone fax machines will probably start to decline in a few years, just as the typewriter market did when word processors came along.

The telephone is another story. For years, telephones have resisted replacement by computers. This is something of a paradox, since modems have been around almost as long as computers have. The telephone's stubborn resistance to replacement is probably due to the fact that it is just too darn convenient. You pick up the receiver, dial, and wait for an answer. Simple. Who needs a computer?

Actually, some people discovered early on that computers could store address books. Early MS-DOS terminate-and-stay-resident (TSR) programs could pop up an address book on the screen at the touch of a key. You could search the address book alphabetically, and then, by pressing another key, you could instruct the computer to dial a specific number using the attached modem. When the other party answered, you would quickly lift the receiver and begin talking. You could even attach a note to an address book entry or instruct the computer to dial a number automatically at a predetermined time. I have my computer remind me to call a certain friend on Thanksgiving. The friend is a vegetarian, and he considers the expression "Turkey Day" off the mark. So I attach a note to his address book entry that flashes on the screen as it dials, "Say Happy Thanksgiving but do not say Turkey Day." Computers are great for this sort of thing.

At the same time, telephones—office phones in particular—are getting extremely complicated. People actually take classes to learn how to use them. Windows 95 includes an API to support all of the neat features in modern phones, called the Telephony API (TAPI). It also includes a Messaging API (MAPI) to handle such things as e-mail and faxes, and it has an improved Serial API for interactive serial communications.

So maybe the computer will eat the telephone (and the answering machine along with it) and maybe it won't. Time will tell, but in the meantime, Windows 95 provides you with the tools to write some killer apps.

If at all possible, you should read this book from front to back. Chapter 1 introduces the Windows 95 communications architecture and provides an overview of communications in Windows 95. It also explains how the various APIs work together. Chapter 2 gets you started writing communications code quickly by showing you how to enable existing applications (in our examples, Microsoft Word) with dialing and messaging capabilities. Chapter 3 covers low-level serial data transfer using Win32c, the Windows 95 32-bit Communications API. It sets the stage for Chapter 4 by developing an application to demonstrate serial communications. Chapter 4 covers the setup and control of phone calls using TAPI. This chapter expands on the example in Chapter 3 to create an application that provides a user interface to configure an attached modem and to make and answer calls. Chapter 5 explains messaging in Windows 95 using MAPI. Messages include faxes, e-mail, and file transfers.

The book's companion disk contains the sample programs from the chapters, including Word macros for placing calls and sending messages; an application to network two computers back to back using the serial ports; and an application that connects two computers over the phone lines, which can also be used for connecting to any online service that has a text interface (such as CompuServe, but not the TCP/IP protocol Internet computers).

Some of the sample files on the companion disk are compressed, so you must install the files onto your hard disk to use them. This will require approximately 1.5 MB of hard disk space. To install the samples, insert the companion disk into your floppy disk drive and type *A:\Setup* (*A* being your floppy disk drive). By default, the files will be installed into a directory called \Communications. The source files are in subdirectories named for the chapter the sample applies to. For example, the samples that are discussed in Chapter 2 are in \Communications\Chapter2. The executable files are also included, so you don't have to compile the programs before running them.

1

Communications and Windows 95: An Overview

The Windows 95 Software Architecture

This chapter begins with a discussion of WOSA, the Windows Open Services Architecture. WOSA is a broad subject, but it's the best place to begin because much of Windows 95 communications is based on the WOSA model. This discussion of WOSA will lead naturally to a question of more substantial interest to developers: why there are so many different communications APIs (application programming interfaces) in Windows.

The WOSA Model

An example of a typical WOSA "component" is the Windows audio driver for Sound Blaster–compatible audio boards. WOSA components come into existence when Microsoft defines an API and then third parties write the drivers to support that API. What is a "third party"? You are a third party, and so are we. So is anyone else who doesn't work for Microsoft. Not exactly an exclusive club, but it's certainly a diverse one.

Third parties have great freedom in how they implement WOSA drivers, but for reasons of compatibility, they must support the general framework defined by Microsoft. Microsoft encourages companies to provide input on what goes into a new WOSA API. The company usually holds a powwow in Redmond, at which everyone sits down and argues about what goes in and what comes out. An extension model that will accommodate unusual vendor-specific features is usually added to the API at this stage. When the dust settles, application writers have a standard API to work with, and hardware vendors have a driver specification.

You can visualize the WOSA model as a stack. The application is on the top, the API sits in the middle, and the driver occupies the bottom. Some people like to call the application the *service requester* and the driver the *service provider* because in some cases, what's on top is not an application. (We'll get to that later.) This terminology is a bit more inclusive, but only because it's vague. So this book will use the terms *application* and *driver* instead of *service requester* and *service provider* wherever possible. Figure 1-1 shows the typical WOSA stack.

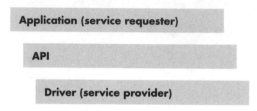

Figure 1-1. *The typical WOSA stack.*

The interface layer between the API and the driver is called the SPI (service provider interface). Unless you are writing drivers, you don't need to know about the SPI. However, a careful study of the SPI can be highly revealing of the API layer above it. Microsoft defines the API and the SPI, and it usually implements a sample application and a sample driver. It then puts all of these pieces together into a developer's kit for the WOSA component.

An example of a top layer of the WOSA stack that is not an application is the MCI (media control interface), which is part of the Multimedia Extensions for Windows. MCI is a high-level driver that sits above the low-level WAVE driver. Applications sit on top of MCI; MCI sits on top of WAVE. If you've never heard of MCI, take a look at Figure 1-2, which captures the spirit. The point is that by stacking a bunch of WOSA layers you can create more generalized functions, such as the MCI *sndPlaySound* function, that are extremely convenient (and often extremely slow). You'll find several functions like these for Windows 95 communications, such as *tapiRequestMakeCall*. In fact, with the right drivers installed, *sndPlaySound* can be a communications function. More on this later.

That's about all you need to know about WOSA. Now let's talk communications.

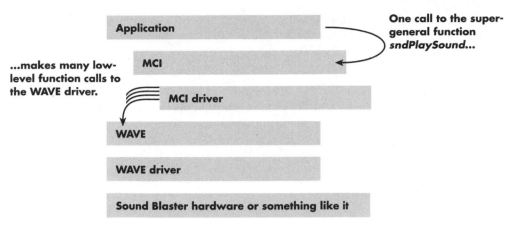

Figure 1-2. *More WOSA layers.*

The Communications Session

The first concept you need to understand is that of the communications session. A communications session involves four stages: configuration, connection, data transfer, and disconnection.

Configuration means preparing the communications hardware and software to behave the way you want. Certain settings seldom change; these are called *static settings*. Examples of static settings are guard tone selection and carrier loss recovery time. For now, don't worry about what the settings are. Just realize that certain settings do not change except in special circumstances, such as transporting the equipment to a foreign country. Of more immediate interest are the settings that change on a daily basis, such as the baud rate and parity method. These are called *dynamic settings*.

Once the hardware and software are configured, a connection is established. Getting connected involves dialing a phone number and having the called party answer the phone call. Nothing mysterious here. In certain situations, some additional configuration might be required after the connection is established.

Next, data is transferred between the connected parties. Sometimes the data is transformed in some way before making the journey; sometimes it goes out "raw." Transformations include compression and filtering. For example, audio data is often filtered (to reduce noise), compressed, and then transmitted.

Transformation is an important step, but it's not a main subject of this book because it's a science unto itself, and because it is typically handled at a low level (usually in the hardware, for speed). Also, data might transition through many protocol layers, which add successive fields for framing, routing, and error recovery. This is also a science unto itself, and not a topic of this book.

The final stage of a session is disconnection. This occurs when the data has been transferred and the connection is no longer required.

Figure 1-3 shows the four stages. In Windows 95, each stage is handled by one or more WOSA components. Each component is covered in this book.

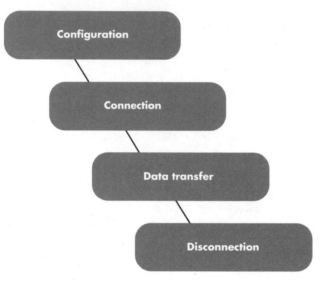

Figure 1-3. *The four stages of any communications session.*

Axioms of Windows 95 Communications

Generalizations about communications are hard to come by. One safe generalization, at least for the purposes of this book, is that the Telephony API (TAPI) is the center of communications in Windows 95. We are really talking about wide area communications here—communications over some form of telephone network. (Local area network communications is a whole different ball game, so put it out of your mind while you read this book.) TAPI is responsible for two of the four stages of a (wide area) communications session: connection and disconnection. In addition, TAPI controls the connection as it is being established. Thus the first axiom of Windows 95 communications is:

TAPI is Call Central in Windows 95.

The other two stages of a session—configuration and data transfer—are less centralized in Windows 95, as you'll learn. These stages are important, of course; communications wouldn't be very useful without data transfer, and data transfer wouldn't work without proper configuration. But TAPI is where it all comes together. That's why the chapter on TAPI, Chapter 4, is the biggest in the book.

Because configuration and data transfer are less centralized, no single WOSA component can do the job. That brings us to the second axiom of Windows 95 communications:

All data is not created equal.

Configuration and data transfer are specialized for different types of data. For example, digital data, such as file transfers, e-mail, and faxes, require error-correcting protocols. In contrast, audio data (digitized sound) can tolerate errors much better than purely digital data can. Audio data has a different problem: It cannot tolerate transmission delays. Video data also has special requirements. Microsoft's approach to this problem has been to define an API for handling each type of data. The API used to transfer one type of data is also used to configure the hardware and software for that type of data. Thus we have the Win32 Communications API for configuring and transferring error-sensitive, non-time-critical data; we have the WAVE API for configuring and transferring audio (error-tolerant, time-sensitive) data; and so forth.

Sometimes communication is personal and interactive, such as logging onto CompuServe and surfing through the forums while reading and posting messages. Other times it is not interactive and involves one-shot (or a series of one-shot) transfers of data. File transfers are a good example of this, as are e-mail and faxes. In fact, it's probably safe to say that most PC-based communications are noninteractive. Even so-called interactive online communications often consists chiefly of the exchange of precomposed messages.

Microsoft has defined one API for all noninteractive communications—the Messaging API (MAPI). The central premise of MAPI is that noninteractive communications consists of a series of messages. A file is a message; so is a fax, and so is e-mail. Any time you collect a bunch of data in one place and send it out together, you are sending a message. It turns out that all messages have certain things in common, and a dedicated API like MAPI makes life easier for programmers. This leads to the third axiom of Windows 95 communications:

Use MAPI for all noninteractive communications.

If you always remember the three axioms, you'll be in good shape to write communications programs in Windows 95. Also, remember how WOSA works as you read the next section on the Windows 95 communications architecture.

The Windows 95 Communications Architecture

The best way to explain the Windows 95 communications architecture is by using examples. A great example is the interactive terminal application, shown in Figure 1-4.

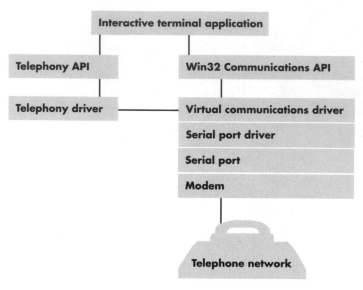

Figure 1-4. *An interactive terminal application.*

The interactive terminal application uses TAPI to connect and disconnect and to control the connection. VCOMM, the Windows Virtual Communications Driver, controls access to the serial port. Historically, modems have connected to the serial port. As a consequence, almost all software that uses modems uses the serial port. Even internal modems emulate a serial port so that existing software will run without problems.

Notice anything unusual about the right side of the figure? That's right, there is no third-party WOSA component for serial communications. The Win32 Communications API bolts right to the Microsoft Windows VCOMM, and third parties cannot replace VCOMM. Serial communications is a closed universe in Windows 95. There is no room for third parties to change the implementation of the Windows 95 serial communications functions.

One of the most complex architectures you'll encounter in Windows 95 is the Messaging API. It is the Taj Mahal of Windows software. Like the Taj Mahal, it is a thing of beauty. It is where all the Windows 95 communications components come together, as shown in Figure 1-5.

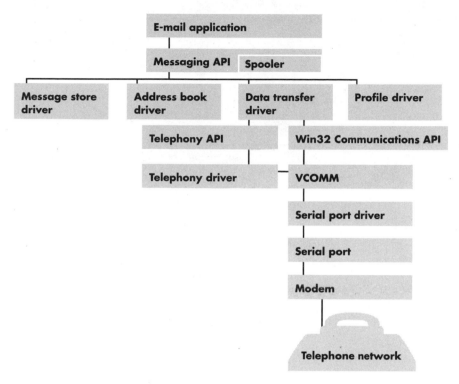

Figure 1-5. *The MAPI architecture (one incarnation).*

MAPI is another case in which the application is not always on top. True, there is a messaging application at the very top of the WOSA hierarchy. Below that is the Messaging API, and below that are drivers. But one of the drivers, the data transfer driver, sits above the Telephony API and the Win32 Communications API. What we have here is another WOSA layer consisting of the data transfer driver on top, the Telephony API in the middle, and the telephony driver on the bottom.

You might have noticed that everything from the data transfer driver on down looks like the interactive terminal program. That's because, at its core, the driver does much the same thing as the interactive terminal; it transmits digital data in a streaming fashion. You can easily modify the interactive terminal program to send files, e-mail, or even faxes. But MAPI does all this anyway. (Remember the third axiom.)

Also notice that since the MAPI data transfer driver is a WOSA component, you can replace it. So, for example, if you want to write a MAPI answering machine to record voice messages in real time, you can replace the data transfer driver in Figure 1-5 with something that resembles an answering machine. (Of course, you'll need special hardware since only voice modems can bring voice data into the computer from a phone line.) The result looks something like Figure 1-6.

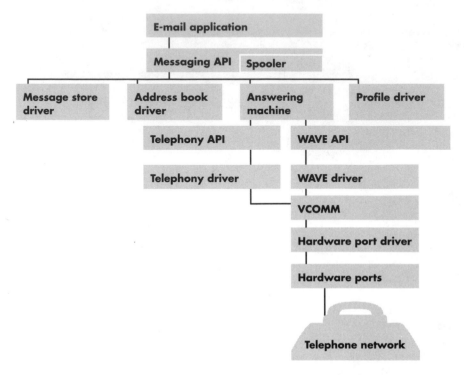

Figure 1-6. *The MAPI architecture (another incarnation).*

A Summary of APIs

You have been introduced to four APIs that are used to write communications programs. Here's a quick summary of which ones to use and when.

■ Use the Win32 Communications API to send or receive data—not in real time, but in a streaming, interactive fashion. Surfing an online service, editing a shared document, and playing a multiplayer game are examples of when this API comes in handy (although Windows 95 offers DirectPlay, which is optimized for interactive gaming).

■ Use the WAVE API to send or receive audio data in real time.

■ Use the Telephony API to connect, disconnect, and control telephone calls.

■ Use the Messaging API to send and receive files, faxes, e-mail, and anything else that is message-based.

The Wide World of Communications

By now you are probably ready to start writing some code, so this section is strictly optional. It is for readers who are curious about the different communications platforms that are possible under Windows 95. The examples are intended to expand your thinking of PC-based communications beyond the basic platform of Hayes-compatible modem plus phone line.

Probably the most common communications platform is the good old Hayes-compatible modem attached to the computer's serial port, as shown in Figure 1-7. A phone line is plugged into the back of the modem. The phone line is one of those old copper wires that make up the public telephone network in most localities.

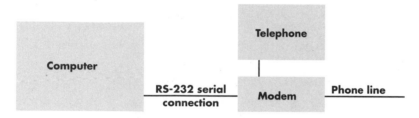

Figure 1-7. *The most common communications platform.*

This configuration is very limited. For example, you cannot implement a telephone answering machine on this platform because Hayes-compatible modems don't handle voice signals well. Remember, *modem* is short for modulator/demodulator, so everything that goes through a modem is modulated or demodulated (mangled). The modem serializes voice signals into ASCII streams, which destroys the quality of audio. Thus you cannot use a PC to record conversations or play audio files over the phone line using this platform. What you can do is transfer files, access a bulletin board system (BBS), play interactive games, and send e-mail—the conventional functions of modems. Another limitation is that the average analog phone line was installed decades ago, before PCs were even invented, so it is too slow for sending or receiving lots of data in a reasonable amount of time. You won't get much more than 56 Kbps of data through an old phone line, no matter how fancy your modem is.

The second type of platform, shown in Figure 1-8 on the next page, is a PCMCIA (Personal Computer Memory Card International Association) modem adaptor inserted into a laptop PC and then plugged into the phone line. The PCMCIA modem adaptor is Hayes-compatible, just like the external modem in the first platform. The phone line is still your typical old analog line. In fact, there is little difference between this platform and the first one except that the hardware is all shrunk down and made portable—and, of course, there is no serial cable or external phone connected to the tiny PCMCIA card. With this platform you can connect to an online service to check your e-mail from any place with a phone line (a hotel, an airport, your parents' house over the holidays).

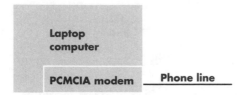

Figure 1-8. *A portable communications platform.*

To enhance either platform with voice capabilities, you must replace the modem with a voice data modem. Unlike a typical modem, a voice data modem passes voices back and forth between the PC and the phone line without mangling the sound quality.

The third platform, shown in Figure 1-9, is for the office. You've probably noticed that your office phone has about a thousand features that your home phone doesn't have—such as call transfer, call conferencing, call park, call pickup, call-back on busy, call forwarding, call you-name-it. You probably never use half of these features, but you might if they were easier to understand. That's where the PC comes in. But is your average Hayes-compatible modem the best tool for the job? Clearly, if the office phone has all of these features that the home phone doesn't have, the two phones are connected to entirely different equipment. The home phone line winds and weaves its way through neighborhoods, over hills, and under rivers until it finally reaches the phone company, where it connects to a machine called a *central office switch.* Don't let the word "office" in the name confuse you; this machine is for connecting home phones to one another. Actually, businesses are also connected to a central office switch, but only when they make outside calls (outside the business, that is). Phones at most businesses and hotels, and even some apartment complexes, are connected to machines called *private branch exchanges,* or *PBXs.* Figure 1-9 shows the connection of a call using two PBXs and a central office switch between phones at different businesses.

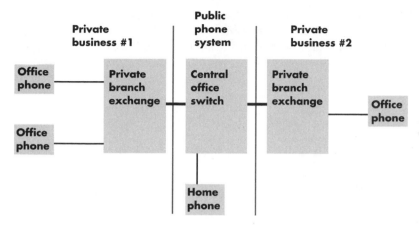

Figure 1-9. *Two businesses connected through both public and private phone systems.*

The call made from a phone in the first business connects to the first private branch exchange. The PBX determines that the call is going outside the business (usually because the caller first dialed a 9), and then routes the call to the public central office switch. Notice the thick black line crossing between the private world of the business and the public phone system? That's called a *trunk*. A trunk is like the phone line into your home, except that it can carry a lot more calls. The central office switch looks at the call and determines that it should go to the trunk connected to the second PBX. The second PBX gets the call from the trunk, looks at the call, and rings the correct phone in the second business. The call can also go to a home phone (such as when someone calls home from work). In that case, the central office switch rings the home phone instead of sending the call to the second PBX.

Where does the PC fit into all of this? Take a look at Figure 1-10 on the next page. Some companies sell boards that connect the PC to the PBX and to the phone. These boards make available all those advanced phone features we talked about, but without making you resort to manuals or confusing phone button sequences. You can dial calls, answer calls, transfer, conference, and so forth using friendly software on the PC. Between two phones in the same business, even more advanced functions are available, such as video conferencing and application sharing. Since an interoffice call within a business never passes through the stodgy old public phone system, data can be transferred much faster than with a regular modem. If you make a call from the office phone to the outside world, you are still limited to the features and data rates provided by the public phone system.

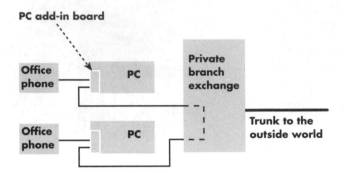

Figure 1-10. *The PC used as a front end to the features of the PBX.*

The final platform, shown earlier in Figure 1-1, is a high-tech combination of the PCMCIA and PBX platforms shown in Figures 1-8 and 1-9. This platform has a PCMCIA adaptor in the computer that is connected to a PBX, but instead of a phone line there is a satellite link to anywhere in the world. The platform has the advantages of full mobility, plus the added features of the office PBX and access to the public phone system. It's possible that no one has actually built one of these things, but it makes for an impressive example.

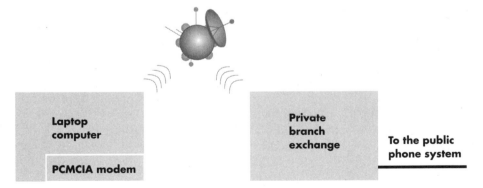

Figure 1-11. *A really impressive platform that probably no one has actually built.*

These are only some of the platforms that Windows 95 supports. These examples are intended to stimulate your imagination.

2

Simple Dialing and Simple Messaging

Writing a full-blown communications program is not easy. As you'll see in later chapters, you must learn many functions, data structures, and messages before you can begin to write a serious communications application. You also have the issues of timing and error handling to consider. Of course, many applications that dial the phone or send messages aren't communications applications at all. Rather, they have some other mission in life, such as word processing, spreadsheet computation, or database management. Wouldn't it be nice if there were a simple way to add dialing and messaging to these applications without learning a bunch of new functions and structures?

As you might have guessed, you do indeed have such a capability with Windows 95. It's easy to add messaging capabilities to applications, and it's even easier to add dialing capabilities. Of course, by simplifying the process you give up a lot of control over the fine details. But for developers who just want the basics, the simple approach can save an enormous amount of time and effort.

Take note: The words "simple" and "basic" are not synonymous with "rudimentary." The simple communications functions that Windows 95 provides are powerful. But they are designed to be simple to use, so you won't find many of the features that power developers would find desirable.

The examples in this chapter are based on enhancing existing noncommunications applications with basic communications. (They are contained in macros in the Ch2.dot template on the companion disk.) The first example shows how to add dialing capabilities to Microsoft Word. The second example shows how to send messages composed in Word.

Simple Dialing

Dialing the phone is actually a tricky business; it requires a certain amount of mental calculation. For example, if you are in your office and you want to dial an outside line, you probably have to first dial 9 or some other prefix digit. If the call is long distance, you have to dial 1 and then the area code. Things are trickier when you travel. A long-distance call to a business associate in Houston might become a local call when you visit Houston for a day of business. And the dialing prefix for an outside line might be 8 instead of 9 when you dial from a hotel room.

"No problem," you say. "I can remember to change the dialing prefix or drop the area code when I'm in the area. I can remember to add the area code to numbers I usually dial locally when I travel." But when dialing with a PC, much of the time you won't be doing the dialing yourself; an application will do it for you. Sometimes the application will ask you to enter the phone number to dial, in which case you can dutifully add or drop the area code and any dialing prefixes. But in other cases the application will *extract* the phone number from somewhere, such as a document, a spreadsheet cell, or a database. This is the real convenience of dialing from the computer. To make the dialing process as smooth as possible, with the least intervention on your part, the application shouldn't have to prompt you for the dialing prefix and area code every time. Ideally, you want to be able to tell Windows where you are calling from and then let the application figure out what to add or subtract from the basic phone number. Windows 95 provides a mechanism for doing exactly this.

You tell Windows about your current location by changing the dialing properties in the Dialing Properties dialog box, shown in Figure 2-1 on page 16. You can open the Dialing Properties dialog box in two ways: by double-clicking the Modems icon on the Control Panel and then clicking the Dialing Properties button in the Modems Properties dialog box, or by selecting Phone Dialer from the Accessories group and then selecting the Dialing Propertics menu option in the Phone Dialer dialog box.

The Dialing Properties dialog box includes controls for changing the area code, country, and dialing prefix of your current location. In certain circumstances, the area code you specify will be removed from the phone number before dialing. For example, suppose you receive a Word memo with a phone number embedded in the text, as shown on the facing page.

Bob,

I have reserved your car and hotel room, but you indicated that you wanted to reserve your own plane tickets. You can reserve tickets by calling Bayshore Travel at

+1 (408) 555 3232

Check into the Airport Hotel upon arriving in Portland....

Sincerely,

Jeff

Suppose you are in the 408 area code and you are browsing through this memo on your laptop PC. You decide to reserve your tickets. First you highlight the phone number:

wanted to reserve your own plane tickets. You can reserve tickets by calling Bayshore Travel at

+1 (408) 555 3232

Check into the Airport Hotel upon arriving in Portland....

Now click the Dial button on the Word toolbar. (The Dial button is not a standard Word feature; you'll learn how to program it into Word in a moment.) Word dials the highlighted number. But wait a second. You are already inside the 408 area code, so won't dialing the highlighted digits cause a dialing error? Don't worry. Windows automatically removes the area code from the dialing string when it matches the area you are in. You tell Windows which area you are in by specifying it in the Dialing Properties dialog box. When Windows gets the phone number, it automatically strips off the +1 (408) prefix. The number it dials is 555 3232, not 1 408 555 3232.

Sometimes you might need to place a long-distance call to a phone number that is within the same area code you are calling from. As we just discussed, if you make a call from within the same area code you are calling to, Windows assumes that you are making a local call and automatically strips off the 1 and the area code. In this case, since your call is actually long distance, it will not be completed. To make a long-distance call from within the same area code, you must specify the number you are calling in such a way that the call can still be completed after the 1 and the area code are stripped. In our example, if you are calling from the 408 area code but the call to Bayshore Travel is still long distance, you need to enter the phone number as +1 (408) 1 408 555 3232. Or, you can configure the 555 local extension as a toll list entry for the 408 area code using the advanced telephony functions. (See the section titled "Canonical and Dialable Addresses" in Chapter 4 for details.)

Now suppose you get on the plane and fly to Portland. On the plane, you take out your laptop (after the plane reaches cruising altitude) and open the Dialing Properties dialog box. (See Figure 2-1.) You change the area code to 503, the area code of Portland. Windows now knows that any dialing will occur from within the 503 area code. When you arrive at your hotel in Portland, you discover that you were assigned to a smoking room instead of the nonsmoking room you requested. You whip out your laptop, plug in your pocket modem, bring up the travel memo in Word, and highlight the phone number of Bayshore Travel. You click the Dial button on the Word toolbar. Since you are no longer dialing from within the 408 area code, Windows does not strip off the 408 area code from the number. Instead, it dials the string 1 408 555 3232. But much to your surprise, this number doesn't work—you get an error tone coming from the modem. Then you remember: You must first dial an 8 for long-distance calls from this particular hotel. You pop back over to the Dialing Properties dialog box and set the external dialing prefix to 8 by placing an 8 in the "To access an outside line, first dial" field. Now when you click the Dial button in Word, the number 8 1 408 555 3232 is dialed. The call goes through, and when the travel agency answers, you pick up the phone receiver and request that they arrange for a new room. Any subsequent external calls from the hotel room will connect with no problems because Windows is now configured to dial out of the hotel.

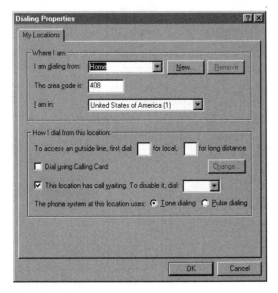

Figure 2-1. *The Dialing Properties dialog box.*

Notice that the Dialing Properties dialog box has fields for accessing a local or a long-distance external line. Some hotels and businesses use a different dialing prefix for a local and for a long-distance call. No problem. Windows adds the long-distance prefix when the number is outside the local area code, and the local prefix otherwise.

The Dialing Properties dialog box also asks you what country you are currently in. You can select from a list of hundreds of countries. Next to each country in the list is a country code, which is like an area code for international calling. Like an area code, the country code is automatically removed by Windows when you dial from within the identified country. For example, suppose you store a number for a friend in Glasgow, Scotland, in the United Kingdom. The country code for the United Kingdom is 44. The area code for Glasgow is 41. So the full number for your friend is +44 (41) SOMENUM. The neat thing about storing the number this way is that if you fly to the United Kingdom on business, you can retrieve the number and dial your friend. Of course, you must configure your location for the United Kingdom when you arrive. You do this by opening the Dialing Properties dialog box and selecting United Kingdom in the "I am in" field. Now when you pass your friend's number to the Telephony API, Windows detects that the country code for the number is the same as the country code for your current location, and it removes the code before dialing the number. When you return to the United States and reconfigure your location for United States of America, Windows automatically adds the U.K. country code to your friend's number the next time you call him. In short, Windows handles the country code in much the same way that it handles the area code.

The *tapiRequestMakeCall* Function

Four functions in Windows make simple dialing possible: *tapiRequestMakeCall*, *tapiRequestMediaCall*, *tapiGetLocationInfo*, and *tapiRequestDrop*. (*tapiRequestMediaCall* and *tapiRequestDrop* are not functional in Win32-based applications). These four functions make up the subset of the Telephony API known as Assisted Telephony. The first and most important function is *tapiRequestMakeCall*. This function dials a phone number—that's all. It does not answer calls, play messages, or transfer files. Once it makes the connection between two telephones, it's up to you to lift the receiver and start talking. The syntax is as follows:

```
LONG tapiRequestMakeCall (lpszDestAddress, lpszAppName,
                          lpszCalledParty, lpszComment)
```

The first parameter, *lpszDestAddress*, is the dial string. In Windows jargon, this is called the *destination address* of the call. This term is generic—it includes phone numbers and e-mail addresses. We'll discuss addresses further in the Chapters 4 and 5. For our present purposes, the destination address means a dial string (like a phone number but with some enhancements). The dial string is a null-terminated string (z-string) of ASCII digits and control characters. Control characters control the dialing behavior. (These are explained in the next section.) The following are examples of valid dial strings:

555 1212

555-1212

1-800-555-1234

9,,555 1313

t9w555 7890

In these examples, the comma (,) and the *t* and *w* characters are control characters. However, for reasons that will become clear in Chapter 4, even though the above examples are all valid dial strings, it is best to store the full phone number (including the country code and area code) in the canonical format. In this format, the number should begin with the + character and the area code should be contained within parentheses. Notice that when using Assisted Telephony it is OK to add spaces and dashes to make the phone number more readable. Dial strings are limited to a size defined by the constant TAPIMAXDEST-ADDRESSSIZE, which is defined in the header file TAPI.H.

The second parameter, *lpszAppName,* is a z-string with the name of the calling application. This name is used by other applications that monitor call activity in the system for call logging purposes. The application name is optional and can be set to NULL, but if it is specified it is limited to TAPIMAXAPPNAMESIZE characters, including the terminating NULL. If you know the name of the party you are calling, you can specify that name in the third parameter, *lpszCalled-Party,* again for logging purposes. In the travel example above, we knew the name of the party: Bayshore Travel. If specified, this parameter is limited to TAPIMAXCALLEDPARTYSIZE characters. Or you can leave the party name NULL if you don't know it or you don't care to specify it. You can also specify an optional comment about the call in the last parameter, *lpszComment.* A comment is limited to TAPIMAXCOMMENTSIZE characters if specified. If it is not specified, it is set to NULL.

If everything goes well, *tapiRequestMakeCall* makes the call and returns 0. Things don't always go well, however, so you should be prepared to handle any errors that arise. If the dial string is flawed in some way, the function returns TAPIERR_INVALDESTADDRESS, which, like all TAPI error codes, is defined in TAPI.H. If one or more of the pointers passed to the function are invalid, the return code is TAPIERR_INVALPOINTER. One error you probably won't see very often is TAPIERR_REQUESTQUEUEFULL. This comes back when you try to make more than one call at a time. People usually have the sense to wait for the first call to complete before trying to dial a second one, but you never know what people will do. (The image of a monkey banging on a keyboard springs to mind.) Another error code that is quite common is TAPIERR_NOREQUESTRECIPIENT. To understand this error, you need to understand how Windows relies on a special kind of application known as a *call manager*.

The call manager is a weird beast. It's like an OLE server for dialing, but it doesn't have an OLE interface. Instead, TAPI translates simple dialing calls to *tapiRequestMakeCall* into messages for the call manager. The call manager translates these messages into low-level TAPI calls. See Figure 2-2 for an illustration of this process. In earlier versions of Windows, a call manager had to be running when you called *tapiRequestMakeCall*, or the function would return an error code of TAPI_NOREQUESTRECIPIENT. In Windows 95, the call manager runs automatically if it isn't running when the function is called. The default call manager application in Windows 95 is called Phone Dialer. You can find Phone Dialer in the Accessories folder. Phone Dialer does other useful things besides enabling simple dialing; it also has a keypad for direct dialing, and it has code for logging all the phone calls that you make from Windows.

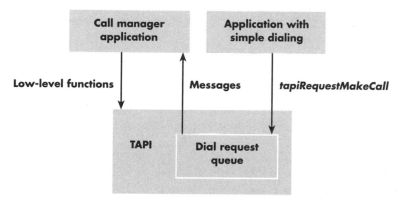

Figure 2-2. *Using a call manager for simple dialing.*

The call to *tapiRequestMakeCall* is entered into the TAPI dialing queue. When previous dialing requests are completed, the dialing request is translated into messages to the call manager. The call manager translates these messages into low-level TAPI function calls to dial the phone. *tapiRequestMakeCall* dials the phone and not much else. All parameters except the dial string are optional. Nonetheless, this is a powerful function because dialing is a tricky business. It is even more powerful because it understands the language of dial strings.

The Language of Dial Strings

Until now, we have treated dial strings as simply a sequence of numerical digits. Dial strings can be more than this, however. For starters, they can include the * and # characters, which correspond to the * and # keys on the telephone keypad. When your computer is connected to a phone line that is set up for touch-tone phones (as opposed to rotary phones, which are quickly becoming obsolete in this country), the dial string can also include the characters *A* through *D,* which correspond to extra tones that cannot be generated using a typical telephone set.

A dial string can also include *control characters*. The ! character is an example of a control character. The ! creates a hookflash—a line signal generated by pressing and releasing the on-hook button (where the receiver rests in the cradle). This can be useful when using phone lines configured with two channels, where the channel is toggled by a hookflash. (Call waiting works like this.)

If you use a rotary phone, your phone service is an old one that requires pulse dialing. To use this type of phone with your PC, you can include the *P* or *p* control character at the beginning of the dial string. This dials all subsequent digits as pulse digits. To ensure that the digits are dialed as touch tones, you can prefix the dial string with *T* or *t*. This is a more common requirement than pulse dialing. However, the Dialing Properties dialog box contains a check box for selecting tone or pulse dialing, so you can let Windows add these characters to the dial string as needed from your current location instead of doing it yourself.

One of the most useful characters in dial strings is the comma. The comma forces the dialing to pause for a period of time (typically between a half-second and a second). Pausing is useful when dialing out of your office or from a hotel room. In these situations, it is often important to give the PBX time to connect to the outside line before dialing the remaining digits. (See Chapter 1 for details on PBXs.) For example, assuming that a comma corresponds to a one-second delay, the following dial string

      8,,1-212-555-1234

dials 8 and then gives the PBX two seconds to connect to the outside line before dialing the remaining 1-212-555-1234.

You can achieve a similar result using *W* or *w*, as shown below.

      8Wt1-212-555-8787

      (dial 8, wait for dial tone, and then using touch tones dial
      1-212-555-8787)

One result of connecting to the external network from a PBX is that the line receives a dial tone from the external network. The *W* character delays dialing of subsequent digits until a dial tone is detected. Unfortunately, not all modems support dial tone detection, and those that do are not terribly reliable. It is usually better to use commas. Determining how many commas provide enough delay involves trial and error, but four seconds is usually plenty for most situations.

ISDN (integrated services digital network) technology provides even more dialing possibilities. ISDN is a new kind of digital phone line that some phone companies are making available to homes and offices. With ISDN, dial strings can include subnumbers and names. A subnumber is like a P.O. box number within a large building; it specifies the destination in greater detail. For example, a home connected to an ISDN line can be accessed by a single main number and three subnumbers, one for each room in the house. Dialing the main number rings all three phones. Each phone can be rung individually by adding a subnumber to the main number, as shown below.

555-2345   (dials all phones in the house)

555-2345|1   (dials phone number one)

555-2345|2   (dials phone number two)

555-2345|3   (dials phone number three)

A name is typically used to identify the caller; this is a sort of personalized caller ID. In Windows 95 you can specify dial strings with subnumbers and names, as in the following example:

555-3456|342^Ed Baxter

The subnumber 342 is separated from the main number 555-3456 by the | character. The name is separated from the subnumber by the ^ character.

With some types of ISDN service, you can specify multiple phone numbers in a single string. Why would you want to do this? Not to dial two or more numbers at once, but rather to support something called *bandwidth allocation*. Bandwidth measures the amount of information that can be forced through the line in a given unit of time. Some new digital phone services let you combine the bandwidth of several digital lines into a single "pipe" for sending information. You might want to do this, for example, when transferring live video information through the phone system. The bandwidth of a single phone line, even a digital one, is usually not adequate for transferring full-motion video with good quality. If your phone service supports it, you can make a video call with twice the bandwidth of a single phone line by specifying something like the following:

555-2345\n555-3456

The \n is translated into a CRLF (carriage return line feed) and separates the two numbers corresponding to the two phone lines. The two lines are combined into one digital pipe.

The language of dial strings turns *tapiRequestMakeCall* into a powerful function indeed. There are, however, a few limitations (which might be eliminated in the future). For one thing, the full alphabet should be supported in dial strings. People find it easier to remember phone numbers when they spell out words. The telephone keypad maps letters to digits; for example, the number 1-800-289-7663 is the equivalent of 1-800-BUY-SOME. It would be convenient to store numbers this way in documents or spreadsheets and to be able to extract them for dialing without extra processing. This chapter includes a little utility function in WordBasic to do this for phone numbers in Word documents. Of course, adding this functionality precludes the use of the *A-D* additional tones mentioned earlier.

Simple Dialing from Microsoft Word

Our first example shows how to enable Microsoft Word (version 6.0 or later) with dialing capabilities. This requires two macros. The first macro, *AddDialButton,* adds a Dial button to Word's Standard toolbar. Clicking the Dial button runs the second macro, *Dialer,* which dials a phone number highlighted in the text. Word documents can thus form a sort of "contextual database" of phone numbers. We saw an example of this earlier, where the phone number of a travel agency was embedded in an office memo.

A knowledge of Word and WordBasic (the Word macro language) is useful but not essential to understanding this example. The example shows how to do simple dialing that can be applied with minor changes to Visual Basic and other macro and scripting environments.

A word of warning: The Dial button that we add to the toolbar can be saved to whatever template the Word document is using. Don't run this macro more than once, because doing so can add multiple Dial buttons to the toolbar. Make a backup of the Normal template before running this macro in documents using Normal; otherwise, the Dial button might display globally. It's best to use a local template for documents with the Dial button on the toolbar, and leave Normal unchanged.

The first macro, which adds the Dial button to the toolbar, is almost trivial.

```
Sub MAIN
DeleteButton "Standard", 1
AddButton "Standard", 1, 2, "Dialer", "Dial", 1
End Sub
```

Every Word macro begins with a *Sub* statement that declares the entry point of the macro. The *End Sub* statement marks the end of the macro. In between are the statements that give the macro its particular functionality. The first statement, *DeleteButton,* deletes a button from the specified toolbar. In this case the Standard toolbar—the one with the buttons for Save, Print, Cut, Paste, and so forth—is specified. The second parameter to *DeleteButton* is the button number to delete, in this case *1,* the first button on the Standard toolbar. The second statement, *AddButton,* adds the Dial button to the toolbar in place of the deleted button. The first and second parameters are the same as they were for *DeleteButton;* they specify the name of the toolbar (Standard) and the button number (1). The third parameter, *2,* tells *AddButton* that clicking the button will result in a call to another macro. The macro called is specified in the fourth parameter; in this example, it is the *Dialer* macro. The text on the face of the button, *Dial,* is specified in the fifth parameter. The last parameter specifies that the toolbar modified with the button be stored into the active template.

Now for the more interesting macro, *Dialer,* which is called when you click the Dial button. The *Dialer* macro looks like this:

```
'Macro to dial the selected phone number

'Declaration of DLL functions called by this macro
Declare Function tapiRequestMakeCall Lib "TAPI32.DLL"(DestAddress$,
AppName$, CalledParty$, Comment$) As Long

Sub MAIN

'Error Return Codes from tapiRequestMakeCall
TAPIERR_INVALPOINTER =         -18
TAPIERR_INVALDESTADDRESS =     -4
TAPIERR_NOREQUESTRECIPIENT =   -2
TAPIERR_REQUESTQUEUEFULL =     -3

'Maximum sizes for function parameters
TAPIMAXDESTADDRESSSIZE = 80

dialstring$ = Selection$()              'Get highlighted text
'Clip dial string to max allowed
'leftmost characters
dialstring$ = Left$(dialstring$, TAPIMAXDESTADDRESSSIZE)
MakeLettersIntoDigits dialstring$       'Turn letters into digits
```

(continued)

```
'Display dialog box to edit the dial string
Begin Dialog UserDialog 370, 92, "Phone Number"
    Text 14, 7, 96, 13, "Phone Number"
    TextBox 14, 23, 160, 18, .dstring$
    OKButton 270, 6, 88, 21
    CancelButton 270, 30, 88, 21
End Dialog

Dim dlg As UserDialog
dlg.dstring$ = dialstring$
choice = Dialog(dlg)

'If the OK button was clicked, then make the call
If choice = - 1 Then

    dialstring$ = dlg.dstring$ 'get dial string from dialog box
    MsgBox "", dialstring$, 48 'display the dial string
    'Make the call and check return value
    lResult = tapiRequestMakeCall \
        (dialstring$, "Microsoft Word 6.0", "", "")

    'handle errors
    If lResult Then
        Select Case lResult
            Case TAPIERR_INVALPOINTER
                MsgBox "", "Bad parameter to dialing function", 48
            Case TAPIERR_INVALDESTADDRESS
                MsgBox "", "Bad dial string", 48
            Case TAPIERR_NOREQUESTRECIPIENT
                MsgBox "", "No Call Manager; " \
                    "Try running Phone Dialer", 48
            Case TAPIERR_REQUESTQUEUEFULL
                MsgBox "", "Another dial is in progress; " \
                    "try later", 48
            Case Else
                MsgBox "", "Dialing Error", 48
        End Select
    End If

End If

End Sub
```

```
'Function to convert letters into dialable digits
Sub MakeLettersIntoDigits(olddialstring$)

newdialstring$ = olddialstring$
For i = 1 To Len(newdialstring$)
    c$ = Mid$(newdialstring$, i, 1)              'get next character
                                                 'in dial string

    Select Case c$
        Case "A", "B", "C", "a", "b", "c"
            c$ = "2"
        Case "D", "E", "F", "d", "e", "f"
            c$ = "3"
        Case "G", "H", "I", "g", "h", "i"
            c$ = "4"
        Case "J", "K", "L", "j", "k", "l"
            c$ = "5"
        Case "M", "N", "O", "m", "n", "o"
            c$ = "6"
        Case "P", "R", "S", "p", "r", "s"
            c$ = "7"
        Case "T", "U", "V", "t", "u", "v"
            c$ = "8"
        Case "W", "X", "Y", "w", "x", "y"
            c$ = "9"
        Case "Z", "Q", "z", "q"
            c$ = "1"             'Q and Z replaced by 1; best guess
        Case Else
            'Take no action
    End Select

    'Insert replacement digit in new dial string
    newdialstring$ = Left$(newdialstring$, i - 1) + c$ + \
                Right$(newdialstring$, Len(newdialstring$) - i)
Next i

olddialstring$ = newdialstring$
End Sub
```

Let's go through it from the top. WordBasic requires that all function calls to Windows DLLs be declared before the calls are made. So right away, outside the body of the macro, we declare the call to *tapiRequestMakeCall:*

```
'Declaration of DLL functions called by this macro
Declare Function tapiRequestMakeCall Lib "TAPI32.DLL"(DestAddress$,
AppName$, CalledParty$, Comment$) As Long
```

The declaration includes the name of the DLL that exports the function—in this case, TAPI32.DLL. It includes all the parameters of the function; the dial string (*DestAddress$*); the application name (*AppName$*); the name of the called party (*CalledParty$*); and the comment (*Comment$*). Notice that each parameter ends with a $. This indicates that each parameter is a string. Finally, the declaration ends with *As Long*. This last phrase declares the type returned by the function—in this case, a LONG value.

Next, the macro declares the return codes of *tapiRequestMakeCall*. We explained these error codes earlier, but you can jog your memory by referring to the switch statement that processes the return code from *tapiRequestMakeCall*:

```
'Error Return Codes from tapiRequestMakeCall
TAPIERR_INVALPOINTER =          -18
TAPIERR_INVALDESTADDRESS =       -4
TAPIERR_NOREQUESTRECIPIENT =     -2
TAPIERR_REQUESTQUEUEFULL =       -3
```

Next, the macro declares the maximum allowable size for the dial string, as shown below. Remember, the dial string that the macro uses is whatever text you highlight in the document, so it's important to make sure it isn't too long.

```
'Maximum sizes for function parameters
TAPIMAXDESTADDRESSSIZE = 80
```

You can also find these constants declared in the TAPI header file, TAPI.H.

Next, the macro retrieves the highlighted text. The special WordBasic function *Selection$* returns the highlighted text in a Word document and places the text into a string variable. The string variable that holds the selected dial string is called *dialstring$*.

```
dialstring$ = Selection$()           'Get highlighted text
```

Now that the text is in a string variable, you need to clip the string to the maximum allowable length by trimming any characters to the right of the maximum length. You accomplish this by using the *Left$* function to take only the maximum allowable leftmost characters of the string and put them back into the string, as shown below.

```
'Clip dial string to max allowed
'leftmost characters
dialstring$ = Left$(dialstring$, TAPIMAXDESTADDRESSSIZE)
```

Now for the fun part. Normally, dial strings cannot contain letters, as in 1-800-BUY-SOME. A call to the subroutine *MakeLettersIntoDigits,* shown below, accepts dial strings with letters and the subroutine converts them to a pure sequence of digits. Any digits in the dial string are left untouched. Any control characters in the dial string are turned into extraneous numbers, so don't call this macro with dial strings that contain control characters. Actually, control characters make a dial string look really confusing, and they change depending on what kind of phone line you are connected to. Phone numbers in Windows should be stored in canonical format, such as the phone number in the travel memo example, without any control characters in them. (See the section titled "Storing Phone Numbers" later in this chapter.) *MakeLettersIntoDigits* accepts one parameter, the dial string, and replaces this parameter with a new dial string containing only digits.

```
MakeLettersIntoDigits dialstring$        'Turn letters into digits
```

MakeLettersIntoDigits uses the following table to map the letters of the alphabet to the digits on a typical telephone keypad:

ABC	2
DEF	3
GHI	4
JKL	5
MNO	6
PRS	7
TUV	8
WXY	9
QZ	1

Notice that the letters *Q* and *Z* map to the digit 1, even though they don't appear this way on the keypad. For some reason, *Q* and *Z* are omitted from the typical telephone keypad (probably because of the infrequent use of these letters in the English language). The macro takes a "best guess" at where they might go, but you might want to avoid using *Q*s and *Z*s in your dial strings, since the meaning is ambiguous.

As you can see by inspecting the *MakeLettersIntoDigits* subroutine in the code listing, lowercase letters are converted according to the same rules as uppercase letters. Once the dial string is converted to all digits, the macro prompts you for any changes to the dial string using a custom dialog box. You can enter delay characters by editing the dial string directly. You can add commas for fixed delay or *W* to wait-for-dial-tone. You can enter commas multiple times any place in the dial string.

After you edit the dial string, you click OK to pass it to *tapiRequestMakeCall*. The macro passes the application name (Microsoft Word 6.0) but leaves the user name and the comment parameters empty, as shown below. It uses a *Select* statement to check the return value from the function and display a message box indicating which error occurred, if any.

```
'Make the call and check return value
lResult = tapiRequestMakeCall\
    (dialstring$, "Microsoft Word 6.0", "", "")
```

For the benefit of C programmers, the companion disk includes C files that, like the Word macros you've seen in this chapter, bring up a dialog box in which you can enter a phone number and dial. You can find these files in the \Chapter2\CSample directory installed from the companion disk. The C calls include the header file TAPI.H, which contains the declaration for *tapiRequest-MakeCall* as well as the error codes and maximum string sizes. The code must be linked to the export library TAPI32.LIB, which exports *tapiRequestMakeCall*.

Storing Phone Numbers

As you've seen, it makes sense to store a phone number without any control characters in it because control characters make the number look messy and they can change depending on the line you're connected to. Another common-sense rule about storing phone numbers is to leave off the dialing prefix. The prefix is not really part of the number. It's just an extra digit or two required to access an external line from inside a business or a hotel. If you use the Dialing Properties dialog box to configure your location when you come and go from work or a hotel, Windows adds or removes the dialing prefix automatically.

Unlike the dialing prefix, the country code and area code should be stored with the phone number. But will you remember to do this? We've written a little Word macro to help you. The macro relies on another simple dialing function called *tapiGetLocationInfo*. The function has the following syntax:

```
LONG tapiGetLocationInfo(LPCSTR lpszCountryCode, LPCSTR lpszCityCode)
```

The function returns the country code and area code configured in the Dialing Properties dialog box. *lpszCountryCode* is a z-string with the country code, and *lpszCityCode* is a z-string with the area code. The macro displays the phone number highlighted in the text, with the country code and area code attached as defaults. If these aren't correct, you can change them to the desired values. When you click OK, the macro places the phone number back into the text, with the country code and area code attached. The strings should both have space for at least eight characters. If you have not configured a country code or area code in the Dialing Properties dialog box, one or both of the strings will be empty.

The macro *GetLocationInfo* is shown below.

```
'Returns the configured location information
'    (area code and country code)
Declare Function tapiGetLocationInfo Lib "TAPI32.DLL"(Country$,
Area$) As Long

Sub MAIN
    lResult = tapiGetLocationInfo(Country$, Area$)
    If (lResult >= 0) Then
        Begin Dialog UserDialog 370, 92, "Phone Number"
            Text 14, 7, 96, 13, "Phone Number"
            TextBox 14, 23, 160, 18, .dialstring$
            OKButton 270, 6, 88, 21
            CancelButton 270, 30, 88, 21
        End Dialog
        Dim dlg As UserDialog
        dlg.dialstring$ = "+" + Country$ + "(" + Area$ + ")" \
                            + Selection$()
        choice = Dialog(dlg)
        If choice = - 1 Then
            EditCut
            Insert dlg.dialstring$
        End If
    Else
        MsgBox "", "Configuration Error", 48
    End If

End Sub
```

The macro starts off with a declaration of the *tapiGetLocationInfo* function. This declaration should look familiar—it's very similar to the one for *tapiRequestMakeCall* in the *Dialer* macro.

```
Declare Function tapiGetLocationInfo Lib "TAPI32.DLL"(Country$,
Area$) As Long
```

The *GetLocationInfo* macro calls the function and checks the return value. If no error occurred, the macro displays a dialog box with the country code and area code attached to the selected phone number. You can accept this default phone number or edit the phone number. When you click OK, the macro deletes the selection (*EditCut*) and inserts in its place the contents of the text box in the dialog box (*Insert dlg.dialstring$*).

tapiGetLocationInfo returns 0 if successful, or a negative error code otherwise. The only possible error, TAPIERR_REQUESTFAILED, indicates a configuration problem; if that error occurs, the macro displays a message box to that effect.

You might have noticed that there is no apparent provision for attaching international access codes to international phone numbers. An international access code is the sequence of digits you must dial in order to make an international call. For example, to call from the United States to a number outside of North America and the Caribbean, you must first dial 011 before dialing the country code, area code, and phone number. Windows configures the international access code automatically when you specify the country you are calling from in the Dialing Properties dialog box.

Simple Messaging

It is often useful to send a message from one computer to another or to a fax machine. A message can be anything—a word, a sentence, a file, or a drawing.

Like dialing the phone, sending a message is actually a complicated process. It is safe to say that sending a message makes dialing look like a stroll through the park. Sending a message requires all four of the communication stages we discussed in Chapter 1: configuration, connection, data transfer, and disconnection. Dialing with *tapiRequestMakeCall* requires only two of the four stages, configuration and connection. The user is responsible for the other two stages—data transfer (speaking) and disconnection (hanging up the phone).

What's more, sending messages is only part of the story. You also need ways of reading messages sent from other computers and for storing and organizing messages. Fortunately, Windows 95 includes about a dozen functions that make sending, receiving, and managing messages a breeze. These are explained in more detail in Chapter 5. The function discussed here is *MAPISendDocuments*. Most of the messaging functions are designed to be called from C or C++ and hence incorporate structures (and often nested structures) within their parameter list. Structured parameters are a pain to use with many macro and scripting languages (including Word and Microsoft Excel macros), so Microsoft designed *MAPISendDocuments* to work without structures. The function declaration looks like this:

```
ULONG MAPISendDocuments(ULONG ulUIParam,
                LPSTR lpszDelimChar,
                LPSTR lpszFilePaths,
                LPSTR lpszFileNames,
                ULONG ulReserved)
```

Notice that none of the parameters is a structure. The calling syntax is actually pretty simple—just the parent window handle (the first parameter), a few strings, and a reserved field that you set to 0.

You can learn a few things about the function just by looking at its declaration. First of all, it is implemented by MAPI, the Messaging API, which was introduced in Chapter 1. This is obvious because the function is prefixed with the letters *MAPI*, in the same way that *tapiRequestMakeCall* is prefixed by *TAPI*. Second, the function requires a window handle, so it probably displays a dialog box of some sort. Also, there are no flags, so you might guess that the behavior of the function is pretty much predetermined. Third, the name of the function, *MAPISendDocuments*, implies that you use it to send e-mail and maybe documents (such as file attachments). You might infer that the function prompts for things like the recipients of the message, since there is no way to specify recipients in the parameter list. Finally, there are a couple of strings for pathnames and filenames that might indicate the names of the files to send.

A message can include almost anything: files, pieces of files, paragraphs, even single words. But what is a *file attachment?* Quite simply, a file attachment is a file. In Windows, when you send a file, you make it an attachment to a message. Text is usually included with the message to explain what the attachment is for. Recipients are the persons to whom the message will be sent. Figure 2-3 makes all of this somewhat clearer.

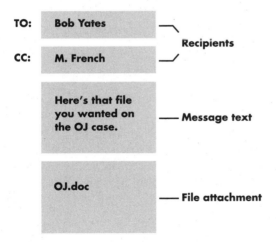

Figure 2-3. *The parts of a message.*

When calling *MAPISendDocuments,* the attachments for the message are specified in the parameters *lpszFilePaths* and *lpszFileNames.* The string *lpszFilePaths* indicates the full pathnames of the files to attach. The string *lpszFileNames* indicates the "friendly" names of the attachments. In other words, *lpszFilePaths* is the name of the file or files to send, and *lpszFileNames* is a new, more descriptive name for them. The pathnames can point to any files that aren't currently open, including the names of temporary files. The names of attachments should be descriptive and related somehow to the purpose or contents of the attachments. Each string can hold multiple names, delimited by the character in *lpszDelimChar*. We're partial to using the comma as a delimiter, but you can use anything except characters that appear in pathnames and filenames. (The backslash obviously can't be used because it appears in pathnames.) If the message has no attachments, specify a NULL or an empty string for both the pathname and the friendly name.

MAPISendDocuments does a clever thing with the attachment name. It looks at the file extension and compares it with a list of file extensions that it is familiar with. It then adds to the message an icon to represent the file type of the attachment. (For example, .xls files get an Excel icon).

MAPISendDocuments displays a dialog box in which you enter the names of recipients and the message text. Also, if the destination is password protected, you will be asked for a name and a password. Most online services are password protected; so are many private BBSs (bulletin board systems). If the destination is a fax machine or an unprotected computer, you probably won't be asked for a name and a password. Be prepared to enter this information when you call *MAPISendDocuments.*

Once the name and password are out of the way, *MAPISendDocuments* invokes the Windows mailing software. In Windows 3.1 this is Microsoft Mail, but in Windows 95 the mailing application is Microsoft Exchange. Here you enter information about the message, including one or more recipients. To make life easier, you can store the names of frequent recipients in an electronic address book. You can also specify people who will receive copies of the message. You can specify a subject for the message and attach files in addition to the ones specified in the function parameters. You can also type in the text of the message at this point. Additional options are covered in more detail in Chapter 5, which deals with messaging in depth.

When you are ready to send, click the Send button. *MAPISendDocuments* sends the message, using your name and password to log on to the destination computer if necessary. It then locates the recipients and sends each of them a copy of the message text and any attachments. Once this is completed, *MAPISendDocuments* logs off (if necessary) and returns. In certain situations, the function might return before completing the sending of the message and complete the send in the background.

Shown below is the *SendMessage* Word macro for sending the highlighted selection in a document to someone on another computer or to a fax machine.

```
'Macro to send the selected text to a user on another computer or to
'a fax machine
Declare Function MAPISendDocuments Lib "MAPI32.DLL" (hwnd as Integer,
delim$, paths$, friendlynames$, reserved As Long)  As Long

Sub Main

'Declare return codes
MAPI_E_INSUFFICIENT_MEMORY = 5
MAPI_E_LOGIN_FAILURE = 3
MAPI_E_USER_ABORT = 1
MAPI_E_TOO_MANY_SESSIONS = 8
MAPI_E_ATTACHMENT_OPEN_FAILURE = 12
SUCCESS_SUCCESS = 0

'Open temporary file
Open "C:\tmp.xyz" For Output As #1
'Write selected text to the temporary file
Print #1, Selection$()
'Close the temporary file
Close #1

'Get a friendly name for the selection from user
Begin Dialog UserDialog 370, 92, "Name the message"
    Text 14, 7, 96, 13, "Attach Name"
    TextBox 14, 23, 160, 18, .name$
    OKButton 270, 6, 88, 21
    CancelButton 270, 30, 88, 21
End Dialog
Dim dlg As UserDialog
choice = Dialog(dlg)
```

(continued)

```
'If the user clicked OK, send the message
If choice = - 1 Then
    'Send the message and check return value
    lResult = MAPISendDocuments(0, ",", "C:\tmp.xyz", dlg.name$, 0)
    Select Case lResult
        Case MAPI_E_INSUFFICIENT_MEMORY
            MsgBox "", "Not enough memory", 48
        Case MAPI_E_LOGIN_FAILURE
            MsgBox "", "Login failure", 48
        Case MAPI_E_USER_ABORT
            MsgBox "", "User aborted the login process", 48
        Case MAPI_E_TOO_MANY_SESSIONS
            MsgBox "", "MAPI is busy; try later", 48
        Case MAPI_E_ATTACHMENT_OPEN_FAILURE
            MsgBox "", "Could not access attachment file", 48
        Case Else
            'Nothing
    End Select

End If

'Delete the temporary file
Kill "C:\tmp.xyz"

End Sub
```

The key to this macro is that it saves the selected text into a temporary file, which is then made into an attachment and sent. (Windows will prompt you for information on how and where to send the text.) The macro prompts you for a friendly name for the attachment. If you click OK, the temporary file is sent as an attachment with the provided name. The macro then deletes the temporary file.

To save the current selection to a temporary file, the macro first opens the temporary file using the *Open* statement. It specifies a filename for this temporary file called *tmp.xyz* in the root directory of the C: drive. It then opens the file for output, creating the file if it doesn't already exist, and wipes out the contents of the file if it does exist.

```
'Open temporary file
Open "C:\tmp.xyz" For Output As #1
```

The *Open* statement specifies a "handle" for the opened file, in this case #1. This handle is used by other statements that reference the file. The macro then writes out the currently selected text to the temporary file using the *Print* statement, shown on the facing page.

```
'Write selected text to the temporary file
Print #1, Selection$()
```

After the macro is done with the file, it closes it with the *Close* statement.

```
'Close the temporary file
Close #1
```

At this point the macro displays a dialog box to prompt you for a friendly name for the temporary file. If you do not specify a friendly name for the attachment, *MAPISendDocuments* permanently assigns it the name *tmp.xyz*, which is pretty obscure. It's a good idea to enter a friendly name to help the recipient of the message figure out what the file contains.

The macro then calls *MAPISendDocuments*, which specifies a NULL window handle. (Any dialog boxes displayed by the function will be system modal.) It also specifies that a comma delimit multiple attachment and friendly names, although this is pretty useless since only one attachment is specified. The pathname of the attachment points to the temporary file, C:\tmp.xyz. The friendly name you entered in the dialog box is used for the friendly name of the temporary file attachment. The reserved parameter of the function is set to 0, as it always should be.

```
'Send the message and check return value
lResult = MAPISendDocuments(0, ",", "C:\tmp.xyz", dlg.name$, 0)
```

MAPISendDocuments returns SUCCESS_SUCCESS if all goes well. This is just a fancy definition that equates to 0, a successful return. The function can fail, however, for a number of reasons. One is when Windows runs out of memory, in which case the return value is MAPI_E_INSUFFICIENT_MEMORY. If the destination requires you to log on and you fail to properly do so, the function returns MAPI_E_LOGIN_FAILURE. If you cancel the logon at the dialog box, the function returns MAPI_E_USER_ABORT. One return value to watch for is MAPI_E_TOO_MANY_SESSIONS. This error code indicates that MAPI is busy doing other things, so you should try again later. Some MAPI drivers don't support multiple sessions, some do. In addition to errors due to low memory, general failures, logon failures, and the like, there are errors that occur when the specified files cannot be attached for some reason. The function returns MAPI_E_ATTACHMENT_OPEN_FAILURE if one or more of the files in *lpszFilePaths* isn't where you said it was.

To learn more about dialing and messaging, see Chapters 4 and 5.

3

Data Transfer with the Win32 Communications API

To accomplish serial data transfer in Windows 95, you use the Win32 Communications API, or Win32c for short. Though not strictly limited to serial data, Win32c is primarily a serial port API. Because of the close historical ties between the serial port and the modem, virtually all data transfer over phone lines involves the serial port. (There are some exceptions for voice modems.) An understanding of serial communications is thus essential to understanding modem communications in Windows.

There are four sample applications in this chapter that demonstrate the different ways serial data can be transferred in Windows 95. Once you know how to transfer data over a serial cable, you'll find it simple to do the same for a modem. The samples require two computers connected back-to-back via their serial ports (using a NULL modem cable). Both computers must be running the sample program (or a terminal program such as Windows HyperTerminal in the Accessories folder) at the same time, and the program settings must be configured alike.

When to Use Win32c

Win32c traces its roots to 16-bit Windows and the Windows COMM API and is highly specialized for serial ports and modems. Modems typically send data sequentially over a single phone line. But Win32c can also be used to send data through parallel devices such as LPT ports and parallel modems (parallel meaning that multiple data bits are sent simultaneously). It is thus difficult to generalize about when to use Win32c.

Win32c is not well suited for communications on a local area network (LAN). True, LANs often serialize the data bits before sending them out on the wire, just as a serial port or a modem does, but LANs often use fewer wires than serial ports do, and they use access, routing, security, and error-correcting protocols that have little in common with serial port protocols. The layers of protocols required for LAN communications makes Win32c less than ideal for these applications. This goes for Internet communications requiring TCP/IP as well.

Win32c doesn't work for real-time communications, either. The quality of real-time communications is timing-dependent. For example, digitized audio is real-time data because the quality of the sound depends on the rate at which it is played back. When audio is recorded (for example, onto a CD-ROM), it is digitized at a particular rate, known as the *sampling rate*. The audio must be played back at the same sampling rate or else it will sound too slow or too fast. Video data is also timing-dependent. If you play video too slowly, the motion looks jerky. Play it too quickly and it's like watching a movie on fast-forward.

Suppose you want to play a sound file (using the Windows Multimedia Extensions) containing a recording of your voice over the phone line, perhaps as the greeting for a software answering machine. (Newer voice modems support this capability.) You should not use Win32c to play the greeting (even if you have a voice modem connected to the serial port) because Win32c cannot transmit audio in real time. But note a subtle distinction here. Even though you cannot use Win32c to send or receive the greeting in real time, you can certainly use it to, say, transmit the greeting in a sound file and then play the sound file locally on the other computer using Microsoft Sound Recorder (an accessory in the Windows 95 Accessories folder). It is not the use of sound data per se that precludes Win32c, but rather the requirement that it be transmitted in real time.

Ruling out LAN, TCP/IP, and real-time communications still leaves plenty of applications for Win32c. Any application that requires a serial port or a modem is a candidate—including e-mail, faxes, file transfers, and interactive applications such as terminal emulation. Automation/control applications that use the serial port to control an external piece of equipment (such as a laserdisc player) are also possibilities. But as we explained in Chapter 1, the Messaging API (MAPI) is preferable for store-and-forward type communications such as e-mail, faxes, and file transfers. So what is left? The answer, more or less by elimination, seems to be interactive and automation/control applications. Automation/control is not very interesting, at least not in terms of the communications involved. That leaves only interactive applications. A general rule might be that if the application is interactive—that is, if it requires a user's continuous supervision and interaction—Win32c is the way to go. This leads to the fourth communications axiom. (See Chapter 1 for the other three.)

> *Use Win32c for interactive, non-real-time communications that don't require many protocol layers.*

Actually, this fourth axiom is a bit misleading. Win32c still has a central role in transmitting and receiving e-mail, faxes, and files. Even though these functions are relegated to MAPI, MAPI relies on Win32c at a low level to actually transmit the data (when a serial port/modem is involved). If you write MAPI drivers for wide area communications, you probably need to use Win32c. Other applications that use Win32c include interactive terminals, front ends to online services, and multiplayer games (although the DirectPlay API in the Windows 95 Game SDK is specialized for multiplayer gaming).

Serial Communications Basics

This chapter assumes a basic knowledge of serial communications. In particular, it assumes that you understand basic concepts such as baud rate, start and stop bits, and parity. It also assumes a familiarity with the basic operation and signaling of RS-232 (EIA RS-232) standard computer ports. For a complete reference on serial communications (with a complete discussion of the basics from the telegraph to modern times) see *The C Programmer's Guide to Serial Communications* by Joe Campbell (SAMS Publishing).

Signal Definitions

This chapter often refers to certain RS-232 signals. These signals form the basis of all serial communications. Definitions of these signals are given below. The term ON is used to refer to a signal in the Asserted or High state, and OFF refers to a signal in the Not Asserted or Low state.

- *RTS (Request to Send)* and *CTS (Clear to Send)*—These signals perform hardware handshaking between the serial port and the attached modem. Not all modems support hardware handshaking. If a modem does not support it, RTS is permanently OFF and CTS is permanently ON. If a modem does support it, RTS is ON when the serial port is ready to receive data from the modem, and CTS is ON when the modem is ready to receive data from the serial port.

- *DSR (Data Set Ready)*—This signal is turned ON when the modem has established a connection with another modem and has performed the necessary handshaking. DSR should be ON before the port attempts to perform any I/O activity.

- *RLSD (Receive Line Signal Detect)*—Also known as *data carrier detect,* this signal is turned ON when the modem receives a carrier signal from another modem.

- *DTR (Data Terminal Ready)*—This signal is used mainly for establishing and maintaining the connection between two modems. DTR is ON for as long as the connection is established. When DTR is turned OFF, the connection immediately drops.

- *RI (Ring Indicator)*—The modem turns this signal ON for the duration of a ring indication (incoming call) on the line.

Opening a Serial Port

In 16-bit Windows, special functions are required to open, close, read, and write to serial ports. These functions are *OpenComm, CloseComm, ReadComm,* and *WriteComm,* respectively. In Windows 95, serial ports and other communications devices are treated like files. Serial ports are opened, closed, read from, and written to using the same functions that are used with files.

A communications session begins with a call to the *CreateFile* function. *CreateFile* "opens" the serial port for read access, write access, or both. True to the Windows tradition, *CreateFile* returns a handle for use in subsequent operations on the opened port.

The *CreateFile* function, shown below, is complex. One reason for its complexity is that it is general-purpose. You can use *CreateFile* to open existing files, create new files, and open devices that aren't files at all, such as serial ports, parallel ports, and modems.

```
CreateFile (szDevice, fdwAccess, fdwShareMode, lpsa, fdwCreate,
            fdwAttrsAndFlags, hTemplateFile);
```

The first parameter, *szDevice,* is the logical name of the serial port to open, such as COM1 or COM2. The second parameter, *fdwAccess,* specifies the type of access for the port. Just as with files, serial ports can be opened for reading, writing, or both. The flag GENERIC_READ opens the port for reading; the flag GENERIC_WRITE opens the port for writing. Joining the two flags with an OR operator, as shown below, opens the port for read/write access. Most serial port communications are bidirectional, so a common setting uses both flags.

```
fdwAccess = GENERIC_READ | GENERIC_WRITE;
```

The third parameter, *fdwShareMode,* specifies the sharing attributes of the port. This parameter is used for files, which can be shared by multiple applications. It must be set to 0 for serial ports, which cannot be shared. This is one of the major differences between files and communications devices. If another application has already opened the port when the current application calls *CreateFile,* the function returns an error because two applications cannot share a port. However, multiple threads of the same application can share the handle to the port returned by *CreateFile,* and, depending on the security attributes settings, this handle can be inherited by children of the application that opened the port.

The fourth parameter, *lpsa,* references a security attribute structure that defines such attributes as how the port handle can be inherited by children of the application that opened the port. Setting this parameter to NULL assigns the default security attributes to the port. The default for inheritance by child applications is that the port cannot be inherited.

The fifth parameter, *fdwCreate,* specifies what to do if *CreateFile* is being called on a file that already exists. Since a serial port always exists, *fdwCreate* must be set to OPEN_EXISTING. This flag tells Windows not to attempt to create a new port, but to open a port that already exists.

The sixth parameter, *fdwAttrsAndFlags,* describes various attributes of the port. For files, many attributes are possible, but for serial ports the only setting of interest is FILE_FLAG_OVERLAPPED. When you specify this setting, port I/O can proceed in the background. (Background I/O—also called asynchronous I/O—is covered later in this chapter.) The last parameter, *hTemplateFile,* specifies the handle to a template file and is not used when opening ports, so it must be set to NULL.

Remember the following exceptions when opening a serial port using *CreateFile:*

- The sharing mode flags must be set to 0 for exclusive access to the modem.

- The create flag must be set to OPEN_EXISTING.

- The template handle must be set to NULL.

Once the port is open, you can allocate a transmit buffer and a receive buffer and perform other initializations by calling *SetupComm,* as shown below. You don't have to call *SetupComm*—Windows allocates default transmit and receive buffers and initializes the port even if you don't—but it's a good way to ensure that the buffer sizes are as large as you need them to be. *SetupComm* takes as parameters, in order, the handle to the open port returned by *CreateFile,* the size of the receive buffers, and the size of the transmit buffer. The sizes you specify are only "recommended" sizes, and Windows is free to allocate any size it wants. This isn't as bad as it sounds. After all, the only reason for specifying particular sizes for the transmit and receive buffers is to try to optimize performance and avoid buffer overruns. Windows will use the sizes you recommend to set up a buffering scheme that provides the performance you would expect from buffers of those sizes. Odds are, Windows will allocate buffers of the size you request.

```
SetupComm (hComm, dwRXBufSize, dwTXBufSize)
```

Closing a Serial Port

Fortunately, closing a serial port is a lot simpler than opening one. You simply call *CloseHandle* (as shown below) with the handle returned by *CreateFile* as the only parameter. Always close a serial port when you are done using it. If you forget to close the port, it stays open and other applications will not be able to open it or use it.

```
CloseHandle (hComm);
```

Configuring a Serial Port

Configuring a serial port is more complicated in Windows 95 than in earlier versions of Windows. But along with this greater complexity comes greater capability. Windows 95 improves the (much maligned) serial port driver and provides greater integration of serial ports and modems. Configuration begins by determining the capabilities of the port. This enables an application to avoid incorrect settings that the port does not support. A port's capabilities are returned in the COMMPROP structure.

The COMMPROP Structure

COMMPROP is perhaps the most interesting and useful addition to the family of data structures for Windows 95 communications. The COMMPROP structure contains the permissible settings for a port—for example, the permitted values for baud rate, number of data bits, number of stop bits, and parity method. If the port is connected to a modem, the COMMPROP structure can include the settings supported by the modem. To retrieve modem information, the port must be opened in a special way. This subject is covered in the section titled "Opening a Modem" in Chapter 4.

Retrieving Port Properties

The function *GetCommProperties,* shown below, fills in the COMMPROP structure with information about the serial port. The COMMPROP structure and *GetCommProperties* are not limited to use with serial ports; they can also be used, for example, to return information about a parallel port. The contents of COMMPROP are static—no application is allowed to change the information returned in this structure—so there is no corresponding function for writing the settings in a COMMPROP structure to the port. The parameters of *GetCommProperties* are the handle to the port and a pointer to the COMMPROP structure.

```
GetCommProperties (hComm, lpCommProp)
```

The COMMPROP structure is shown below:

```
typedef struct _COMMPROP {        // cmmp
    WORD  wPacketLength;          // structure size, in bytes
    WORD  wPacketVersion;         // structure version
    DWORD dwServiceMask;          // services implemented
    DWORD dwReserved1;            // reserved, do not use
    DWORD dwMaxTxQueue;           // max Tx bufsize, in bytes
    DWORD dwMaxRxQueue;           // max Rx bufsize, in bytes
    DWORD dwMaxBaud;              // max baud rate, in bps
    DWORD dwProvSubType;          // specific provider type
    DWORD dwProvCapabilities;     // capabilities supported
    DWORD dwSettableParams;       // changeable parameters
    DWORD dwSettableBaud;         // allowable baud rates
    WORD  wSettableData;          // allowable byte sizes
    WORD  wSettableStopParity;    // stop bits/parity allowed
    DWORD dwCurrentTxQueue;       // Tx buffer size, in bytes
    DWORD dwCurrentRxQueue;       // Rx buffer size, in bytes
    DWORD dwProvSpec1;            // provider-specific data
    DWORD dwProvSpec2;            // provider-specific data
    WCHAR wcProvChar[1];          // provider-specific data
} COMMPROP, *LPCOMMPROP;
```

Notice the last member of COMMPROP, the one called *wcProvChar*. This member is declared as an array of characters, yet it consists of only a single character. This rather strange construction can be found elsewhere in Windows; for example, you might encounter it when programming Device Independent Bitmaps (DIBs) and palettes. The member is intended to be used as the starting byte for extra data that will be appended to the structure by Windows. In some cases, it is up to the application to allocate the memory for the extra data, and to fill in the values of the data. With COMMPROP, the application still allocates the memory for the extra data, but Windows, not the application, fills in the values. This creates a problem because the application won't know how much memory to allocate for the extra data.

There are two ways to solve this problem: the right way and the lazy way. The lazy way wastes memory, but it's fast and easy. The problem, to restate, is that the application must allocate the memory for the COMMPROP structure plus any extra data, but it doesn't know how much extra data Windows will return. The lazy way of getting around this is to allocate more memory than Windows could possibly need. COMMPROP itself is only 64 bytes (unpacked), so it seems safe to assume that allocating 1000 bytes (as shown below) should more than accommodate any extra data that Windows might return.

```
LPCOMMPROP lpCommProp = (LPCOMMPROP)malloc (1000);
```

Fortunately, there is a better way. The trick is to call *GetCommProperties* twice, as shown below. The first time the application calls *GetCommProperties,* the function fills in the *wPacketLength* member of COMMPROP with the total number of bytes required for the structure, including the extra data. The application checks this value to allocate the correct amount of memory, and calls *GetCommProperties* a second time to retrieve the extra data.

```
LPCOMMPROP lpCommProp = (LPCOMMPROP)malloc (sizeof(COMMPROP));
lpCommProp.wPacketLength = sizeof(COMMPROP);
GetCommProperties(hComm, lpCommProp);
dwSize=lpCommProp.wPacketLength;
free(lpCommProp);
lpCommProp = (LPCOMMPROP)malloc (dwSize);
lpCommProp.wPacketLength = dwSize;
GetCommProperties(hComm, lpCommProp);
```

In the above example, before the application calls *GetCommProperties* the first time, it sets *wPacketLength* to *sizeof(COMMPROP).* This is a necessary step because Windows will assume *wPacketLength* bytes of total space available for copying data into. (If *wPacketLength* is set to more than the amount of space available, a memory overwrite can occur.) Windows then sets *wPacketLength* to the number of bytes required for the COMMPROP structure, including all of the extra data. Finally, the application reallocates the correct amount of space for the structure and calls *GetCommProperties* again. You won't have to worry about extra data until you attempt to use the port in connection with a modem.

Port Properties Defined

We've discussed how to retrieve values from COMMPROP (*GetCommProperties*), and we've explored the first and last members (*wPacketLength* and *wcProvChar*) of the structure. In this section we'll discuss some more members.

The *wPacketVersion* member specifies the version of the COMMPROP structure. Different versions of Windows and other Microsoft operating systems use different versions of COMMPROP with different member interpretations, so check this member first to ensure that you are interpreting the structure correctly. In Windows 95, the version is set to 0xffff. The *dwServiceMask* member broadly defines the functionality of the port. This member is set to SP_SERIALCOMM for serial ports.

dwMaxTxQueue and *dwMaxRxQueue* contain the maximum permitted sizes (in bytes) of the port's output buffer and input buffer, respectively. If these members return 0, it means that the port places no restrictions on the buffer sizes. Because Windows might set these members to 0 to indicate that there is no maximum value, you should always check for a 0 instead of blindly interpreting these members as the allowable buffer sizes. *dwMaxBaud* is the maximum data rate the port supports, in bits per second (bps). This number can be fixed or programmable. If programmable baud rates are supported, *dwMaxBaud* is set to BAUD_USER. Otherwise it is set to one of the values shown below.

BAUD_075	75 bps
BAUD_110	110 bps
BAUD_134_5	134.5 bps
BAUD_150	150 bps
BAUD_300	300 bps
BAUD_600	600 bps
BAUD_1200	1200 bps
BAUD_1800	1800 bps
BAUD_2400	2400 bps
BAUD_4800	4800 bps
BAUD_7200	7200 bps
BAUD_9600	9600 bps
BAUD_14400	14400 bps
BAUD_19200	19200 bps
BAUD_38400	38400 bps
BAUD_56K	56 Kbps
BAUD_57600	57600 bps
BAUD_115200	115200 bps
BAUD_128K	128 Kbps

dwProvSubType specifies the type of communications device in greater detail than *dwServiceMask*. For serial ports, this field is set to PST_RS232. Other supported devices are listed below.

PST_FAX	Fax device
PST_LAT	LAT protocol
PST_MODEM	Modem device
PST_NETWORK_BRIDGE	Unspecified network bridge
PST_PARALLELPORT	Parallel port
PST_RS422	RS-422 port
PST_RS423	RS-423 port
PST_RS449	RS-449 port

PST_SCANNER	Scanner device
PST_TCPIP_TELNET	TCP/IP Telnet protocol
PST_UNSPECIFIED	Unspecified
PST_X25	X.25 standards

Note: A bit of magic occurs when the serial port is attached to a modem (PST_MODEM). In a sense, the serial port *becomes* the modem. The properties of the port and the modem are merged into a single logical space. We'll see how this works in the next chapter.

Now for the most useful members—the ones that make COMMPROP really interesting. *dwProvCapabilities* describes the capabilities supported by the port. Each value specifies a single bit in the *dwProvCapabilities* member. The values and their corresponding capabilities are shown below.

PCF_16BITMODE	Special 16-bit mode is supported.
PCF_DTRDSR	DTR (data-terminal-ready)/DSR (data-set-ready) is supported.
PCF_INTTIMEOUTS	Interval timeouts are supported.
PCF_PARITY_CHECK	Parity checking is supported.
PCF_RLSD	RLSD (receive-line-signal-detect) is supported.
PCF_RTSCTS	RTS (request-to-send)/CTS (clear-to-send) is supported.
PCF_SETXCHAR	Settable XON/XOFF is supported.
PCF_SPECIALCHARS	Special characters are supported.
PCF_TOTALTIMEOUTS	Total (elapsed) timeouts are supported.
PCF_XONXOFF	XON/XOFF flow control is supported.

Standard RS-232 serial ports and the Windows serial port driver support most of the capabilities shown above, with the exception of PCF_16BITMODE and PCF_SPECIALCHARS.

The member *dwSettableParams* specifies which port settings are configurable. The flag values and interpretations for this member are shown below.

SP_BAUD	Baud rate is configurable.
SP_DATABITS	Number of data bits is configurable.
SP_HANDSHAKING	Handshaking (flow control) is configurable.
SP_PARITY	Parity mode is configurable.
SP_PARITY_CHECK	Parity checking enabled/disabled is configurable.
SP_RLSD	RLSD (receive-line-signal-detect) is configurable.
SP_STOPBITS	Number of stop bits is configurable.

dwSettableParams is one of the most important members for an application to check. Common sense dictates that an application must check whether a setting is configurable before attempting to change the setting. Standard RS-232 serial ports and the Windows serial port driver support configuration of all of the settings listed above.

The members *dwSettableBaud, wSettableData,* and *wSettableStopParity* contain the allowable settings for the baud rate, number of data bits, number of stop bits, and parity mode. The settable baud rates for the port and port driver are one or more of the values listed on page 45. The Windows 95 port driver allows up to 38 Kbps on standard serial ports. Windows reports a maximum settable baud rate of 56 Kbps for a standard RS-232 serial port. The number of data bits can range from 5 to 16. The allowable values for the number of data bits are shown below. The Windows 95 serial port driver supports all of these settings for standard serial ports, with the exception of the 16-bit settings.

DATABITS_5	5 data bits
DATABITS_6	6 data bits
DATABITS_7	7 data bits
DATABITS_8	8 data bits
DATABITS_16	16 data bits
DATABITS_16X	Special wide path through serial hardware lines

The members *dwCurrentTxQueue* and *dwCurrentRxQueue* contain the current size of the transmit buffer and the receive buffer, respectively.

The members *dwProvSpec1, dwProvSpec2*, and *wcProvChar* are not used with RS-232 serial ports. *dwProvSpec1* and *dwProvSpec2* are not used by modems, either. But as you'll see in the next chapter, *wcProvChar* has special significance when opening a modem attached to a serial port.

Now that you know how to determine which settings are supported by a port, the next step is to actually read and write port settings. The next section explains how to retrieve the current settings for a port and how to use COMMPROP to change those settings to one of the supported settings.

The DCB Structure

The COMMPROP structure tells you which settings the port supports. COMMPROP is purely informational; it cannot be used to change the port settings. This is where the Device Control Block, or DCB, comes in. The DCB serves the same purpose in Windows 95 that it does in earlier versions of Windows—it is a container for the current port settings that can be used to programatically configure a port. The DCB for each version is shown on the following pages.

Windows 95 DCB:

```
typedef struct _DCB {
    DWORD DCBlength;
    DWORD BaudRate;
    DWORD fBinary: 1;
    DWORD fParity: 1;
    DWORD fOutxCtsFlow: 1;
    DWORD fOutxDsrFlow: 1;
    DWORD fDtrControl: 2;
    DWORD dDsrSensitivity: 1;
    DWORD fTXContinueOnXoff: 1;
    DWORD fOutX: 1;
    DWORD fInX: 1;
    DWORD fErrorChar: 1;
    DWORD fNull: 1;
    DWORD fRtsControl: 2;
    DWORD fAbortOnError: 1;
    DWORD fDummy2: 17;
    WORD wReserved;
    WORD XonLim;
    WORD XoffLim;
    BYTE ByteSize;
    BYTE Parity;
    BYTE StopBits;
    char XonChar;
    char XoffChar;
    char ErrorChar;
    char EofChar;
    char EvtChar;
    WORD wReserved1;
} DCB;
```

Windows 3.1 DCB:

```
typedef struct tagDCB{
    BYTE Id;
    UINT BaudRate;
    BYTE ByteSize;
    BYTE Parity;
    BYTE StopBits;
    UINT RlsTimeout;
    UINT CtsTimeout;
    UINT DsrTimeout;
    UINT fBinary        :1;
    UINT fRtsDisable    :1;
    UINT fParity        :1;
```

```
        UINT fOutxCtsFlow     :1;
        UINT fOutxDsrFlow     :1;
        UINT fDummy           :2;
        UINT fDtrDisable      :1;
        UINT fOutX            :1;
        UINT fInX             :1;
        UINT fPeChar          :1;
        UINT fNull            :1;
        UINT fChEvt           :1;
        UINT fDtrflow         :1;
        UINT fRtsflow         :1;
        UINT fDummy2          :1;
        char XonChar;
        char XoffChar;
        UINT XonLim;
        UINT XoffLim;
        char PeChar;
        char EofChar;
        char EvtChar;
        UINT TxDelay;
} DCB;
```

As you can see, the DCB in Windows 95 is quite different from the earlier DCB. The *Id, RlsTimeout, CtsTimeout, DsrTimeout, fChEvt,* and *TxDelay* members were omitted in the Windows 95 version or were moved to other areas of the communications API. The *fRtsDisable* and *fRtsflow* members were incorporated into the *fRtsControl* member, and the *fDtrDisable* and *fDtrflow* members were incorporated into the *fDtrControl* member. *fPeChar* and *PeChar* were renamed *fErrorChar* and *ErrorChar,* respectively, and *fDummy* was renamed *wReserved.* There are also new members: *DCBlength, fDsrSensitivity, fTXContinueOnXoff,* and *fAbortOnError.* Overall, the amount of information is greater than before. The member definitions of the Windows 95 DCB are shown below:

DCBlength	Specifies the size, in bytes, of the DCB structure.
BaudRate	Specifies the current baud rate.
fBinary	Specifies whether binary mode is enabled. In Windows 3.1, FALSE means that nonbinary mode is enabled, and the character specified by *EofChar* is recognized on input as the end of data. This member must be TRUE in Windows 95.
fParity	Specifies whether parity checking is enabled.
fOutxCtsFlow	Specifies whether CTS is monitored for transmission flow control. When this member is TRUE and CTS is OFF, transmission is suspended until CTS is turned ON.

fOutxDsrFlow	Specifies whether DSR is monitored for transmission flow control. When this member is TRUE and DSR is OFF, transmission is suspended until DSR is turned ON.
fDtrControl	A value of DTR_CONTROL_DISABLE turns DTR OFF. A value of DTR_CONTROL_ENABLE turns DTR ON, and a value of DTR_CONTROL_HANDSHAKE enables DTR handshaking. (See the explanation of DTR handshaking later in this section.)
fDsrSensitivity	When this member is TRUE, bytes received while DSR is OFF are ignored.
fTXContinueOnXoff	Specifies whether transmission stops when the receive buffer is full and the driver has transmitted the *XoffChar* character. When this member is TRUE, transmission continues after the receive buffer has come within *XoffLim* bytes of being full and the driver has transmitted the *XoffChar* character to stop receiving bytes. When this member is FALSE, transmission continues when the receive buffer is within *XonLim* bytes of being empty and the driver has transmitted the *XonChar* character to resume reception.
fOutX	When this member is TRUE, transmission stops when the *XoffChar* character is received and starts again when the *XonChar* character is received.
fInX	When this member is TRUE, the *XoffChar* is sent when the receive buffer comes within *XoffLim* bytes of being full, and the *XonChar* character is sent when the receive buffer comes within *XonLim* bytes of being empty.
fErrorChar	When this member is TRUE and *fParity* is TRUE, bytes received with parity errors are replaced with the character specified by the *ErrorChar* member.
fNull	When this member is TRUE, null (zero valued) bytes are discarded when received.
fRtsControl	RTS is turned OFF when this value is set to RTS_CONTROL_DISABLE. RTS is turned ON when this value is RTS_CONTROL_ENABLE. A value of RTS_CONTROL_HANDSHAKE tells the port driver to turn RTS ON when the receive buffer is less than half full and to turn RTS OFF when the receive buffer is more than three-quarters full. A value of RTS_CONTROL_TOGGLE turns RTS ON when there are bytes remaining in the receive buffer and turns the default RTS OFF otherwise. A value of 0 is

	equivalent to RTS_CONTROL_HANDSHAKE. (See the explanation of RTS handshaking later in this section.)
fAbortOnError	When this member is TRUE, read and write operations terminate when an error occurs.
fDummy2	Not used.
wReserved	Not used; must be 0.
XonLim	Specifies the minimum number of bytes allowed in the receive buffer before the XON character is sent.
XoffLim	Specifies the minimum number of available bytes allowed in the receive buffer before the XOFF character is sent.
ByteSize	Specifies the number of data bits currently used by the port.
Parity	Specifies the parity method currently used by the port. The possible values are EVENPARITY, MARKPARITY, NOPARITY, and ODDPARITY.
StopBits	Specifies the number of stop bits currently used by the port. The possible values are ONESTOPBIT, ONE5STOPBITS, and TWOSTOPBITS.
XonChar, XoffChar	Specifies the value of the XON and XOFF characters to use for both transmitting and receiving.
ErrorChar	This character value replaces characters received with a parity error.
EofChar	This character signals the end of data when binary mode is not used.
EvtChar	An event is generated when this character is received.
wReserved1	Do not use.

Changing Port Settings

To read the DCB settings for the current port, you call *GetCommState*. This function accepts a handle to the open port and a pointer to a DCB structure where the information is returned. The complement of *GetCommState* is *SetCommState*, which also requires a port handle and pointer to a DCB. *SetCommState* writes the contents of the DCB structure to the port settings. The two function calls are shown below.

```
BOOL GetCommState(hComm, &dcb);
BOOL SetCommState(hComm, &dcb);
```

Changing the port settings isn't as simple as reading with *GetCommState*, changing select settings, and then writing the settings back with *SetCommState*.

One additional step is required: comparing the new settings with the allowable settings for the port. You'll recall that the allowable settings are in the COMMPROP structure. If the new settings are supported, they are placed into the DCB and written with *SetCommState*. The following example changes the baud rate to 19.2 Kbps.

```
GetCommProperties(hComm, &commprop);
GetCommState(hComm, &dcb);
/* if 19.2 Kbps is supported, make setting, otherwise no change */
if (commprop.dwSettableBaud & BAUD_19200)
    dcb.dwBaudRate = 19200;
SetCommState(hComm, &dcb);
```

Handshaking and Flow Control

Most of the members of the DCB structure are easy to understand, but the members that specify handshaking and flow control can be confusing. Let's start with the *fDtrControl* member, which is used to turn DTR ON or OFF or to specify DTR handshaking. When the port is used with a modem, turning DTR ON tells the modem that the port is ready to receive bytes. DTR acts as an enable signal so that when DTR is turned OFF the modem stops sending bytes to the port. The port driver thus turns DTR OFF when the receive buffer gets close to full, suspending reception until the receive buffer is serviced. For example, if port1 is connected to port2 using a NULL modem cable, DTR at port1 is usually connected to DSR at port2, and vice versa. When port1 turns DTR ON, DSR is turned ON at port2, telling port2 that port1 is ready to receive bytes. Port2 can then transmit bytes to port1 until port1 turns DTR OFF. *fDtrControl* can be used with *fOutxDsrFlow* to control the transmission and reception of bytes to and from a port. Figure 3-1 illustrates the transmission flow of the above process that can result from the following code:

```
fOutxDsrFlow = TRUE;
fDtrControl = DTR_CONTROL_HANDSHAKE;
```

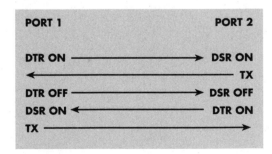

Figure 3-1. *Transmission flow between two ports.*

If DTR handshaking is used, *fDsrSensitivity* should be set to TRUE. This way, bytes received when DSR is OFF are ignored.

Many members of the DCB structure relate to XON/XOFF flow control. This flow control uses special *embedded signals* to control the transmission and reception of bytes between two ports. Embedded signals are special characters used *within the data stream* to tell the port when to transmit and receive. For example, when the receive buffer is full, you can send ASCII character 19 to tell the remote port to stop sending bytes. A special character with this purpose is called XOFF. When there is once again room in the receive buffer, you can send ASCII 17 to tell the remote port to resume transmitting bytes. A special character with this purpose is called XON. The XOFF and XON characters are specified by *XoffChar* and *XonChar*.

You can set the member *fOutX* to TRUE to tell the port driver to suspend transmission of bytes when the remote port sends XOFF. Transmission resumes when the remote port sends XON. Or you can set member *fInX* to TRUE to tell the port driver to send XOFF to the remote port when the number of bytes in the receive buffer exceeds a certain threshold. This threshold is specified by *XoffLim*. *XoffLim* does not actually specify the maximum number of bytes allowed in the receive buffer before XOFF is sent. Rather, it specifies the minimum number of *available* bytes permitted to remain unfilled in the receive buffer before XOFF is sent. The maximum number of bytes permitted in the receive buffer is computed by subtracting *XoffLim* from the total buffer size (*buffsize*). *XoffLim*, sometimes called the *high-water mark*, is the threshold that triggers a shutoff of data transfer while the receive buffer is read down. Setting *fInX* to TRUE also tells the port driver to send XON to resume transmission once the number of bytes in the receive buffer falls below a certain threshhold, specified in *XonLim*. *XonLim* is sometimes called the *low-water mark*.

When *fInX* is TRUE, XOFF is sent when the number of bytes in the receive buffer exceeds the high-water mark defined by *XoffLim*, as shown in Figure 3-2.

RECEIVE BUFFER

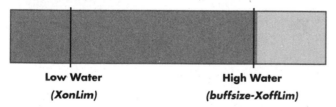

Low Water

(XonLim)

High Water

(buffsize-XoffLim)

Figure 3-2. *The receive buffer filled above the high-water mark.*

XON is sent when the number of bytes in the receive buffer falls below the threshold value specified by *XonLim,* as shown in Figure 3-3.

RECEIVE BUFFER

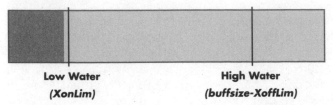

Low Water	High Water
(XonLim)	(buffsize-XoffLim)

Figure 3-3. *The receive buffer read down below the low-water mark.*

When the member *fTXContinueOnXoff* is set to TRUE, transmission is not affected by the above operations. In other words, transmission continues even after XOFF has been received. When *fTXContinueOnXoff* is set to FALSE, transmission is suspended and resumed in sync with reception.

The final type of handshaking that can be specified in the DCB is RTS/CTS handshaking. This is the "classic" hardware flow control of RS-232 serial communications. Using the member *fRtsControl,* RTS can be turned ON (RTS_CONTROL_ENABLE) or OFF (RTS_CONTROL_DISABLE), or RTS handshaking can be enabled (RTS_CONTROL_HANDSHAKE). With RTS handshaking enabled, a port turns RTS ON to tell the remote port or the attached modem that it is ready to receive bytes. The port turns RTS OFF when the receive buffer is full, to tell the remote port or attached modem to stop sending bytes. The remote port or the attached modem turns CTS ON to indicate that it is ready to receive bytes. When CTS is OFF, the remote port or the attached modem is not prepared to receive bytes, so the port does not transmit until CTS is turned ON. With RTS/CTS handshaking, the member *fOutxCtsFlow* is set to TRUE to tell the port not to transmit any bytes when CTS is OFF.

Changing Common Settings

The most commonly changed settings in the DCB are baud rate, parity method, and number of data and stop bits. A convenient function for changing these settings is *BuildCommDCB:*

```
BuildCommDCB(szSettings, &DCB);
```

The parameters of *BuildCommDCB* are a string containing the new settings and a pointer to a DCB structure into which the settings are applied. You might wonder why a string is used to pass the settings to the DCB structure; the answer is that a string is both convenient and familiar. The string has the same format as the Mode command string in MS-DOS or Microsoft Windows NT, as in the following example:

```
"baud=12 parity=N data=8 stop=1"
```

This string changes the baud rate to 1200 bps, turns off parity checking, sets the number of data bits to 8 and the number of stop bits to 1. Do not include the serial port name in the string as you would in MS-DOS or Windows NT—the function does not actually change the settings of the port, so the port need not be identified. Instead, the new settings are simply copied into the supplied DCB structure. To make the new settings active, use *SetCommState*. Notice that the *Retry* parameter of the Mode command has no meaning in Windows 95 and should be omitted from the string. Note also that you can omit the parameter identifiers from the string, passing the settings by their position in the string. The above example can thus be shortened to the following:

"12,N,8,1"

Figure 3-4 shows the valid values for each parameter in the control string passed to *BuildCommDCB*.

You should check COMMPROP to ensure that the serial port supports a setting before you attempt to change it with *BuildCommDCB* and *SetCommState*. As you can see from the table, the short form of the baud rate settings (11, 15, 30. . .) are limited to those available to the DOS Mode command. To specify baud rates above 19200 bps, you must use the long form. For example, to specify a baud rate of 38400 bps, use *baud=38400,* not *baud=38*. If *Build-CommDCB* does not recognize the baud rate specified as one of the short forms, it copies the literal value into the baud rate field of the DCB. *Baud=38* results in a baud setting of 38 bps. Now *that* will test your patience!

Baud (short form options)	Parity (case-insensitive)	Data Bits	Stop Bits
11 or 110 = 110 bps	n = none	5	1
15 or 150 = 150 bps	e = even	6	1.5
30 or 300 = 300 bps	o = odd	7	2
60 or 600 = 600 bps	m = mark	8	
12 or 1200 = 1200 bps	s = space		
24 or 2400 = 2400 bps			
48 or 4800 = 4800 bps			
96 or 9600 = 9600 bps			
19 or 19200 = 19200 bps			

Figure 3-4. *The valid values for each parameter in the control string passed to* BuildCommDCB.

The COMMCONFIG Structure

Another configuration structure worth mentioning briefly is COMMCONFIG. COMMCONFIG contains a DCB structure that is identical in all respects to the one returned by *GetCommState*. COMMCONFIG is also important when the port is attached to a modem. The structure is shown below.

```
typedef struct _COMMCONFIG {
    DWORD dwSize;                /* Size of the entire structure */
    WORD  wVersion;             /* version of the structure */
    WORD  wReserved;            /* alignment */
    DCB   dcb;                  /* device control block */
    DWORD dwProviderSubType;    /* ordinal value for identifying
                                   provider-defined data structure
                                   format*/
    DWORD dwProviderOffset;     /* Specifies the offset of provider
                                   specific data field in bytes from
                                   the start */
    DWORD dwProviderSize;       /* size of the provider-specific
                                   data field */
    WCHAR wcProviderData[1];    /* provider-specific data */
} COMMCONFIG, *LPCOMMCONFIG;
```

COMMCONFIG comes with a handy function for configuring the port, called *CommConfigDialog*. This function displays a dialog box for changing the baud rate, data bits, parity method, stop bits, and flow control method for the port. It also contains a button for restoring the default settings. The dialog box is shown in Figure 3-5.

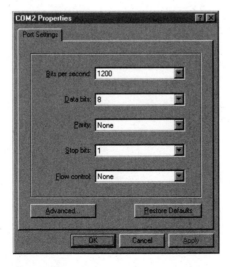

Figure 3-5. *The Properties dialog box for configuring a port.*

The settings selected are returned in the *dcb* member of COMMCONFIG when the function returns. A typical call to *CommConfigDialog* is shown below.

```
CommConfigDialog (lpszComName, hWnd, &cc)
```

The first parameter is the name of the port to configure, the second is the handle to the window that will own the dialog box, and the third points to the COMMCONFIG structure. *CommConfigDialog* does not actually change the settings of the port. (The handle to the open port is not passed as a parameter.) The following code shows how to change the port settings with a subsequent call to *SetCommState*. The example does not show the part where the settings returned in COMMCONFIG are checked against the supported settings in COMMPROP, but you should include this in your code.

```
COMMCONFIG cc;
#define WINDOWS95_COMMCONFIG_VERSION          0x100
⋮
cc.dwSize = sizeof(COMMCONFIG);
cc.wVersion = WINDOWS95_COMMCONFIG_VERSION;
if (!CommConfigDialog ("COM2", hWnd, &cc))     /* function returns
                                                  FALSE if error */
     break;
⋮
/* NOT SHOWN - check returned settings against COMMPROP settings to
make sure they are supported */
⋮
dcb.BaudRate = cc.dcb.BaudRate;
dcb.BaudRate = cc.dcb.ByteSize;
dcb.BaudRate = cc.dcb.StopBits;
dcb.BaudRate = cc.dcb.Parity;
SetCommState (hComm, &dcb);
```

Timeout Settings

A major concern facing any developer of a communications application is how to handle unexpected events that occur while reading or writing data. What if the connection drops in the middle of receiving bytes, or if the other side simply stops transmitting? What happens when bytes are transmitted and a handshake is expected, but it never comes? Unless you are careful, these circumstances can hang the I/O thread (or at least block its execution indefinitely). Fortunately, Windows 95 provides a safeguard against this type of problem. It lets you specify how long a read or write function waits before giving up. You do this through timeout settings, using the COMMTIMEOUTS structure, shown on the next page.

```
typedef struct _COMMTIMEOUTS {
    DWORD ReadIntervalTimeout;            /* maximum time between read
                                             chars */
    DWORD ReadTotalTimeoutMultiplier;  /* multiplier of chars */
    DWORD ReadTotalTimeoutConstant;    /* constant in milliseconds */
    DWORD WriteTotalTimeoutMultiplier; /* multiplier of chars */
    DWORD WriteTotalTimeoutConstant;   /* constant in milliseconds */
} COMMTIMEOUTS, *LPCOMMTIMEOUTS;
```

There are two types of timeouts. The first type, called an *interval timeout,* applies only to reading from the port. It specifies how much time can elapse between the reading of two characters. Windows starts an internal timer each time a character is received. If the timer exceeds the interval timeout before the next character arrives, the read function gives up. The second type of timeout, the *total timeout,* applies to both reads and writes from the port. This timeout is triggered when the total time required to read or write a specific number of bytes exceeds a threshold. For example, if the total timeout is set at 10 ms (milliseconds), and an application tries to read 10 bytes from the port, the total timeout is triggered if it takes more than 10 ms to read all 10 bytes. It doesn't matter if 9 of the 10 bytes have been read by the time 10 ms is up. The timeout is still triggered, and the read function returns only 9 bytes.

Timeout Equations

Timeout values are specified in milliseconds. The interval timeout applies only to reads from the port and is specified in the *ReadIntervalTimeout* member. Total timeouts are specified independently for reads and writes, and they are specified in two parts, using a constant and a multiplier. Windows computes the total timeouts for reading and writing from the constant and the multiplier using the following formulas:

```
ReadTotalTimeout = (ReadTotalTimeoutMultiplier * bytes_to_read) +
                   ReadTotalTimeoutConstant;
WriteTotalTimeout = (WriteTotalTimeoutMultiplier * bytes_to_write) +
                    WriteTotalTimeoutConstant;
```

This equation makes the total timeout a flexible tool. Instead of a fixed value, the total timeout "floats" according to the number of bytes to read or write. As a starting point, consider only the writing of bytes. When *WriteTotalTimeoutConstant* is set to 0, the formula for the total write timeout reduces to the following:

```
WriteTotalTimeout = WriteTotalTimeoutMultiplier * bytes_to_write;
```

The result is that if the *average* value of the time to write each byte exceeds *WriteTotalTimeoutMultiplier/bytes_to_write,* the timeout is triggered. This is a great way to specify a mean performance requirement when transmitting bytes.

Now consider what happens when *WriteTotalTimeoutConstant* is added to the formula. The total timeout is still directly related to the mean performance of the write function, but now the mean performance has an *upper threshold* defined by the constant. For example, consider what happens when there is only one byte to write. The formula for *WriteTotalTimeout* reduces to the following:

```
WriteTotalTimeout = WriteTotalTimeoutMultiplier +
                    WriteTotalTimeoutConstant;
```

If the constant is much greater than the multiplier, the total timeout approaches the constant value as the number of bytes to write decreases. This formula takes into account the greater inefficiencies of writing fewer bytes while still retaining mean performance characteristics for larger numbers of bytes.

Finally, the *WriteTotalTimeoutMultiplier* can be 0. In this case, the total timeout is specified by the constant. This might be useful in situations in which the write must complete within a fixed time regardless of the number of bytes involved.

If you don't want to use timeouts at all, set all members of the COMMTIMEOUTS structure to 0. This is risky, however, because if you don't use timeouts, a read or write function will not complete until all of the requested bytes are read or written. If any problems occur that prevent the transfer from completing, the read or write function will simply remain pending. The result this will have on applications will vary, but chances are it won't be a result you want.

You can also use your application's read function to check for bytes waiting in the receive queue. If no bytes are waiting, your read function returns immediately and the thread continues executing. The trick is to set *ReadInterval-Timeout* to MAXDWORD, and to set the read timeout multiplier and constant to 0.

Now for some examples. First we want to set the timeout for writing bytes, such that the mean time allowed for writing any one byte is approximately 5 ms. We also want to set a threshold so that the total timeout for a write never falls below 50 ms. The following settings achieve this result:

```
WriteTotalTimeoutMultiplier=5;
WriteTotalTimeoutConstant = 50;
```

Suppose we want to read incoming bytes in a loop. If it takes longer than 5 ms to read consecutive bytes, we want the read function to return so that the thread can continue execution. The settings are as follows:

```
ReadIntervalTimeout = 5;
```

To force the read function to return immediately when no bytes are waiting in the receive queue, use the following:

```
ReadIntervalTimeout = MAXDWORD;
```

Do not use:

```
ReadIntervalTimeout = 0;
```

It seems counterintuitive that the largest possible setting (MAXDWORD) for the timeout interval causes the function to return most quickly, while a value of 0 causes the function to wait indefinitely. But that's how it works.

Implementing Timeout Settings

Once you decide on the timeout settings, call *SetCommTimeouts* to implement them. *SetCommTimeouts* takes a handle to the open port and a pointer to the COMMTIMEOUTS structure that contains the settings. To change only some settings and leave the others unchanged, first call *GetCommTimeouts* to fill the COMMTIMEOUTS structure with the current settings. Change the particular settings, and then call *SetCommTimeouts* to implement them, as shown below.

```
GetCommTimeouts (hComm, &timeouts);
timeouts.ReadIntervalTimeout = 5
SetCommTimeouts (hComm, &timeouts);
```

Remember *BuildCommDCB,* that convenient function for changing the settings in the DCB structure? Well, Windows 95 has a function that not only fills up your DCB but also fills up your COMMTIMEOUTS. This function, shown below, is called *BuildCommDCBAndTimeouts*. The string that is passed in the first parameter to the function includes all the values for setting the DCB fields, plus more for setting the COMMTIMEOUTS members.

```
BuildCommDCBAndTimeouts(lpszString, &dcb, &timeouts);
```

Always check the *dwProvCapabilities* member of COMMPROP to ensure that timeouts are supported before you try to set them. The flag PCF_INTTIMEOUTS is set when read interval timeouts are supported. The flag PCF_TOTALTIMEOUTS is set if total timeouts for both read and write are supported.

Reading and Writing Data

In Windows 95, reading and writing to a port are accomplished using the same functions as for reading and writing to files. There are as many techniques for reading and writing to a port as for reading and writing to files. We will examine four methods here: polling, synchronous I/O, asynchronous (background) I/O, and event-driven I/O.

Polling

Polling is the most straightforward technique for reading from a port. A thread continually polls (attempts to read from) the port. If bytes are present in the port's receive buffer, they are read. Otherwise, the thread continues. Polling takes up a lot of CPU time because the thread is always executing, looking for bytes—even when there aren't any. The advantage of polling is that it is straightforward and simple to understand. The following code, which is included in the sample application in \Chapter3\Ex3-1, shows how to poll bytes from the port.

```
COMMTIMEOUTS to;
    ⋮
DWORD ReadThread (LPDWORD lpdwParam1)
{
BYTE inbuff[100];
DWORD nBytesRead;
    /* The next two lines check to make sure that interval
    timeouts are supported by the port */
    if (!(cp.dwProvCapabilities & PCF_INTTIMEOUTS))
        return 1L;  /* error;  can't set interval timeouts */
    /* the next three lines tell the read function to return
    immediately when no bytes are waiting in the
    port's receive queue */
    memset (&to, 0, sizeof(to));
    to.ReadIntervalTimeout = MAXDWORD;
    SetCommTimeouts (hComm, &to);

    /* this loop polls the port reading bytes until the
    control variable bReading is set to FALSE by the
    controlling process */
    while (bReading) {
        /* poll the port and read bytes if available */
        if (!ReadFile(hComm, inbuff, 100, &nBytesRead, NULL)) {
            /* handle error */
            locProcessCommError(GetLastError ());
        } /* end if (error reading bytes) */
        else {
            /* if there were bytes waiting,
            display them in a TTY window */
            if (nBytesRead)
                locProcessBytes(inbuff, nBytesRead);
        }
    } /* end while (thread active) */

    /* clean out any pending bytes in the receive buffer */
    PurgeComm(hComm, PURGE_RXCLEAR);

    return 0L;
} /* end function (ReadThread) */
```

The polling code has some familiar parts and some unfamiliar parts. First the familiar parts. The code configures the timeouts of the port so that the read function returns immediately when no bytes are in the receive buffer. It does this by setting the read interval timeout to the magic value MAXDWORD. Notice how the code checks COMMPROP with the line *if (!(cp.dwProvCapabilities & PCF_INTIMEOUTS))* to make sure that interval timeouts are supported before attempting to set them.

Now the unfamiliar part. A loop is used to read from the port by continuously calling the function *ReadFile,* as shown below. As the name suggests, *ReadFile* is used to read from files. But it is also used to read from ports.

```
ReadFile (hComm,  inbuff, nBytes, &nBytesRead, &overlapped)
```

The first parameter of *ReadFile* is the handle to the open port. The second parameter is the buffer where the bytes will be returned. Be sure to allocate enough space for all the bytes you want to read. The third parameter is the number of bytes to read, and the fourth parameter is the number actually read. There are many reasons why the number of bytes read might be less than the number requested. An error might occur before all of the bytes are read, for example, or the timeout interval might expire before all of the bytes are read. Never assume that all the bytes have been read; always check *nBytesRead* for the actual number. The last parameter points to an overlapped structure. (We'll get to that structure later on.) The example reads the number of bytes available in the receive queue, up to a maximum of 100.

If an error occurs, it is processed by *locProcessCommError.* Functions with the *loc* prefix are local (to the application), as distinguished from the Windows 95 library functions. When *ReadFile* returns successfully, if *nBytesRead* is nonzero the bytes are processed using the local function *locProcessBytes.* In the examples on the companion disk, the bytes are displayed only in the client area of the window. The loop calls *ReadFile* again for as long as the control variable *bReading* is TRUE. *bReading* is set by the controlling thread. When the controlling thread no longer wants to read bytes, it sets *bReading* to FALSE, and the loop ends.

When the read loop ends, the thread calls the function *PurgeComm* as a final step before terminating. *PurgeComm* is a clean-up function. It can terminate any pending background reads or writes, and it can also flush the I/O buffers. The code uses *PurgeComm,* as shown below, to flush the input buffer of any unread bytes by specifying the action as PURGE_RXCLEAR.

```
PurgeComm (hComm, PURGE_RXCLEAR);
```

Other possible values for the action are PURGE_TXABORT, which terminates all background writes; PURGE_RXABORT, which terminates any background reads; and PURGE_TXCLEAR, which flushes the transmit buffer. If you want to exit without flushing (an inconsiderate habit) after writing to the port, call *FlushFileBuffers*. This function waits until all data in the transmit buffer has been sent before it returns.

One disadvantage of the polling technique is that it always tries to read exactly *nBytes* bytes (100 in our example) every time *ReadFile* is called. This is inefficient because there might be times when more than 100 bytes are available, in which case *ReadFile* must be called multiple times to read all of the bytes. A better technique checks the number of bytes available in the receive buffer and reads exactly that number—no more, no less. But how do you determine the number of bytes in the receive buffer?

You call the *ClearCommError* function, as shown below, to determine the number of bytes waiting in the port's receive buffer. The name of this function is something of a misnomer, because the function has a dual purpose. Its first purpose is, as the name suggests, to clear away error conditions. Its second purpose is to determine the status of the port. We are most interested in the latter purpose right now.

```
ClearCommError(hComm, &dwErrorMask, &comstat)
```

The first parameter of *ClearCommError* is the handle to the open port. The second parameter points to a mask of possible error conditions that are returned by the function. (These error conditions are covered in detail in the section titled "Errors" later in this chapter). The last parameter is the one we care about; it points to a COMSTAT structure that holds useful information about the status of the port. The structure is shown below.

```
typedef struct _COMSTAT {
    DWORD fCtsHold : 1;          /* Tx waiting for CTS signal */
    DWORD fDsrHold : 1;          /* Tx waiting for DSR signal */
    DWORD fRlsdHold : 1;         /* Tx waiting for RLSD signal */
    DWORD fXoffHold : 1;         /* Tx waiting, XOFF char received */
    DWORD fXoffSent : 1;         /* Tx waiting, XOFF char sent */
    DWORD fEof : 1;              /* EOF character sent */
    DWORD fTxim : 1;             /* character waiting for Tx */
    DWORD fReserved : 25;        /* reserved */
    DWORD cbInQue;               /* bytes in input buffer */
    DWORD cbOutQue;              /* bytes in output buffer */
} COMSTAT, *LPCOMSTAT;
```

The first five members of COMSTAT provide information about the cause of a transmission stall. Bad things can happen to applications, and these members tell you why the bytes in the transmit buffer aren't moving. Depending on the type of handshaking involved, transmission can stall when CTS is OFF, DSR is OFF, or RLSD is OFF. The members that indicate these conditions are, respectively, *fCtsHold, fDsrHold,* and *fRlsdHold.* If XON/XOFF flow control is used, *fXoffHold* and *fXoffSent* indicate if transmission is waiting because XOFF was received or because XOFF was sent. The latter case only occurs when *fTXContinueOnXoff* is FALSE in the DCB structure.

As an example, suppose the port is configured for RTS/CTS hardware flow control. It will not transmit bytes until CTS is turned ON. A problem occurs, and the bytes in the transmit buffer just sit there, not moving out as they are supposed to. How can you tell? By calling *ClearCommError* and checking the *cbOutQueue* member, which contains the number of bytes waiting in the transmit buffer. If this number remains unchanged for a long period of time (a fraction of a second or so), transmission has stalled. The application then checks *fCtsHold* to see if the port is waiting for CTS to be turned ON. If *fCtsHold* is set to TRUE, the remote port (or attached modem) has not turned CTS ON.

Other members of COMSTAT include *fEof,* which is set to TRUE if the end-of-file character was received (in non-binary mode), and *fTxim,* which specifies whether data is waiting in the transmit buffer. Finally, there is *cbInQue,* which specifies the number of bytes in the receive buffer that are waiting to be read.

Synchronous I/O

Now that you've seen an example of using polling to read from a port, let's look at a similar example using synchronous processing. The following code is included in the sample application in \Chapter3\Ex3-2.

```
COMMTIMEOUTS to;
   :
DWORD ReadThread (LPDWORD lpdwParam1)
{
BYTE inbuff[100];
DWORD nBytesRead, dwErrorMask, nToRead;
COMSTAT comstat;

    /* the next two lines check to make sure that total timeouts
    are supported */
    if (!cp.dwProvCapabilities & PCF_TOTALTIMEOUTS)
        return 1L;

    /* the next four lines set the total timeout interval */
    memset (&to, 0, sizeof(to));
    to.ReadTotalTimeoutMultiplier = 5;
    to.ReadTotalTimeoutConstant = 50;
    SetCommTimeouts (hComm, &to);

    while (bReading) {
        ClearCommError (hComm, &dwErrorMask, &comstat);
        /* check if there was an error */
```

```
    if (dwErrorMask) {        /* handle error */
        locProcessCommError(dwErrorMask);
    } /* end if (error) */
    /* if too many bytes to read, just read the maximum */
    if (comstat.cbInQue > 100)
        nToRead = 100; /* maximum that inbuff can hold */
    else
        nToRead = comstat.cbInQue; /* otherwise read them all */

    /* if no bytes to read, continue */
    if (nToRead == 0)
        continue;

/* read the bytes */
    if (!ReadFile(hComm, inbuff,
            nToRead, &nBytesRead, NULL)) {
        locProcessCommError(GetLastError ());
    } /* end if (error reading bytes) */
    else {
        if (nBytesRead)
            locProcessBytes(inbuff, nBytesRead);
    }
} /* end while (thread active) */

    return 0L;
} /* end function (ReadThread) */
```

This second example looks a lot like the first one, but there are significant differences. First of all, the timeouts are set differently. The interval timeout is set to 0, but the total timeout is specified. As a result of this apparently minor change, the *ReadFile* function becomes *synchronous*—that is, when *ReadFile* is called, it does not return until either the number of bytes specified are read or the total timeout interval expires. For example, if *ReadFile* is called to read 1000 bytes but only 100 bytes are in the receive buffer, *ReadFile* does not return control to the calling thread until the 1000 bytes are read or until 5050 milliseconds (50+5*1000) have expired. As you can see, the potential exists for blocking the execution of the calling thread for long intervals of time (5 seconds in this case).

Blocking the thread can create problems. Other parts of the program that depend on the received bytes sit idle while the thread waits for *ReadFile* to return. To avoid this problem, the code checks the *cbInQue* member of COMSTAT to determine the exact number of bytes waiting in the receive buffer. The code reads exactly this number with *ReadFile,* up to the maximum allowed in the buffer (100), so the function returns immediately with the bytes. If no bytes are waiting, the code does not call *ReadFile* because there is nothing for it to do. You might wonder why you should bother to set the timeouts at all; after all, the code knows how many bytes are available before calling *ReadFile,* so it will never time out. You should set timeouts because it's good programming practice to do so, and because you can never be 100 percent confident that unanticipated situations will not cause *ReadFile* to hang the thread.

Asynchronous I/O

Asynchronous (background) I/O is another tool for reading and writing from a port. Using asynchronous I/O, an application can read (or write) data in the background while doing something else in the foreground. An application can, for example, initiate a read of 1000 bytes and then continue execution. When the 1000 bytes are read, Windows generates a signal that the application can alert itself to. This can be useful in situations in which a thread does not want to spend a lot of time polling the port. It can also be very useful when the thread needs to write (transmit) large chunks of bytes but needs to continue execution while the write proceeds in the background. The latter situation is probably the more common application of asynchronous I/O.

Asynchronous I/O requires revisiting an earlier topic, namely *CreateFile*. Remember that *CreateFile* has a parameter called *fdwAttrsAndFlags*. When this parameter is set to FILE_FLAG_OVERLAPPED, the port is opened for asynchronous I/O. When the port is opened this way, an OVERLAPPED structure can be specified in the last parameter of *ReadFile* to make the reading of bytes occur in the background. Windows 95 includes many variations of asynchronous I/O. We discuss only one of them here, but you can find the other variations in the Microsoft Win32 SDK or Microsoft Developer Network (MSDN) documentation. The OVERLAPPED structure is shown below.

```
typedef struct _OVERLAPPED {
    DWORD Internal;
    DWORD InternalHigh;
    DWORD Offset;
    DWORD OffsetHigh;
    HANDLE hEvent;
} OVERLAPPED;
```

None of the first four members of the OVERLAPPED structure is used with ports. The first two members are reserved for use by Windows. The next two members are used to specify a beginning point in a file from which to begin reading or writing data. These members must be 0 when dealing with ports. The last member, *hEvent,* specifies a manual-reset event that Windows signals when the asynchronous I/O completes. The manual-reset event is created and initialized to the nonsignaled state, and the handle to this event is placed in *hEvent*. In the following example, the other members are implicitly set to 0 by declaring OVERLAPPED as a static variable. This example is included in the sample application in \Chapter3\Ex3-3.

```
COMMTIMEOUTS to;
⋮
DWORD ReadThread (LPDWORD lpdwParam1)
{
BYTE inbuff[100];
DWORD nBytesRead, endtime, lrc;
static OVERLAPPED o;

    /* the next two lines check to make sure that total timeouts
    are supported */
    if (!cp.dwProvCapabilities & PCF_TOTALTIMEOUTS)
        return 1L;

    /* the next four lines set the total timeout interval */
    memset (&to, 0, sizeof(to));
    to.ReadTotalTimeoutMultiplier = 5;
    to.ReadTotalTimeoutConstant = 1000;
    SetCommTimeouts (hComm, &to);

    /* create a manual-reset event */
    o.hEvent = CreateEvent (NULL,  /* lpsa */
                            TRUE,  /* manual reset */
                            FALSE, /* init state non sig */
                            NULL);

    /* read loop */
    while (bReading) {
        /* try to read 10 bytes */
        if (!ReadFile(hComm, inbuff, 10, &nBytesRead, &o)) {
            /* if there are not ten bytes waiting in read buffer,
            then ERROR_IO_PENDING is returned */
            /* if ReadFile failed, the number of returned bytes not
            valid, so zero out and wait to get correct number from
            GetOverlappedResult */
            nBytesRead = 0;
            if ((lrc=GetLastError()) == ERROR_IO_PENDING) {
                /* do additional processing */
                endtime = GetTickCount() + 1000;
                /* wait for overlapped I/O to complete */
                while (!GetOverlappedResult(hComm, &o, &nBytesRead,
                        FALSE)){
                    /* make sure timeout has not expired */
                    if (GetTickCount() > endtime) {
                        break;
                    }
```

(continued)

```
            } /* end while (I/O still pending) */

            /* if I/O retrieved some bytes, then process
            bytes */
            if (nBytesRead) {
                locProcessBytes(inbuff, nBytesRead);
            }
        } else {
            /* handle error */
            locProcessCommError(GetLastError ());
        }
    } /* end if (error reading bytes) */
    else {
        if (nBytesRead)
            locProcessBytes(inbuff, nBytesRead);
    }
    /* manually reset event */
    ResetEvent (o.hEvent);
} /* end while (reading bytes) */

/* clean out any pending bytes in the receive buffer */
PurgeComm(hComm, PURGE_RXCLEAR);

return 0L;

} /* end function (ReadThread) */
```

The call to *ReadFile* looks pretty much the same as before, except that the last parameter points to the OVERLAPPED structure. If *ReadFile* returns FALSE, the code checks the error code using *GetLastError*. An error value of ERROR_IO_PENDING from *GetLastError* indicates that asynchronous I/O was initiated successfully. Any other error is bad news and is treated as such by calling *locProcessCommError*. (Refer to the sample applications in the \Chapter 3 directory for a look at *locProcessCommError,* which simply logs the error and returns.)

After asynchronous I/O is initiated, the code falls into a loop in which additional foreground processing is performed. The loop is broken two ways. First, it is broken if the *GetOverlappedResult* function returns TRUE. *GetOverlappedResult* returns FALSE for as long as the asynchronous I/O is pending. When *GetOverlappedResult* returns TRUE, the I/O is complete and the contents of *inbuff* are processed. Note that when *ReadFile* returns, the value *nBytesRead* is not valid because the number of bytes read is undetermined until asynchronous I/O completes. *GetOverlappedResult* returns the number of bytes actually read, which will either be the number of bytes requested or less if an error or a timeout occurs. The loop is also broken if you exceed the timeout threshold. If the asynchronous I/O takes longer than 10 seconds to collect the 10 bytes, it's time to give up and try again.

Notice that the code handles the situation when *ReadFile* returns TRUE. This is because *ReadFile* might return TRUE even when asynchronous I/O is requested. If all 10 bytes are already in the receive buffer, the function does not have to wait for anything and returns the bytes immediately, as shown below.

```
while (bReading) {
    if (!ReadFile(hComm, inbuff, 10, &nBytesRead, &o)) {
        if ((lrc=GetLastError()) == ERROR_IO_PENDING) {
            if (GetOverlappedResult(hComm, &o, &nBytesRead,
                TRUE)) {
                if (nBytesRead)
                    locProcessBytes(inbuff, nBytesRead);
            } else {
                locProcessCommError(GetLastError ());
            }
        } else {
            /* handle error */
            locProcessCommError(GetLastError ());
        }
    } /* end if (error reading bytes) */
    else {
        if (nBytesRead)
            locProcessBytes(inbuff, nBytesRead);
    }
    /* reset event */
    ResetEvent (o.hEvent);
} /* end while (thread active) */
```

This example saves CPU cycles by telling *GetOverlappedResult* to wait for the I/O to complete before returning. Simply specify TRUE for the last parameter, and the function will not return until all of the bytes are received.

Writing Bytes

The techniques available for writing bytes are the same as the ones for reading bytes. The only real difference is that instead of calling *ReadFile* you call *WriteFile,* as shown below.

```
WriteFile (hComm, outBuff, nToWrite, &nActualWrite, &overlapped);
```

The first parameter is the handle to the open port. The second parameter points to the buffer where the data to be written is stored. The third parameter is the number of bytes to write, the fourth parameter points to the number actually written, and the fifth parameter points to an OVERLAPPED structure.

When transmitting large amounts of data, it is handy to have a means of suspending transmission without disturbing the contents of the transmit buffer. The *SetCommBreak* function serves this purpose—it immediately suspends transmission even if the transmit buffer is full of bytes. The contents of the transmit buffer are not affected by calling *SetCommBreak*. To resume normal transmission, call *ClearCommBreak*. You can use another function, *Transmit-CommChar*, to transmit a single character ahead of any data that's waiting in the transmit buffer. This is most useful for transmitting characters caused by keypresses that have the top priority. (For example, Ctrl-C could have the top priority.) All three of these functions can be called as shown here.

```
SetCommBreak (hComm)
ClearCommBreak (hComm)
TransmitCommChar (hComm, cChar)
```

Both reading and writing can also be driven by events, as demonstrated in the next section.

Event-driven I/O

Sometimes it is useful to know when certain conditions occur without having to check on the status of the port. For example, it would be nice if Windows could indicate when certain signals change state so that you can take appropriate action. Not surprisingly, there is a way to do this. Windows 95 can notify your application when certain conditions, known as *events,* occur.

The events that Windows 95 can report to an application are returned by the function *GetCommMask*. To add to or otherwise modify the list of events that Windows reports, use *SetCommMask*. Calls to these functions are shown below.

```
GetCommMask (hComm, &dwMask)
SetCommMask (hComm, dwMask)
```

The first parameter is the handle to the open port. The second parameter is a mask of one or more events to wait for. These events are described below.

EV_BREAK	A break was detected on input.
EV_CTS	The CTS (clear-to-send) signal changed state.
EV_DSR	The DSR (data-set-ready) signal changed state.
EV_ERR	A line-status error occurred. Line-status errors are CE_FRAME (framing error), CE_OVERRUN (receive buffer overrun), and CE_RXPARITY (parity error).
EV_RING	A ring was detected.
EV_RLSD	The RLSD (receive-line-signal-detect) signal changed state.
EV_RXCHAR	A character was received and placed in the input buffer.
EV_RXFLAG	The event character (the *EvtChar* member of the DCB structure) was received and placed in the input buffer.
EV_TXEMPTY	The last character in the output buffer was sent.

For example, to set up an event when CTS changes state, use the following:

```
SetCommMask (hComm, EV_CTS);
```

After the events of interest are specified with *SetCommMask,* an application waits for an event to occur by calling *WaitCommEvent,* as shown below.

```
WaitCommEvent (hComm, &dwEvent, &overlapped)
```

WaitCommEvent, like *ReadFile* and *WriteFile,* can operate synchronously or asynchronously depending on whether the OVERLAPPED structure is specified in the third parameter. When a NULL pointer is specified instead, the function becomes synchronous and does not return until one of the events specified in *SetCommMask* occurs. *WaitCommEvent* then returns the event in *dwEvent.*

The following example shows how to use events to read from the port. This can be useful when the bytes are received infrequently or erratically. By using events, an application does not need to constantly monitor the port for received bytes, consuming valuable CPU time. Instead, the thread enters a wait state, consuming very few CPU cycles, until *WaitCommEvent* returns. The following example is included in the sample application in \Chapter3\Ex3-4.

```
COMMTIMEOUTS to;
  ⋮
DWORD ReadThread (LPDWORD lpdwParam1)
{
BYTE inbuff[100];
DWORD nBytesRead, dwEvent, dwError;
COMSTAT cs;

    /* generate event whenever a byte arrives */
    SetCommMask (hComm, EV_RXCHAR);

    /* read a byte whenever one is received */
    while (bReading) {
        /* wait for event */
        if (WaitCommEvent (hComm, &dwEvent, NULL)){
            /* read all available bytes */
            ClearCommError (hComm, &dwError, &cs);
            if ((dwEvent & EV_RXCHAR) && cs.cbInQue) {
                if (!ReadFile(hComm, inbuff, cs.cbInQue,
                            &nBytesRead, NULL)){
                    /* handle error */
                    locProcessCommError(GetLastError ());
                } /* end if (error reading bytes) */
```

(continued)

```
                else {
                    if (nBytesRead)
                        locProcessBytes(inbuff, nBytesRead);
                }
            }
        } else {
            locProcessCommError (GetLastError());
        }
    } /* end while (reading bytes in loop) */
    /* clean out any pending bytes in the receive buffer */
    PurgeComm(hComm, PURGE_RXCLEAR);
    return 0L;
} /* end function (ReadThread) */
```

The code tells Windows to generate an event whenever a byte is received, by calling *SetCommMask* with the event EV_RXCHAR.

After *WaitCommEvent* returns, the code checks that the received event was EV_RXCHAR. It does this by comparing the event mask returned by *Wait-CommEvent* with EV_RXCHAR. If EV_RXCHAR was received, at least one byte is waiting in the receive buffer. The code determines the number of received bytes by calling *ClearCommError* with the COMSTAT structure.

What if the event never comes? Does *WaitCommEvent* wait forever? It is not subject to the timeout values set for *ReadFile* and *WriteFile,* so what can you do to terminate the *WaitCommEvent?* Call *SetCommMask* a second time using a different event mask to change what *WaitCommEvent* is waiting for. For example, *SetCommMask (hComm, 0)* terminates *WaitCommEvent* immediately.

When events are generated for changes in the state of a signal, it is often helpful to know the new state. For example, if an event is generated when CTS changes state (EV_CTS), it is helpful to know whether CTS went from OFF to ON, or vice versa. The function *GetCommModemStatus* can help. *GetComm-ModemStatus* returns the status of CTS, DSR, RING, and RLSD. The example below shows how to detect when CTS is turned ON. Notice that the code first checks that the port supports CTS signaling before attempting to set the event.

```
if (cp.dwProvCapabilities & PCF_RTSCTS) {
    SetCommMask (hComm, EV_CTS);
    WaitCommEvent (hComm, &dwMask, NULL);
    if (dwMask & EV_CTS) {
        GetCommModemStatus(hComm, &dwStatus);
        if (dwStatus & MS_CTS_ON) {
            /* CTS transition OFF-ON */
        } else {
            /* CTS transition ON-OFF */
        }
    }
}
```

Shown below are the status values returned by *GetCommModemStatus*. Be sure to check COMMPROP to ensure that these signals are supported before attempting to read their status with *GetCommModemStatus*. Otherwise, you might get fooled into thinking that the status values mean something when actually they are not supported at all.

MS_CTS_ON	CTS is on
MS_DSR_ON	DSR is on
MS_RING_ON	RING is on
MS_RLSD_ON	RLSD is on

Errors

Communications is a complicated business, and errors can occur for a variety of reasons. When errors do occur, you should always call *ClearCommError* to determine precisely what went wrong. You can use *ClearCommError* to determine status information about the port or to obtain details about what can go wrong when sending or receiving bytes. The function is called as follows:

```
ClearCommError (hComm, &dwErrorMask, &comstat)
```

The second parameter contains a mask of errors that occurred. This mask can include one or more of the values shown below.

CE_BREAK	Break condition.
CE_FRAME	Framing error.
CE_IOE	General I/O error. This error will often be set in conjunction with a more detailed error flag.
CE_MODE	The requested mode is not supported, or the communication handle is invalid. If this value is specified, ignore all other error flags. Always check for this error first.
CE_OVERRUN	A buffer overrun has occurred. The next character is lost.
CE_RXOVER	A receive buffer overrun has occurred. There is either no room in the input buffer or a character was received after the end-of-file (EOF) character. The EOF character is the one specified in the DCB member *EofChar*, and it is only detected when not in binary mode (when the DCB *fBinary* flag is not set).
CE_RXPARITY	Parity error.
CE_TXFULL	The transmit buffer is full.
CE_DNS	The parallel device is not selected.
CE_PTO	A timeout occurred on a parallel device.
CE_OOP	The parallel device is out of paper.

If the *fAbortOnError* member of the DCB structure is set, you *must* call *ClearCommError* whenever any communications function indicates an error by returning FALSE (unless the function call was made asynchronously). When *fAbortOnError* is set, a communications error immediately terminates any pending reads or writes, and no new reads or writes are permitted until *ClearCommError* is called.

Control Commands

Some programmers like to get down and dirty with the hardware. That's not so easy to do in Windows 95, but one function brings you just a bit closer to total control: *EscapeCommFunction* (as in an escape from pure hardware abstraction). Calling *EscapeCommFunction,* as shown below, lets you turn individual hardware signals ON or OFF and lets you simulate the receipt of XON and XOFF characters. *EscapeCommFunction* can also set or clear a break condition when transmitting bytes. In this last capacity, it functions identically to *SetCommBreak* and *ClearCommBreak*.

```
EscapeCommFunction (hComm, dwFunction)
```

The value of *dwFunction* determines how the function behaves. The possible values of *dwFunction* and the resulting behavior are shown below. Note that these are flags and that more than one can be set at a time.

CLRDTR	Turns DTR OFF.
CLRRTS	Turns RTS OFF.
SETDTR	Turns DTR ON.
SETRTS	Turns RTS ON.
SETXOFF	Simulates receipt of the XOFF character.
SETXON	Simulates receipt of the XON character.
SETBREAK	Causes a break in transmission (same as *SetCommBreak*).
CLRBREAK	Clears a break in transmission (same as *ClearCommBreak*).

In this chapter you've learned how to transfer data between two computers using the Win32 Communications API. In the next chapter, you'll learn how to apply this knowledge to send data across the phone line. You'll also have to set up a phone connection between the two computers and learn how Windows 95 configures modems.

4

The Telephony API

The previous chapter showed you how to send and receive data using serial ports. In this chapter, you'll learn about the next step, which is transferring data over phone lines. Transferring data over phone lines requires modems and the Telephony API (TAPI). When you use TAPI, you can communicate with anyone who has access to the public phone network.

Lines, Phones, Addresses, and Calls

In this section, you'll learn about some of the basic features behind all telephony communications: lines, phones, addresses, and calls. These features are closely related and are all necessary for any kind of TAPI application you will build.

Logical Line Devices

A *logical line device* represents a phone line. The features of a logical line device depend on the features of the physical phone line it represents. A typical phone line, such as the one in most residential homes, is called a POTS line. POTS is short for Plain Old Telephone Service. In Windows 95, a POTS line is represented by a single logical line device. Some digital phone lines (such as ISDN) contain multiple "channels," or information paths, that can be used to simultaneously transfer different kinds of data. These multichannel digital lines are often represented by multiple logical line devices, with one logical line device per channel. The standard Windows 95 telephony driver, Unimodem, does not support multichannel digital lines; it supports only the less sophisticated POTS lines found in most homes today. (Note: In this chapter we are referring to the initial release of Unimodem with Windows 95. Future releases, including Unimodem for voice modems, might have additional capabilities that are not covered in detail in this chapter.)

Logical Phones

A *logical phone* represents a phone. A phone typically includes both a *hookswitch* and a *transducer*. A hookswitch is the switch that connects and disconnects the phone from the line. A transducer is a device that consists of a speaker and a microphone that convert sound energy into electrical energy, or vice versa. A phone can have several transducers, such as a handset, speakerphone, and headset. A phone can control the volume of the speakers and the gain of the microphones. Virtually all phones have a ringer and buttons for dialing. Some digital phones use LCDs to display messages, and some include lamps that flash to indicate the state of a call, such as whether the call is on hold. Some advanced phones can be programmed from a computer through a serial cable. These phones include program memories.

Unimodem supports only basic phone features—nothing fancy like displays, flashing buttons, or program memories. But if you have an advanced digital phone and the right Windows drivers, you can have a lot of fun making the lamps blink on and off, the ringer ring, and the display show brief messages. (Phone devices are implemented in a later version of Unimodem called UnimodemV. They are not discussed in this chapter.)

Addresses and Calls

Addresses are strings of letters, digits, and control characters that define paths to phones, modems, or computers. Addresses can be almost anything, from phone numbers to LAN addresses to Internet addresses. For the purposes of this chapter, addresses are just phone numbers. A logical line device can be assigned one or more addresses. A POTS line typically has a single address, which is the phone number for that line. It is not unusual for other kinds of lines to have several phone numbers. For example, digital lines in large businesses often have separate phone numbers for internal calls and external calls.

Lines, phones, and addresses are static—they have some permanence. The lines or phones connected to the computer do not change very often, and neither does the phone number of a line. *Calls,* on the other hand, are dynamic—they come and go with each new connection. Technically, calls are the connections by which data is exchanged between two or more parties over the line. More simply, calls are just phone calls. One or more calls can exist on a line simultaneously, as anyone familiar with call waiting knows. With call waiting, an existing call is interrupted by the arrival of a second call. The person with call waiting flashes (presses and releases) the hookswitch to put the first call on hold and begin the second call.

The relationship between lines, addresses, and calls can be complex. Figure 4-1 shows some of the possible relationships. The relationship Unimodem supports is POTS lines—one line, one address per line, and one call per address.

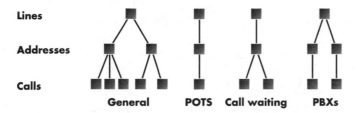

Figure 4-1. *Relationships between lines, addresses, and calls on different phone systems.*

Calls are where the action is. Calls can be connected, placed on hold, transferred, conferenced, "parked," "picked up," and more. Of course, even Windows can't make your phone line do things it isn't designed for. Most POTS lines don't support conferencing or call transfers, for example. What Windows does provide is information about installed telephony drivers and the services supported by the connected line.

Each call transitions through a number of states over its lifetime. Windows informs the controlling application when a call changes state. Call states include DIALTONE, RINGING, CONNECTED, and so forth. The CONNECTED state is of primary importance because once the call reaches that state, data can be transferred over the line and it will reach the destination party. A call that has been disconnected or has not been started is in the IDLE state.

Opening a Modem

Opening a modem is nothing like opening a COM port—Windows opens the modem for you. To use the modem, your application requests a copy of the handle to the open modem. The application can use the handle just as if it had opened the modem itself. While your application has the modem handle, it and it alone can transfer data over the phone line. You can close the modem by calling *CloseHandle* from your application, just as you do to close the handle to a COM port. (See the section titled "Closing a Serial Port" in Chapter 3.) The call to *CloseHandle* is shown below.

```
CloseHandle (hModem);
```

The *lineGetID* Function

You use the function *lineGetID,* shown below, to request a handle to the modem from Windows. You don't have to specify which COM port the modem is attached to; Windows knows this information already from the settings specified using the Modems applet on the Control Panel.

```
lineGetID(hLine, dwAddressID, hCall, dwSelect, lpDeviceID,
        lpszDeviceClass);
```

The first parameter of *lineGetID, hLine,* is a handle to the logical line associated with the modem. For the moment, ignore the question of where the line handle comes from. The second and third parameters, *dwAddressID* and *hCall,* specify the address and call handles associated with the modem, respectively.

The fourth parameter, *dwSelect,* selects which of the first three parameters *lineGetID* should consider when retrieving the modem handle. A value in *dwSelect* of LINECALLSELECT_LINE tells *lineGetID* to consider the modem associated with the line handle. A value of LINECALLSELECT_ADDRESS tells the function to consider both the line handle and address ID when retrieving the modem handle. For lines that support multiple addresses, this is a way to distinguish among several addresses on the same logical line device. A value of LINECALLSELECT_CALL tells the function to consider the call handle *hCall* and return the handle of the modem to use to make or answer that call. *hCall* should only be specified when a call is already connected on the line, the application you're calling *lineGetID* from owns the call, and the application wants a handle to the modem so that it can transfer data over the phone line using Win32c.

The fifth parameter, *lpDeviceID,* points to a variable-sized structure of the type VARSTRING. *lpDeviceID* is also where Windows returns a handle to the open modem. The other parameters of *lineGetID,* including the last parameter, *lpszDeviceClass,* give Windows information that it needs to know before returning the handle. *lpszDeviceClass* tells Windows the format of the device handle to return in *lpDeviceID*. To retrieve a modem handle that can be used with Win32c, set *lpszDeviceClass* to *comm/datamodem.* Later in this chapter, you'll learn about some of the other device classes that you can specify in *lineGetID* to get modem handles that can be used with Windows data transfer APIs other than Win32c (for example, an NDIS-compatible modem handle).

The VARSTRING structure

Windows uses VARSTRING as a flexible container for returning information to the application. The VARSTRING structure, shown on the facing page, is used when Windows, not the application, knows how much memory needs to be allocated for the returned information. This happens because the calling application is ignorant of the length of the returned data. For example, if the calling application wants to retrieve the name of the modem from Windows, it has no idea how many bytes to allocate for the string to hold the name. The application can allocate 1000 bytes, more space than any reasonable name can consume, but this is wasteful. A better way is to let Windows tell the application how much space is required so that the application can allocate just the right amount of memory. Remember the variable-sized structures that we mentioned in the previous chapter? VARSTRING is another example of one of these.

```
typedef struct varstring_tag {
    DWORD  dwTotalSize;
    DWORD  dwNeededSize;
    DWORD  dwUsedSize;
    DWORD  dwStringFormat;
    DWORD  dwStringSize;
    DWORD  dwStringOffset;
} VARSTRING, FAR *LPVARSTRING;
```

Think of VARSTRING as a container for information that Windows will return. You don't know how big the container will be until Windows tells you. So you start with a container of the minimum size, and then make it bigger if Windows tells you to. The *dwTotalSize* member of the VARSTRING structure contains the size of the container when you pass the value of *dwTotalSize* to Windows. Windows reads this value and decides if the space is sufficient. A good starting size is *sizeof(VARSTRING)*, the size of the basic structure. Windows sets the *dwNeededSize* member to the size actually needed to hold all of the information. Then, if necessary, the application reallocates VARSTRING to hold *dwNeededSize* bytes. You don't need to bother with the member *dwUsedSize;* it contains the number of bytes in the structure holding useful information, but we've never discovered any use for this member once the value of *dwNeededSize* is known. Windows sets the *dwStringFormat* member to indicate the format of the string. Possible values are STRINGFORMAT_UNICODE for Unicode wide-character formats, STRINGFORMAT_DBCS for double-byte strings, STRING-FORMAT_ASCII for ASCII strings, and STRINGFORMAT_BINARY for anything else. "Anything else" includes integer arrays, structures, and mixtures of strings and other data types. The returned string (or structure, or whatever) is located by referring to the *dwStringSize* and *dwStringOffset* members. These members contain the size of the returned string and its offset relative to the first byte of the VARSTRING structure.

Retrieving the Modem Handle

Usually, an application will need the modem handle after a call has been connected so that it can exchange data with the person or computer on the other end of the call. Because we haven't yet discussed how to make calls for exchanging data, the following example shows how to use *lineGetID* to retrieve the modem handle before a call has been connected.

```
/* structure returned by Windows, which contains modem handle and
modem name */
typedef struct tagCommID {
    HANDLE hModem;
    char szModemName[1];
} CommID;
```

(continued)

```c
HANDLE GetModemHandle ()
{
CommID FAR *cid;
VARSTRING  *vs;
LONG lrc;
DWORD dwSize;
HANDLE hModem;

    /* the next four lines prepare a VARSTRING structure
    to pass to Windows through lineGetID */
    vs = (VARSTRING *) malloc (sizeof(VARSTRING));
    if (!vs)
        return NULL;
    vs->dwTotalSize = sizeof(VARSTRING);

    do {
        /* get modem handle associated with the line */
        if (((lrc = lineGetID(hLine, 0L, NULL, LINECALLSELECT_LINE,
                            vs, "comm/datamodem")) == 0 &&
                            (vs->dwTotalSize < vs->dwNeededSize)) {

            /* the next six lines reallocate the VARSTRING
            structure with the amount of space that Windows
            indicates is needed to return all of the information */
            dwSize = vs->dwNeededSize;
            free (vs);
            vs = (VARSTRING *) malloc(dwSize);
            if (!vs)
                return NULL;
            vs->dwTotalSize = dwSize;
        } /* end if (need more space) */
        else if (lrc < 0) {
            /* handle error */
        } /* end else if (error getting comm device handle) */
        else
            break; /* success  */
    } while (TRUE);

    cid = (CommID FAR *) ((LPSTR)vs + vs->dwStringOffset);
    lstrcpy (szModemName, &cid->szModemName[0]);

    hModem = cid->hModem;
    free(vs);
    return hModem;

} /* end function (GetModemHandle) */
```

Let's take a closer look at the call to *lineGetID,* shown here.

```
lrc = lineGetID(hLine, 0L, NULL, LINECALLSELECT_LINE, vs,
                "comm/datamodem")
```

As we stated earlier, *lineGetID* lets you select from among three ways of asking for the modem handle. You can specify *hLine* and get the modem associated with a logical line device. You can specify *hLine* and *dwAddress* and get the modem associated with an address on that line. Or you can specify *hCall* and get the modem associated with a call. Remember, in theory a logical line device can have multiple addresses attached to it, and each address can have multiple calls. In practice, a POTS line has one line with one address and a maximum of one call at a time. In our example, the address ID is meaningless because we do not specify LINECALLSELECT_ADDRESS, and the call handle *hCall* doesn't exist yet because we haven't made a call. Therefore, the address ID and call handle parameters are not used, so we set them to 0 and NULL, respectively. As a result, we need to use a line handle in the call to *lineGetID* and specify LINECALLSELECT_LINE. (We haven't yet discussed how to get the line handle.)

Once you retrieve a pointer to the VARSTRING structure from *lineGetID,* you can find the handle to the modem. Windows appends the modem handle and the modem name to the VARSTRING structure. The format of this appended information is as follows:

```
typedef struct tagCommID {
    HANDLE hModem;
    char szModemName[1];
} CommID;
```

The length of the appended modem name is actually longer than the single byte shown in the structure above. The member *szModemName* is merely a placeholder for the first byte of the modem name. The following example shows how to access the full modem name. You cast a pointer with the CommID format to the extra data that Windows appends to the VARSTRING structure. Then you perform a simple string copy to copy the NULL-terminated *szModemName* member to the local variable.

```
cid = (CommID FAR *) ((LPSTR)vs + vs->dwStringOffset);
lstrcpy (szModemName, &cid->szModemName[0]);
```

The modem handle is returned by accessing the *hModem* member of the CommID structure, as shown here.

```
hModem = cid->hModem;
```

The modem name string contains the name of the modem selected from the Modems applet on the Control Panel. However, the format of the CommID structure that contains the name and is appended to VARSTRING is STRING-FORMAT_BINARY since it is a structure and not a true string.

Before making a call, an application needs the modem handle to retrieve important information about the modem's configuration and capabilities. However, it should return the modem handle to Windows using *CloseHandle* once this information is retrieved, so that the modem is available to other applications. Once an application makes or answers a call, it should retrieve the modem handle again (this time using the call handle, not the line handle), in order to send and receive data over the phone line once the call is connected.

Exploring Modems

An application can learn a great deal about the modem by reading the COMMPROP and COMMCONFIG structures. These are the same structures that return information about the COM port. (See the section titled "Configuring a Serial Port" in Chapter 3.) Associated with COMMPROP and COMMCONFIG are two structures that are specific to modems only: MODEMDEVCAPS and MODEMSETTINGS.

Retrieving Modem Properties

To retrieve the MODEMDEVCAPS structure, you must first retrieve the COMMPROP structure. You retrieve the COMMPROP structure for a modem in the same way that you do for COM ports—using a call to *GetCommProperties*—but instead of passing the COM port handle to *GetCommProperties,* you pass the modem handle. The information returned in COMMPROP is the capabilities of the modem. There are noticeable differences between the information returned when you call *GetCommProperties* with the COM port handle and when you call it with the modem handle. For a modem handle, the value of *dwProvSubType* is PST_MODEM, as opposed to PST_RS232 for a COM port handle. Also, the transmit buffer size *dwCurrentTxQueue* can be different for modem handles since the telephony drivers can use different buffering schemes from the port drivers.

When you call *GetCommProperties* with a modem handle, Windows puts additional information about the modem into a structure and appends the structure to the end of COMMPROP. This appended structure is the MODEMDEVCAPS structure, shown on the facing page, which contains information about the capabilities of the modem.

```
typedef struct _MODEMDEVCAPS {
    DWORD   dwActualSize;
    DWORD   dwRequiredSize;
    DWORD   dwDevSpecificOffset;
    DWORD   dwDevSpecificSize;
    // product and version identification
    DWORD   dwModemProviderVersion;
    DWORD   dwModemManufacturerOffset;
    DWORD   dwModemManufacturerSize;
    DWORD   dwModemModelOffset;
    DWORD   dwModemModelSize;
    DWORD   dwModemVersionOffset;
    DWORD   dwModemVersionSize;
    // local option capabilities
    DWORD   dwDialOptions;            // bitmap of supported values
    DWORD   dwCallSetupFailTimer;     // maximum in seconds
    DWORD   dwInactivityTimeout;      // maximum in deciseconds
    DWORD   dwSpeakerVolume;          // bitmap of supported values
    DWORD   dwSpeakerMode;            // bitmap of supported values
    DWORD   dwModemOptions;           // bitmap of supported values
    DWORD   dwMaxDTERate;             // maximum value in bit/s
    DWORD   dwMaxDCERate;             // maximum value in bit/s
    // Variable portion for proprietary expansion
    BYTE    abVariablePortion [1];
} MODEMDEVCAPS, *PMODEMDEVCAPS, *LPMODEMDEVCAPS;
```

Retrieving the MODEMDEVCAPS structure is a bit tricky. We touched on this in Chapter 3, in the discussion of the COMMPROP structure. The *wPacketLength* member of COMMPROP specifies the number of bytes available to Windows to return information. Remember, the application, not Windows, allocates the memory for COMMPROP, so if you don't tell Windows how much memory is available, the results can be unpredictable and unpleasant. To retrieve the modem capabilities, you must first allocate enough memory, as shown below.

```
cp = (COMMPROP *) malloc(sizeof(COMMPROP) + sizeof(MODEMDEVCAPS));
```

Next, you include a line like the following to set the *wPacketLength* member to the size of the container.

```
cp->wPacketLength = sizeof(COMMPROP) + sizeof(MODEMDEVCAPS)
```

You then set the *dwProvSpec1* member to COMMPROP_INITIALIZED. This tells Windows that *wPacketLength* contains the available memory for returning information. Then you call *GetCommProperties,* as shown here.

```
GetCommProperties (hModem, cp);
```

The *wcProvChar* member of COMMPROP now contains the first byte of the MODEMDEVCAPS structure that Windows appended to COMMPROP. Casting a pointer to this member, as shown below, provides access to the MODEMDEVCAPS members.

```
MODEMDEVCAPS *mdc;
⋮
mdc = (MODEMDEVCAPS *)&cp->wcProvChar;
```

This is not quite the end of the story, however. MODEMDEVCAPS, like COMMPROP, is a variable-sized structure. Windows appends additional information to the end of MODEMDEVCAPS, as long as the application allocates enough memory for the extra information. Upon the first call to *GetCommProperties,* an application has no idea how much extra information Windows will attach to MODEMDEVCAPS. Windows sets the *dwRequiredSize* member of MODEMDEVCAPS to the number of bytes required to hold all the extra information available. An application should reallocate the amount of memory for COMMPROP and call *GetCommProperties* a second time, as in the following code segment.

```
dwRequiredSize = mdc->dwRequiredSize+sizeof(COMMPROP);
free (cp);
cp = (COMMPROP *) malloc(dwRequiredSize);
cp->wPacketLength = (WORD)dwRequiredSize;
if (!GetCommProperties(hModem, cp)) {
    /* handle error */
}
mdc = (MODEMDEVCAPS *) &cp->wcProvChar;
```

The memory allocated by the application now contains a COMMPROP structure, followed by a MODEMDEVCAPS structure, followed by extra data about the modem. (See Figure 4-2.) You can verify that Windows returned all of the available information by checking the *dwActualSize* member of MODEM-DEVCAPS against the *dwRequiredSize* member. If they are the same, all available information was returned.

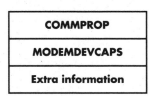

Figure 4-2. *Memory containing COMMPROP, MODEMDEVCAPS, and extra information about the modem.*

As we've stated, the MODEMDEVCAPS structure contains information about the capabilities of the modem. The *dwModemProviderVersion* member contains the version number of the Windows modem driver. The *dwDialOptions* member contains special dialing options that the modem supports. Dialing options are some of the most important options for the modem. The possible values are:

DIALOPTION_DIALBILLING	Modem supports wait-for-billing-tone ($).
DIALOPTION_DIALQUIET	Modem supports wait-for-quiet (@).
DIALOPTION_DIALDIALTONE	Modem supports wait-for-dial-tone (W).

If the modem supports waiting for a billing tone, dial strings can take advantage of the billing tone that long-distance phone carriers make available to customers with calling cards. Suppose a person with a calling card wants to make a long-distance call. The normal process is to dial a prefix code, followed by the area code and phone number. The caller then waits to hear a "bong" on the line (the billing tone). After hearing the bong, the caller enters the calling card number. A modem that supports DIALOPTION_DIALBILLING automatically detects the bong for the caller using sophisticated signal processing algorithms. After it detects the bong, the modem dials the digits that follow the wait-for-billing-tone (sometimes called wait-for-bong) character in the dial string. These digits are typically the digits of the calling card number. The following example shows a dial string for making a long-distance call from Windows using a calling card.

```
if (mdc->dwDialOptions & DIALOPTION_DIALBILLING)
    dialstring = "0 408 555 2345 $ 12345678991234"
else
    dialstring = "1 408 555 2345"
```

The code checks to see if the modem supports wait-for-billing-tone. If it does, a 0 is appended to the dial string rather than the 1 prefix that is used for direct dialing. When Windows receives this dial string, it dials 0 408 555 2345 and then waits for the modem to detect a bong. The $ character in the dial string tells Windows to pause until the modem detects the bong, and then dial the digits of the calling card, which are 12345678991234. If the modem does not support wait-for-billing-tone, the dial string is set to dial the long-distance number directly without accessing the calling card system.

Another dialing option, wait-for-quiet, is supported by the modem when the DIALOPTION_DIALQUIET flag is set. Wait-for-quiet tells the modem to detect "quiet" on the line, which usually means no tones (such as ringing or busy tones) and no other sounds (such as human voices). A modem that supports wait-for-quiet is useful for making calls to automated phone systems, such as voicemail systems and automated banking systems.

Suppose you want to dial your automated banking system to find out your current account balance. The system might work as follows:

1. You dial the automated bank system computer.

2. The computer answers the phone and prompts you for your account number.

3. You enter your account number.

4. The computer prompts you for your password.

5. You enter your password.

6. The computer prompts you to press 3 to hear the current account balance.

7. You press 3.

If your modem supports wait-for-quiet, you can automate this entire sequence with the following dial string:

```
if (mdc->dwDialOptions & DIALOPTION_DIALQUIET)
    dialstring = "555 4523 @ 123456789,,333,,3"
else
    dialstring = "555 4523"
```

This dial string causes Windows to first dial the number of the automatic banking computer, 555-4523. The @ following the phone number tells Windows to wait for quiet after dialing the phone number. When the computer answers, several things happen. First, the ringing tone on the line goes away because the call has connected. Second, the bank computer prompts for the account code. After that, there is silence on the line while the bank computer waits for the account code to be entered. The modem detects the silence and dials the account code digits, which are 123456789 in this example. The modem then pauses twice as long as the amount specified by a comma (,), which at a half-second per comma is a total of 1 second. (Delay times for the comma can vary; see Chapter 2 for a discussion of commas in dial strings.) This one-second delay gives the computer time to prompt for the password. Windows then dials the password digits, which are 333 in this example. Finally, Windows waits one second and then dials 3 to access the current account balance.

In the wait-for-quiet example above, both the @ and the comma are used for pauses. Typically, you should use the @ when you are unsure of the length of the pause or when the length of the pause can change, and you should use commas when the length of the pause is consistent and rarely changes. In the banking example, you might hear a message that includes upcoming bank closures, changes in hours, or other information bank customers might be interested in. Since this information could change at any time, you would want to use the @ to wait for the message to finish, as we did in this example. The other prompts after the initial message rarely change, so you can use the commas with confidence that the call will be completed successfully.

Another dial option is wait-for-dial-tone. If a modem supports this option, it pauses after a *W* character in the dial string until it detects a dial tone. Once it detects a dial tone, it dials any remaining digits after the *W*. This option is especially useful in hotels or large businesses, where it is usually necessary to dial a special prefix digit, such as an 8 or a 9, to reach an outside line. The following example uses wait-for-dial-tone:

```
if (mdc->dwDialOptions & DIALOPTION_DIALDIALTONE)
    dialstring = "9 W 555 3434";
```

Windows dials 9, and then the modem waits to detect a dial tone. Once the modem detects a dial tone, Windows dials the remaining digits. (See Chapter 2 for more information on using wait-for-dial-tone in dial strings.)

The *dwCallSetupFailTimer* member of the MODEMDEVCAPS structure specifies the maximum timeout value, in seconds, supported by the modem for call setup. After the modem dials a phone number, Windows waits for an indication from the answering modem that the call has connected. If this indication is not forthcoming within the interval specified by *dwCallSetupFailTimer,* Windows hangs up. Unimodem allows a maximum timeout value of 255 seconds (a little over four minutes).

The *dwInactivityTimeout* member specifies, in seconds, the amount of inactivity time that Windows will tolerate before it disconnects a call. If a call is established between two modems but no information is exchanged for an excessive period of time, Windows assumes that the user has abandoned the call or that the application making or receiving the call has crashed for some reason. To save on toll charges, it disconnects the call. Unimodem supports a maximum inactivity timeout of 15,300 seconds, or 255 minutes.

The *dwSpeakerVolume* member specifies the speaker volume settings supported by the modem. If the modem does not provide a speaker, this member can be 0. Otherwise, Windows reports that the modem supports three levels of volume:

MDMVOLFLAG_LOW	Low volume
MDMVOLFLAG_MEDIUM	Medium volume
MDMVOLFLAG_HIGH	High volume

The volume levels are not defined in terms of actual decibels; rather, they are relative levels of volume, with LOW being the softest. Actual decibel levels depend on the particular modem.

The *dwSpeakerMode* member defines the supported speaker modes. If the modem does not have a speaker, this member is 0. Otherwise, it is one or more of the following flags:

MDMSPKRFLAG_OFF	The speaker is always off.
MDMSPKRFLAG_DIAL	The speaker is on while a call is set up, except during dialing.
MDMSPKRFLAG_ON	The speaker is always on.
MDMSPKRFLAG_CALLSETUP	The speaker is always on, except during call setup.

The *dwModemOptions* member specifies miscellaneous features that the modem supports. If the corresponding flag is set, the feature is supported.

MDM_COMPRESSION	Modem supports compression protocols.
MDM_ERROR_CONTROL	Modem supports error control protocols.
MDM_FORCED_EC	Model supports forced error control.
MDM_CELLULAR	Modem supports cellular error control protocols.
MDM_FLOWCONTROL_HARD	Modem supports hardware RTS/CTS flow control.
MDM_FLOWCONTROL_SOFT	Modem supports XON/XOFF software flow control.
MDM_CCITT_OVERRIDE	Modem supports non-CCITT (International Telegraphy and Telephony Consultative Committee) modulations, which can be turned off for a call.
MDM_SPEED_ADJUST	Modem speed negotiation behavior can be changed. (The modem can be set to fall back to lower baud rates in order to connect.)
MDM_TONE_DIAL	Dialing mode of modem can be toggled between tone and pulse.
MDM_BLIND_DIAL	Modem dial tone detection behavior can be changed.
MDM_V23_OVERRIDE	Modem supports CCITT modulations V.23. MDM_CCITT_OVERRIDE must also be set for CCITT V.23 support.

The members *dwMaxDTERate* and *dwMaxDCERate* specify the maximum data transfer rate, in bits per second, that can be transferred through the serial port and the modem, respectively. The smaller of these two values controls the maximum data transfer rate that can be achieved using the serial port with the modem. For example, if *dwMaxDTERate* is 57600 bps, it means the COM port can transfer data at a maximum rate of 57.6 Kbps. If, however, *dwMaxDCErate* is only 14400 bps, the modem can transfer at a maximum rate of only 14.4 Kbps. The maximum rate that data can be sent over the phone line is 14.4 Kbps, since this is the lesser of the two data rates.

Remember the extra data about the modem that Windows returns? We had to reallocate the COMMPROP structure and call *GetCommProperties* twice to get that extra data, which is appended to the end of the MODEMDEVCAPS structure. Eight members of MODEMDEVCAPS specify where this information is and how much to retrieve. The members come in pairs, consisting of a size and an offset. The size member specifies how many bytes of extra information are available. The offset member specifies where this information is relative to the beginning of the MODEMDEVCAPS structure. So, for example, a size of 10 and an offset of 80 indicate 10 bytes of data at an offset of 80 bytes from the beginning of the structure.

The name of the modem manufacturer, the model name of the modem, and the model version are among the extra data at the end of the structure. This data is stored as strings. The size and offset of the modem manufacturer name are specified by the members *dwModemManufacturerOffset* and *dwModemManufacturerSize*. The following code can be used to retrieve the manufacturer name:

```
strncpy (szManufacturerName,
        (LPSTR)((LPSTR)mdc+mdcc->dwModemManufacturerOffset),
        mdc->dwModemManufacturerSize);
szManufacturerName[mdc->dwModemManufacturerSize] = 0;
```

Notice that the *strncpy* function, not the *strcpy* function, is used to copy the string. The reason *strcpy* cannot be used is that the manufacturer name is not NULL-terminated. The characters in the string are copied to *szManufacturerName,* and then the string is explicitly NULL-terminated.

Similarly, the model name of the modem can be retrieved using the members *dwModemModelOffset* and *dwModemModelSize,* and version information can be retrieved using the members *dwModemVersionOffset* and *dwModemVersionSize.* Any other manufacturer-specific information about the modem is specified by the members *dwDevSpecificSize* and *dwDevSpecificOffset*. There is no standard definition for the information specified by these last two members; the information is modem-specific.

If the size, offset, or both are 0 for any one of the variable length members we just discussed, no corresponding extra information for these members exists. As a result, Windows doesn't append the extra information after the structure and the variable length members can be safely ignored.

Modem Settings

The MODEMDEVCAPS structure is to modems what the COMMPROP structure is to COM ports. Both structures are read-only and return information about the capabilities of the device. The structures do not return information about the current settings of a device. For a COM port, the COMMCONFIG structure is used to return information about the current settings of the COM port. Windows appends the MODEMSETTINGS structure to the end of the COMMCONFIG structure when you call the *GetCommConfig* function with a modem handle. The modem handle represents the unified COM port and modem device. The DCB settings in COMMCONFIG are the unified settings for the COM port and the modem. In other words, the baud rate, parity method, and number of stop bits in the DCB are used by both the port and the modem. The COMMCONFIG structure with the MODEMSETTINGS appended is retrieved in a manner similar to the one used to retrieve the COMMPROP structure with MODEMDEVCAPS appended.

To receive the MODEMSETTINGS structure, you first allocate a COMMCONFIG structure with enough space to hold a MODEMSETTINGS structure at the end:

```
cc = (COMMCONFIG *) malloc(sizeof(COMMCONFIG) +
                           sizeof(MODEMSETTINGS));
```

Next, you set the *wSize* member to the size of the container:

```
cc->dwSize = sizeof(COMMCONFIG) + sizeof(MODEMSETTINGS);
```

You call *GetCommConfig,* as shown below, by passing the modem handle, container, and size.

```
size = cc->dwSize;
if (!GetCommConfig (hModem, cc, &size))
    /* handle error */
;
```

When *GetCommConfig* returns, the *wcProviderData* member of COMMCONFIG contains the first byte of the MODEMDSETTINGS structure, which Windows appends to COMMCONFIG. Casting a pointer to this member as in the example below provides access to the MODEMSETTINGS members.

```
MODEMSETTINGS *ms;
    :
ms = (MODEMSETTINGS *)&cc->wcProviderData;
```

Windows returns the required size of the container in the third parameter of *GetCommConfig,* which is called *size* in this example. Because Windows might return some extra data about the modem and append the information to the MODEMSETTINGS structure, it is a good idea to compare the required size to the actual size of the container. If the required size is greater, you should reallocate the container to the required size and call *GetCommConfig* again to retrieve the extra data, as follows:

```
if (size > cc->dwSize) {
    free (cc);
    cc = (COMMCONFIG *) malloc(size);
    cc->dwSize = size;
    if (!GetCommConfig (hModem, cc, &size))
        /* handle error */
        ;
}
```

The COMMCONFIG structure returned for a modem handle differs slightly from the one returned for a COM port handle. The structure version number in the *wVersion* member can be set to 1 for Windows 95 device drivers. Also, the communications driver subtype, *dwProviderSubType,* is set to PST_MODEM for a modem handle, and PST_RS232 for a COM port. There are also two members in COMMCONFIG that define the size and offset of any extra data that Windows returns about the modem, *dwProviderSize* and *dwProviderOffset.* The extra data is appended to the MODEMSETTINGS structure. Often, however, Windows does not return any extra data. If one or both of the size and offset members are set to 0, Windows does not return extra data. If both members are nonzero, Windows retrieves the extra information in the same manner that it retrieves the extra information from the COMMPROP structure. The extra information can be anything, depending on the model and manufacture of the modem. Unless you have "inside" knowledge of the format of a manufacturer's extra information, just ignore it.

The format of the MODEMSETTINGS structure is as follows:

```
typedef struct _MODEMSETTINGS {
    DWORD    dwActualSize;
    DWORD    dwRequiredSize;
    DWORD    dwDevSpecificOffset;
    DWORD    dwDevSpecificSize;

    // static local options (read/write)
    DWORD    dwCallSetupFailTimer;      // seconds
    DWORD    dwInactivityTimeout;       // deciseconds
    DWORD    dwSpeakerVolume;           // level
    DWORD    dwSpeakerMode;             // mode
    DWORD    dwPreferredModemOptions;   // bitmap

    // negotiated options (read only) for current or last call
    DWORD    dwNegotiatedModemOptions;  // bitmap
    DWORD    dwNegotiatedDCERate;       // bit/s

    // Variable portion for proprietary expansion
    BYTE     abVariablePortion [1];
} MODEMSETTINGS, *PMODEMSETTINGS, *LPMODEMSETTINGS;
```

The *dwActualSize* and *dwRequiredSize* members of MODEMSETTINGS define the actual number of bytes returned and the required number of bytes (including any extra information appended to the end of the structure), respectively. These two members should have the same value if Windows returned all of the extra information available; if *dwRequiredSize* is greater than *dwActualSize,* you must reallocate the container and call *GetCommConfig* a second time, as shown here.

```
if (ms->dwRequiredSize > ms->dwActualSize) {
    free (cc);
    size = cc->wSize + ms->dwRequiredSize;
    cc = (COMMCONFIG *) malloc(size);
    if (!GetCommConfig (hModem, cc, &size))
        /* handle error */
    ;
}
```

The size returned in the third parameter of *GetCommConfig* should always indicate the required size, including the extra data, but comparing the actual and required size is a good way to double-check that you are getting all the information Windows has to offer.

The members of MODEMSETTINGS correspond closely to the members of MODEMDEVCAPS. *dwCallSetupFailTimer* specifies the amount of time (in seconds) that Windows should wait after dialing for a connection to be established. This member of MODEMSETTINGS contains the actual value that will be used when a call is made. The value cannot exceed the maximum allowable timeout value specified in the *dwCallSetupFailTimer* member of the MODEMDEVCAPS structure. The *dwInactivityTimeout* member specifies, in seconds, how much time can elapse without activity on the line before Windows hangs up the call. The value of this member cannot exceed the maximum inactivity timeout specified by the *dwInactivityTimeout* member of MODEMDEVCAPS. Before setting either of these members, you should check that you are not exceeding the maximum allowed values, as shown below. (The *dwInactivityTimout* member of MODEMDEVCAPS and the *dwInactivityTimeout* member of MODEMSETTINGS are specified in seconds.)

```
SetupTimeoutToUse     = min(mdc->dwCallSetupFailTimer,
                            DesiredSetupTimeout);
InactivityTimeoutToUse = min(mdc->dwInactivityTimeout,
                            DesiredInactivityTimeout);
```

The *dwSpeakerVolume* and *dwSpeakerMode* members specify the current settings of the modem speaker volume and mode, respectively. The volume can be either low, medium, or high, as specified by one of the following constants:

MDMVOL_LOW	Low volume
MDMVOL_MEDIUM	Medium volume
MDMVOL_HIGH	High volume

Possible settings for the speaker mode are as follows:

MDMSPKR_OFF	The speaker is always off.
MDMSPKR_DIAL	The speaker is on during call setup, except during dialing.
MDMSPKR_ON	The speaker is always on.
MDMSPKR_CALLSETUP	The speaker is always on, except during call setup.

You can change the modem settings by first changing the setting in MODEM-SETTINGS and then calling *SetCommConfig* to make the new settings active.

```
SetCommConfig (hModem, cc, size)
```

The *cc* parameter of *SetCommConfig* points to the COMMCONFIG structure with the MODEMDEVCAPS and extra data appended to it. The *size* parameter indicates the total size of COMMCONFIG and MODEMSETTINGS and the extra data. Remember to always check MODEMDEVCAPS to confirm that a setting is supported before you change a setting in MODEMSETTINGS. For example, to change the speaker mode of the modem, use code such as the following:

```
/* check MODEMDEVCAPS supports call-setup speaker mode*/
MODEMDEVCAPS *mdc;
MODEMSETTINGS *ms;
    :
if (mdc->dwSpeakerMode & MDMSPKRFLAG_CALLSETUP)
    ms->dwSpeakerMode = MDMSPKR_CALLSETUP;
```

Modem Negotiation

After a call is established, a negotiation occurs between the modem making the call and the modem answering the call. Each modem begins with a negotiating position, which includes all of the communication options that it prefers to have in place when a call is established. After the negotiation is over, each modem usually has some of the options it wants, and a working connection is established with the agreed-upon set of options. The options include flow control (hardware or software), compression format, and error control protocol. The *dwPreferredModemOptions* member of MODEMSETTINGS defines the modem's preferred options. An application should set this member with a bitmask of the MDM_ flags (see the *dwModemOptions* member of MODEM-DEVCAPS on page 88). After a call is established, the agreed-upon options are contained in the *dwNegotiatedModemOptions* member and are represented by a bitmask of the MDM_ constants. The modems also negotiate a data transfer rate that they both support. This can be less than, but never greater than, the maximum data rate supported by the calling modem and defined in the *dwMaxDCERate* member of MODEMDEVCAPS. For example, if a 14.4 Kbps modem calls a modem with a maximum data rate of 9600 bps, the two modems will likely negotiate a data rate of 9600 bps. The negotiated data rate is stored in the *dwNegotiatedDCERate* member of MODEMSETTINGS.

Exploring Lines

MODEMDEVCAPS and MODEMSETTINGS are rich in information about the modem. You access these structures using the modem handle returned by *lineGetID*. Once a call is established, you use the modem handle with the Win32c functions to transfer data using the serial port and the modem. However, the modem handle has one serious deficiency: You cannot use it to actually make a call. To actually dial the phone and connect to another computer, your application must use TAPI.

AT Commands

Before TAPI became part of Windows, applications that used the modem could make calls using AT commands—strings of ASCII characters written to the COM port to which a modem is known to be attached. These commands make up the famous AT command set, a standard language for controlling modems. Virtually all modems contain internal microcode for interpreting AT commands. As long as the modem is in a special operating mode called *command mode,* strings of characters recognized as AT commands are read and acted upon by the modem. Once a call is established, the modem switches into *data mode,* in which AT commands no longer affect the behavior of the modem. Switching from command mode to data mode is very important, because otherwise byte sequences in the transferred data that correspond to AT commands will cause unpredictable behavior in the modem.

AT commands have not disappeared. The Windows telephony drivers still use them to control the modem at a low level. But they are not appropriate for use in Windows applications for a couple of reasons. First, many modem manufacturers have added variations to the "standard" AT command set, which makes it difficult for an application to maintain full compatibility with all of the modems on the market. Windows 95 maintains a database of commercial modems and the variations of the AT command set that each modem implements. TAPI functions access this database, so an application that uses the standard TAPI functions to make calls and control the modem doesn't need to know the details of the AT command set.

The second reason to use TAPI instead of AT commands is that Windows treats modems as shared resources. Bypassing TAPI by using AT commands to control the modem directly bypasses the resource sharing code in Windows. This can cause problems when more than one application needs access to the modem. More on this later.

The *lineInitialize* Function

To begin using TAPI, an application first calls *lineInitialize,* as shown below. *lineInitialize* allocates certain internal resources that are necessary to support use of a logical line device. It also registers a callback function to which Windows returns messages to the application regarding the status of the line. *lineInitialize* returns the number of logical line devices implemented by Windows. Unimodem supports POTS lines, and therefore implements one line device. (See the discussion of POTS lines at the beginning of this chapter in the section titled "Logical Line Devices.")

```
lineInitialize (&hTAPI, hInstance, lpfnCallbackFunction, szAppName,
            &numLines)
```

The first parameter of *lineInitialize, hTAPI,* is an API handle returned by Windows. This handle keeps track of which applications are using the modem. An application should save this handle until it is done using TAPI. The second parameter, *hInstance,* is the instance handle of the application. The third parameter, *lpfnCallbackFunction,* points to a function in your application known as a callback function. Windows sends messages about the line to the application through this function. A callback function has the following syntax. (The call to *lineInitialize* and the callback function should be located within the same thread of the application.)

```
void FAR PASCAL CallbackFunction (DWORD dwDevice, DWORD dwMessage,
    DWORD dwInstanceData, DWORD dwParam1, DWORD dwParam2,
    DWORD dwParam3)
```

The first parameter to the callback function, *dwDevice,* identifies the line device (or the call, as we'll see later) to which the message applies. The second parameter, *dwMessage,* identifies the message, and the third parameter, *dwInstanceData,* identifies application data that Windows will pass unchanged to the callback. The last three parameters contain extra data for a message, and their meaning depends on the message being sent. (The parameters to the callback are explained more fully later in this chapter.) It's a good idea to call *MakeProcInstance* on the pointer to the callback (*lpfnCallbackFunction*) before passing it to *lineInitialize.* This minimizes the required changes for porting the application to 16-bit Windows. Also note that for 16-bit Windows, the callback should be declared with the __export option. (The __export option is obsolete in Windows 95.)

Getting back to *lineInitialize,* the fourth parameter, *szAppName,* is a NULL-terminated string that contains the name of the calling application. Windows passes this string back to the calling application and other applications that use the modem, to keep track of which applications initiate or answer calls. This parameter is useful for generating phone records. It can be left NULL, in which case Windows uses the calling application filename by default. The last parameter, *dwNumLines,* returns the number of logical line devices supported by the Windows drivers. This is always 1 when you are using Unimodem.

An application should always check the return value of *lineInitialize* because this is one of the best ways to discover configuration problems with the Windows telephony system. LINEERR_INIFILECORRUPT is returned if the TAPI configuration file, telephon.ini, is damaged or corrupt. telephon.ini contains telephony configuration information and is normally maintained by Windows. Users and applications should not modify telephon.ini except under extraordinary circumstances. If one of the Windows telephony drivers is missing or damaged, *lineInitialize* returns LINEERR_NODRIVER. If you have not installed a telephony driver from the Windows Control Panel, it returns LINEERR_NODEVICE.

Conversely, if you have somehow installed multiple instances of the Windows telephony drivers, it returns LINEERR_NOMULTIPLEINSTANCE.

Another error occurs when you add or remove the telephony driver (using the Modems applet) while at least one application is using the modem. Windows sends a message to each application, telling it to temporarily stop using the modem so your changes can take effect. Each application should terminate its use of the modem when it receives this message. It might take some time for all of the applications to stop using the modem; in the meantime, all applications will be blocked from using the modem. If an application calls *lineInitialize* while Windows is still waiting for another application to stop using the modem, *lineInitialize* returns LINEERR_REINIT. This is not a fatal error. Rather, it is an indication that the application should try again later. LINEERR_REINIT is the only nonfatal error returned by *lineInitialize*. The following code shows how errors from this function should be handled:

```
tc = GetTickCount();
while ((lrc=lineInitialize(&hTAPI, hInstance,
        (LINECALLBACK)MakeProcInstance((FARPROC)CallbackFunction,
        hInstance), "MyProcess", &numLines)) == LINEER_REINIT) {
    /* wait five seconds, then ask if want to retry */
    if (GetTickCount() - tc >= 5000) {
        if (MessageBox(hWnd, "Telephone System is Reinitializing - \
            Click Cancel to Abort", "Error", MB_RETRYCANCEL) ==
            IDCANCEL)
        break;
    }
    tc = GetTickCount();
} // while
if (lrc < 0)
    ProcessTAPIError(lrc);
```

Like most TAPI functions, *lineInitialize* returns 0 if the function call is successful, and it returns a negative error code if an error occurs.

In the above example, if a LINEERR_REINIT error occurs, the application waits five seconds for the other applications that are using the modem to stop using it. After five seconds, the application asks you whether you want to continue attempting to use the modem. If you click Retry, *lineInitialize* is called again. At this point, all of the other applications that are using the modem have probably stopped doing so, and it will be safe for your application to start using the modem. Any other error that *lineInitialize* returns is handled by the function *ProcessTAPIError,* which is a local function that prints out an error message. Of course, you might want to throw a *PeekMessage* function call into the loop so that the application window can continue to process messages.

The complementary function to *lineInitialize* is *lineShutDown*. When an application is done using the line device, it should call *lineShutDown*, as shown below, to free the resources allocated for the line device.

```
lineShutDown (hTAPI);
```

The single parameter to *lineShutDown, hTAPI,* is the API handle returned by *lineInitialize*.

Version Negotiation

After an application calls *lineInitialize* to retrieve an API handle and the number of supported logical line devices, the next step is to negotiate a TAPI version with Windows. The concept of version negotiation is probably unfamiliar to most Windows programmers. TAPI is one of the only Windows APIs that requires version negotiation (WinSock 2.0 is another example). Basically, it works like this:

1. An application is written to work with the functions, structures, and messages that are supported by the latest version of TAPI.

2. Microsoft makes changes to the functions, structures, and messages in a subsequent version of TAPI.

3. Users install the later version of TAPI (perhaps in a Windows upgrade), but they continue to run the application written for the older version of TAPI.

4. When the application runs, the application and the subsequent version of TAPI agree to use the functions, structures, and messages of the older version of TAPI so that TAPI appears like the older version. To other applications written for the latest version of TAPI, it appears like the latest version.

Version negotiation is not a bad idea, when you think about it. An application can use the functions, structures, and messages available at the time without worrying that later changes to TAPI will render it incompatible, or worse, cause a software crash. But version negotiation is not automatic. This functionality must be programmed into each application that wants to support version negotiation. The version number is negotiated by calling the function *lineNegotiate-APIVersion,* as shown below.

```
lineNegotiateAPIVersion (hTAPI, dwDeviceID, dwLowVersion,
                         dwHighVersion, &dwVersionToUse,
                         &extensions)
```

The first parameter, *hTAPI,* is the API handle returned by *lineInitialize.* The second parameter, *dwDeviceID,* identifies the logical line device for which to negotiate the version. An application can negotiate versions for any logical line device supported by TAPI, so in theory each application must negotiate a version for each logical line device that it uses. Again, this requirement is meant to increase compatibility with future versions of TAPI; a future version might support today's versions of the functions, structures, and messages with one logical line device, and subsequent versions of the functions, structures, and messages with a second logical line device. Older applications could use the first logical line device, while applications written for the future version of TAPI could use the second logical line device.

There are two methods of specifying logical line devices in TAPI. The first method is with an integer; this is the method used by *lineNegotiateAPIVersion.* Recall that *lineInitialize* returns the number of logical line devices (*numLines*) supported by TAPI. Unimodem supports only one logical line device. When a logical line device is specified using an integer, the integer must be within the range of 0 to *numLines*–1. Therefore, to specify the single logical line device supported by Unimodem, use the integer 0.

The second method of specifying logical line devices is with line handles, which specify open line devices only. Recall that a line handle was used to specify the line when retrieving the modem handle using *lineGetID.* This implies that the line device was already open before *lineGetID* was called. *lineInitialize* and *lineNegotiateAPIVersion* must be called before the line can be opened. Until the line is opened, the line device must be specified using an integer instead of the line handle.

The third and fourth parameters to *lineNegotiateAPIVersion, dwLowVersion* and *dwHighVersion,* specify the range of TAPI versions that the application is compatible with. Windows selects the highest version in this range that is supported by the installed telephony software, and it returns that version in the fifth parameter, *dwVersionToUse.*

In Figure 4-3 on the next page, the highest version supported by Windows is not supported by the application. However, the highest version supported by the application is within the range of versions supported by Windows. This is the version returned in the *dwVersionToUse* parameter of *lineNegotiateAPIVersion.* The initial release of Windows 95 supports TAPI version 0x00010004.

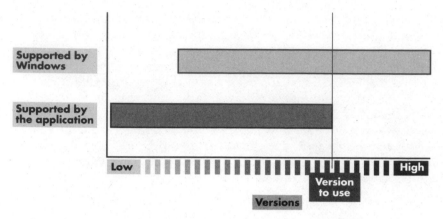

Figure 4-3. *The range of TAPI versions supported by Windows and an application.*

The last parameter of *lineNegotiateAPIVersion, extensions,* identifies extensions to standard TAPI that are supported by the drivers. Unimodem does not support API extensions, so this parameter can be safely ignored (but not omitted) by the application when calling *lineNegotiateAPIVersion*. The following is an example of how to call *lineNegotiateAPIVersion* for Windows 95.

```
lrc = lineNegotiateAPIVersion
    (hTAPI,
    0,             /* identifies first and only supported line
                   device */
    0x00010004,    /* low version */
    0x00010004,    /* high version */
    &dwVersionToUse,
    &extensions);
if (lrc)
    ProcessTAPIError(lrc);
```

lineNegotiateAPIVersion returns 0 if it is successful or a negative error code in the case of an error. If Windows does not support any versions in the range specified in the function call, LINEERR_INCOMPATIBLEAPIVERSION is returned.

If the installed Windows telephony drivers support extensions to standard TAPI, your application must also negotiate an extension version that is compatible with the drivers. You can accomplish this by calling another function, *lineNegotiateExtVersion,* which is similar to *lineNegotiateAPIVersion*.

Future versions of the Windows telephony drivers might implement more than one logical line device, so you should design your applications to handle this situation. When more than one logical line device is implemented, the code should negotiate a version for each line until it finds a line that is compatible with the version it implements, as in the following example.

```
for (dwLine=0, vercnt=0; dwLine < dwNumLines; ++dwLine) {
    if (!lineNegotiateAPIVersion(hTAPI, dwLine,
        dwApplicationAPIVersion, dwApplicationAPIVersion,
        &dwVersionToUse, &extensions))
        versionLines[vercnt++] = dwLine;
} //for
versionLines[vercnt] = -1;
```

In this example, *dwNumLines,* which was returned by a call to *lineInitialize,* is the number of logical line devices supported by the Windows drivers. *dwApplicationAPIVersion* is the TAPI version for which the application was designed. The loop checks each line to find any that support the application version. The line numbers of compatible lines are stored in an array. These are the lines your application can use to make and control phone calls.

The LINEDEVCAPS Structure

An application can discover a huge amount of information about a logical line by calling the function *lineGetDevCaps,* as shown below. This function returns a structure called LINEDEVCAPS, which is a treasure chest of useful information about the line.

```
lineGetDevCaps(hTAPI, dwLine, dwVersionToUse, dwExtVersion,
                &linedevcaps)
```

The first parameter, *hTAPI,* is the TAPI handle. The second parameter, *dwLine,* identifies the line to retrieve information on. *dwLine* is a small integer in the range of 0 to *numLines*–1, where *numLines* is returned by *lineInitialize.* The use of an integer instead of a handle to identify the line implies that *lineGetDevCaps* is meant to be called before the line is opened. This is indeed the case. The information returned by this function is invaluable in helping an application determine whether a line has the capabilities the application requires. If the line has the required capabilities, it is opened; otherwise, it is not. *lineGetDevCaps* can be called by an application at any time, even after the line is opened, so long as an integer is used to specify the line device.

The third parameter to *lineGetDevCaps, dwVersionToUse,* is the negotiated version number you retrieved in your call to *lineNegotiateAPIVersion. lineGetDevCaps* is a good example of why version negotiation is important. The amount of information returned in LINEDEVCAPS is so large and so varied that LINEDEVCAPS will probably be changed in future versions of Windows. If not for the version information passed to *lineGetDevCaps,* Windows would not know which version of LINEDEVCAPS to return to the application.

The fourth parameter, *dwExtVersion,* is the extension version number you obtained from *lineNegotiateExtVersion.* Unimodem does not support extensions, so this parameter should be set to 0 when Unimodem is installed. The last parameter points to a LINEDEVCAPS structure where the information about the line is returned. The format of LINEDEVCAPS is as follows:

```
typedef struct linedevcaps_tag {
    DWORD      dwTotalSize;
    DWORD      dwNeededSize;
    DWORD      dwUsedSize;

    DWORD      dwProviderInfoSize;
    DWORD      dwProviderInfoOffset;

    DWORD      dwSwitchInfoSize;
    DWORD      dwSwitchInfoOffset;

    DWORD      dwPermanentLineID;
    DWORD      dwLineNameSize;
    DWORD      dwLineNameOffset;
    DWORD      dwStringFormat;

    DWORD      dwAddressModes;
    DWORD      dwNumAddresses;
    DWORD      dwBearerModes;
    DWORD      dwMaxRate;
    DWORD      dwMediaModes;

    DWORD      dwGenerateToneModes;
    DWORD      dwGenerateToneMaxNumFreq;
    DWORD      dwGenerateDigitModes;
    DWORD      dwMonitorToneMaxNumFreq;
    DWORD      dwMonitorToneMaxNumEntries;
    DWORD      dwMonitorDigitModes;
    DWORD      dwGatherDigitsMinTimeout;
    DWORD      dwGatherDigitsMaxTimeout;

    DWORD      dwMedCtlDigitMaxListSize;
    DWORD      dwMedCtlMediaMaxListSize;
    DWORD      dwMedCtlToneMaxListSize;
    DWORD      dwMedCtlCallStateMaxListSize;

    DWORD      dwDevCapFlags;
    DWORD      dwMaxNumActiveCalls;
    DWORD      dwAnswerMode;
    DWORD      dwRingModes;
    DWORD      dwLineStates;
```

```
    DWORD     dwUUIAcceptSize;
    DWORD     dwUUIAnswerSize;
    DWORD     dwUUIMakeCallSize;
    DWORD     dwUUIDropSize;
    DWORD     dwUUISendUserUserInfoSize;
    DWORD     dwUUICallInfoSize;

    LINEDIALPARAMS     MinDialParams;
    LINEDIALPARAMS     MaxDialParams;
    LINEDIALPARAMS     DefaultDialParams;

    DWORD     dwNumTerminals;
    DWORD     dwTerminalCapsSize;
    DWORD     dwTerminalCapsOffset;
    DWORD     dwTerminalTextEntrySize;
    DWORD     dwTerminalTextSize;
    DWORD     dwTerminalTextOffset;

    DWORD     dwDevSpecificSize;
    DWORD     dwDevSpecificOffset;
    DWORD     dwLineFeatures;
} LINEDEVCAPS, FAR *LPLINEDEVCAPS;
```

A good way to learn about logical line devices is to go through this structure member by member. But first you must understand the important distinction between analog phone lines and digital phone lines.

Analog lines vs. digital lines

Analog lines are old technology. Most phone networks that connect residential homes and small businesses consist of analog lines. Analog lines have certain physical characteristics that make them well-suited for carrying human voice information over long distances but limit their usefulness for carrying bits of information from a computer. Basically, bits of information are converted to a form that more resembles human voice information, in a process called *modulation*. A modem modulates and then demodulates the bits of information sent out over the analog line. (Hence the name *modem,* which is short for modulator/demodulator.)

Some confusion has arisen over the use of the term *modem*. It is most aptly used to describe devices that convert digital signals to analog and vice versa, using modulation and demodulation, but the term is also used to describe devices that send digital data over digital lines. To distinguish between the two types of modem, the terms *analog modem* and *digital modem* are often used. An analog modem is a true modulator/demodulator. A digital modem transmits digital information, but it does not use modulation or demodulation because the information is never converted to analog data. (Similarly, an analog [G3] fax device sends fax information over an analog line. A G4 fax also sends fax data, but it does so over a digital line.)

Because digital lines transmit information as digital bits from one end of the line to the other, modulation and demodulation are unnecessary. This results in digital lines having fewer physical limitations than analog lines. Also, digital lines are faster and generally more efficient than analog lines for sending bits of information between two computers.

TAPI was designed to support both analog lines and the more versatile digital lines, which will someday replace analog lines as the standard. TAPI is full of functions and structure members that apply only to digital lines. As a general rule, these are not implemented by the Unimodem telephony driver in the initial release of Windows 95. Therefore, they are not covered in this book. Microsoft might implement a telephony driver with all-digital functionality in a later version of Windows, once digital lines become more common and once a clear digital standard emerges. (ISDN, though hampered by a slow introduction, might someday become the digital standard in the United States.)

Members of LINEDEVCAPS

Let's begin our discussion of the LINEDEVCAPS structure with the first three members. You should recognize these members by now as the size members of a variable-sized structure. The member *dwTotalSize* defines the total size of the container for holding the base structure and any extra data that is appended to the base structure. The calling application should initialize this member before passing the structure to *lineGetDevCaps*. Calling *lineGetDevCaps* causes Windows to check the value of *dwTotalSize* to determine how much memory the application has allocated for the structure. Windows then sets the member *dwNeededSize* to indicate how much memory is required to return all available information. Your application should always compare *dwNeededSize* to *dwTotalSize* to determine whether Windows needs more memory to return all of the available information. If *dwNeededSize* is greater than *dwTotalSize*, the container should be reallocated with *dwNeededSize* worth of memory, *dwTotalSize* should be set to *dwNeededSize*, and *lineGetDevCaps* should be called again. The following code shows how this can be done:

```
LINEDEVCAPS *ldc;
 :
ldc = (LINEDEVCAPS *) calloc(sizeof(LINDEVCAPS), 1);
ldc->dwTotalSize = sizeof(LINEDEVCAPS);
while ((lrc = lineGetDevCaps(hTAPI,
                            0,              /* line id */
                            dwVersionToUse,
                            0,              /* no extensions */
                            ldc)) ==0) {
```

```
    if (ldc->dwNeededSize > ldc->dwTotalSize) {
        dwNeededSize = ldc->dwNeededSize;
        free (ldc);
        ldc = (LINEDEVCAPS*) calloc(dwNeededSize, 1);
        ldc->dwTotalSize = dwNeededSize;
    } //if
    else
        break;
} //while
if (lrc)
    ProcessTAPIError(lrc);
```

Windows also sets the member *dwUsedSize* to indicate how much of the allocated container actually contains useful information. *dwUsedSize* is equal to *dwNeededSize* when the application allocates as much as or more memory for the structure than Windows needs. *dwUsedSize* is less than *dwNeededSize* if the application allocates too few bytes for the container.

Now let's look at some of the more important members of LINEDEVCAPS. The member *dwStringFormat* specifies the character string formats supported by the line device. We first encountered string formats earlier in this chapter when using the VARSTRING structure to retrieve the modem handle. Unimodem supports both ASCII and Unicode string formats (STRINGFORMAT_ASCII and STRINGFORMAT_UNICODE).

The member *dwNumAddresses* indicates the number of addresses supported by the logical line device. Unimodem supports a single address on the line. The member *dwAddressModes* defines how an application should identify the address of the line. Your application can identify the address of a line in two ways: by the phone number of the address or by an integer. When an integer is used, it must be within the range of 0 to *dwNumAddresses*–1. Because *dwNumAddresses* is 1 for Unimodem, the value 0 should be used to identify the single address on the line. Unimodem does not support specifying the address using the phone number. Several TAPI functions that we'll examine later require that the address of the line be specified using an integer.

The member *dwBearerModes* specifies the bearer modes that are supported by the line. Bearer mode is one of the more difficult telephony concepts to grasp. The bearer mode defines, in general terms, the types of data that can be reliably transmitted over the line. For example, lines that support the *voice bearer mode* can reliably transmit human voices. Such lines can also transmit modem and fax data because modem and fax data are, through modulation, suited for analog lines that are designed to transmit voice data. Not all analog lines that support the reliable transmission of voices will reliably transmit modem and fax data, however. Some lines are designed to make the widest range of human voices sound as clear as possible by using special signal processing and compression techniques (such as companding, echo cancellation, and filtering). These special techniques wreak havoc on modem and fax data because they actually add and remove bits from the data. Lines that do this support what is called the *speech bearer mode*. Unimodem supports lines with the voice bearer mode but does not support the speech bearer mode. The LINEBEARER-MODE_VOICE flag is set in the *dwBearerModes* member for lines using the voice bearer mode. Several other bearer modes, including unrestricted data mode, alternate speech and data mode, and multiuse mode, apply only to digital lines and are currently not supported. These bearer modes might be supported in future versions of Windows.

Before attempting to send or receive data with the modem or fax, an application should always check that the line supports the voice bearer mode, as in the following code example:

```
if (!(ldc->dwBearerModes & LINEBEARERMODE_VOICE))
    MessageBox (hWnd, "Error - Line does not support voice bearer \
              mode", "ERROR", MB_OK);
```

As we've stated, the bearer mode specifies, generally, the types of data transfer that the line supports. An application can determine specifically which types of data transfer the line supports by checking the *dwMediaModes* member. For example, the voice bearer mode includes support for human voice data, analog modem data, and G3 fax data. The media mode defines specifically whether one or more of these three data types are supported. A setting of LINEMEDIAMODE_INTERACTIVEVOICE in the *dwMediaModes* member specifies that the line supports the transfer of human voice information. Human voice calls are the kind of calls that we made in Chapter 2 using *tapiRequestMakeCall*. A setting of LINEMEDIAMODE_DATAMODEM indicates that the line supports the transfer of analog modem data. LINEMEDIAMODE-_G3FAX indicates that the line supports the transfer of G3 (analog) fax data.

Unimodem supports human voice data and analog modem data. To indicate this support, the *dwMediaModes* member is set to LINEMEDIAMODE_INTER-ACTIVEVOICE | LINEMEDIAMODE_DATAMODEM. *dwMediaModes* will *not* indicate that the line supports fax data, even if a fax modem is attached. What is going on here? Well, you can send and receive faxes in Windows 95, but you should use the Messaging API to send and receive fax data, for the reasons set forth in Chapter 1. Microsoft has designed Windows 95 so that the MAPI drivers and the telephony drivers are integrated at a low level. Applications cannot answer fax calls using TAPI. Only MAPI drivers have this privilege. Applications can make outgoing fax calls using TAPI, but this practice is discouraged. Thus, LINEMEDIAMODE_G3FAX is not supported by the line device specified in the call to *lineGetDevCaps*.

Unimodem does not support the transfer of digital modem or digital fax data types. The flags for these unsupported media modes are LINEMEDIAMODE_DIGITALDATA and LINEMEDIAMODE_G4FAX, respectively. Digital modem data and digital fax data require lines that transfer data digitally from one end to the other. POTS lines transfer data in an analog form. Currently, Unimodem supports only POTS lines, although this might change in the future.

Another media mode that is currently not supported by Unimodem but will likely be supported in the future is the *automated voice* media mode. (The Unimodem voice modem extensions support this mode.) Automated voice is specified by the flag LINEMEDIAMODE_AUTOMATEDVOICE. The automated voice media mode is used by software answering machines, voicemail systems, and any application that plays or records audio messages over the phone line. The difference between the automated voice media mode and the interactive voice media mode is subtle but important. You might wonder how a line can support the transfer of human voices and yet not support the human voice messages that are played and recorded by answering machines. The reason is that for the automated voice media mode, the audio data must actually originate from or terminate within the computer. To send a voice message, an answering machine application must somehow take the information stored in a sound file, such as a Windows .wav file, and play this information over the phone line in real time. (Recall the discussion in Chapter 1 about the difference between real-time and non-real-time data). Likewise, to record a message, the answering machine application must somehow record the audio data from the phone line in real time and then save it to a file. This all requires special hardware, which in turn requires special software, which is not currently implemented by Unimodem. However, future versions of Windows will likely offer standard support for automated voice, and in the meantime third-party hardware and drivers can do the job.

An application should call *lineGetDevCaps* for each logical line device until it identifies a line that supports the type of data the application is interested in. Once it identifies a compatible line, it should open that line, as described in the next section. The following code shows how an application can test each line supported by Windows until it finds one that supports the type of data that the application works with.

```
LINEDEVCAPS *ldc;
⋮
lrc = lineInitialize(&hTAPI, hInstance, CallbackFunction, "",
                     &numLines);
if (lrc)
    ProcessTAPIError(lrc);
```

(continued)

```
for (i=0; i < numLines; i++) {
    ldc = (LINEDEVCAPS *) calloc(sizeof(LINEDEVCAPS), 1);
    ldc->dwTotalSize = sizeof(LINEDEVCAPS);
    while ((lrc = lineGetDevCaps(hTAPI,
                                i,          /* line id */
                                dwVersionToUse,
                                0,          /* no extensions */
                                ldc)) ==0) {
        if (ldc->dwNeededSize > ldc->dwTotalSize) {
            dwNeededSize = ldc->dwNeededSize;
            free (ldc);
            ldc = (LINEDEVCAPS*) calloc(dwNeededSize, 1);
            ldc->dwTotalSize = dwNeededSize;
            continue;
        } //if
        else {
            if (ldc->dwMediaModes & LINEMEDIAMODE_DATAMODEM)
                goto done;
            else
                continue;
        }
    } //while
    if (lrc)
        ProcessTAPIError(lrc);
    free (ldc);
}
done:
    if (i<numLines) {
        /* found a compatible line! */
        dwLineToUse = i;
        free(ldc);
    }
```

In this example, *lineGetDevCaps* is called for each line device on the PC supported by Windows until a line that supports analog modem calls (LINEMEDIAMODE_DATAMODEM) is located. The number of supported lines, *numLines,* is returned by *lineInitialize*. When a compatible line is located, the integer identifying the line is saved in the variable *dwLineToUse* for later use by the application.

Two members of LINEDEVCAPS, *dwNumAddresses* and *dwMaxNumActiveCalls,* define the number of addresses and the number of simultaneous calls that the line supports, respectively. For the POTS lines supported by Unimodem, both fields are set to 1. In other words, the line has one phone number and supports one *active* call at a time. This does not preclude call waiting, because with call waiting only one call is active at a time. That is, only one call at a time is actually used to transfer human voices. With call waiting, the call that is waiting is effectively placed on hold.

The member *dwMaxRate* specifies the maximum data rate supported by the modem, which is the same value as the *dwMaxDCERate* member of MODEMDEVCAPS.

Configuring a Line

An application can configure a line before opening it by calling the function *lineConfigDialog,* as shown below. This function displays a Properties dialog box with tabs that contain configuration information for the line. With Unimodem, this information is simply the modem settings. These are not the same settings that would be displayed by a call to *CommConfigDialog;* these settings relate to how the modem sets up calls and transfers data, whereas *CommConfigDialog* displays the settings for the port to which the modem is attached. The dialog box returned by *lineConfigDialog* is the same dialog box that is displayed when you click the Properties button in the Modems Properties dialog box, with one exception: *lineConfigDialog* displays an extra tab, called Options, with additional dialing options. This extra tab is not displayed by the Modems applet on the Control Panel.

```
lineConfigDialog (dwLine, hWnd, lpszDeviceClass);
```

The first parameter, *dwLine,* is an integer that identifies the line device. The second parameter, *hWnd,* is a handle to the window of the calling application. The last parameter, *lpszDeviceClass,* can be used to specify which type of media device you want to configure the modem for. With Unimodem, this last parameter should be set to NULL. You can use device classes such as COMM and comm/datamodem to specify that the modem be configured to work with a serial media device such as the COM port. However, when calling the function with Unimodem, this will not change the behavior of the function, since Unimodem assumes that the modem is used with a serial port. Calling the function with unsupported device names results in an error.

The General tab of the Properties dialog box lets you specify the COM port to which the modem is attached, the volume setting of the modem speaker, and the maximum data rates to use with the modem. (See Figure 4-4 on the next page.) A word of warning: The data rates displayed in this setting are those supported by the COM port and the port driver, and might not correspond to what your modem supports. If the displayed maximum data rate clearly exceeds the maximum rate supported by your modem, select the listed value that is nearest (but not greater than) your modem's maximum rate. Selecting a higher rate than what your modem supports is not fatal as long as your application checks the *dwMaxDCERate* member against the *dwBaudRate* member of the DCB and uses the lesser one. Also, when selecting the baud rate, bear in mind that your modem might use compression to achieve data rates that are not listed for the COM port. For example, a 9600 baud modem might achieve data rates of 14.4 Kbps by using compression.

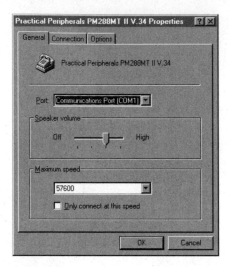

Figure 4-4. *The General tab of the Properties dialog box for a Practical Peripherals modem.*

The Connection tab of the dialog box, shown in Figure 4-5, has settings for the modem baud rate (data bits), parity method, and number of stop bits. These are the settings that will be used to transfer data between the two modems once a connection is made; these settings should match those specified for the serial port in the DCB structure. The Connection tab also has settings to tell the modem to wait for a dial tone before dialing (the same as including a *W* before any digit in a dial string), and settings for call setup fail timer and inactivity timeout. Changing these last two settings changes the values in the *dwCallSetupFailTimer* and *dwInactivityTimeout* members of the MODEMSETTINGS structure.

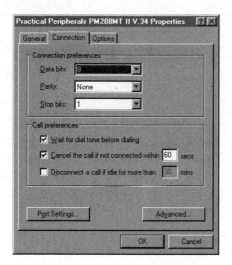

Figure 4-5. *The Connection tab of the Properties dialog box for a Practical Peripherals modem.*

On the Connection tab, you can click the Port Settings button, which brings up a dialog box that lets you specify buffering preferences for receiving and transmitting bytes. Also on the Connection tab, you can click the Advanced button to display a dialog box containing advanced connection settings, as shown in Figure 4-6 on the next page. You can specify whether to use error control protocols and compression when transferring data with the modem and whether to use hardware or software flow control between the port and the modem. You can also specify the low-speed modulation type to use with slow modems. (You should generally ignore this unless you are connecting at a very low speed [1200 or 300 baud].)

One of the most interesting fields in the Advanced Connection Settings dialog box is called Extra Settings. This is where clever users can tell Windows to send extra initialization commands to the modem during initialization (when the line device is opened by a first application). These modem initialization commands usually take the form of AT command strings, and they can be used to make the modem execute functions that are not supported by Windows, especially if the modem is an unusual model or brand that Windows does not recognize.

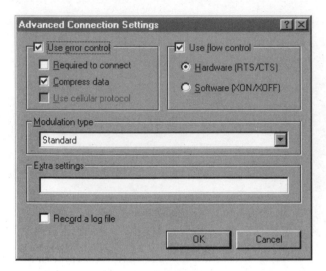

Figure 4-6. *The Advanced Connection Settings dialog box.*

The Advanced Connection Settings dialog box also includes a check box for recording a log file, called MODEMLOG.TXT, in the Windows home directory. This is an incredibly useful feature for troubleshooting when you are having trouble making a call. The following listing is an example of this log file. It was generated by attempting to use the Phone Dialer application in the Accessories folder to make a call on a U.S. Robotics Sportster 14400 fax modem. The phone line was deliberately disconnected so that Windows would not receive a dial tone when it attempted to dial the phone. A word of warning: You should disable the log file setting after you locate the problem. Otherwise, the log file will continue to accumulate information every time you use the modem, and it might grow quite large.

```
07-13-1995 13:48:43.33 - Sportster 14400 FAX in use.
07-13-1995 13:48:43.43 - Modem type: Sportster 14400 FAX
07-13-1995 13:48:43.43 - Modem inf path: MDMUSRSP.INF
07-13-1995 13:48:43.43 - Modem inf section: Modem2
07-13-1995 13:48:43.71 - 38400,N,8,1
07-13-1995 13:48:44.59 - 38400,N,8,1
07-13-1995 13:48:44.61 - Initializing modem.
07-13-1995 13:48:44.61 - Send: AT<cr>
07-13-1995 13:48:44.62 - Recv: AT<cr>
07-13-1995 13:48:44.77 - Recv: <cr><lf>OK<cr><lf>
07-13-1995 13:48:44.77 - Interpreted response: Ok
07-13-1995 13:48:44.77 - Send: AT&FE0V1&A3&B1&D2&S0<cr>
```

```
07-13-1995 13:48:44.80 - Recv: AT&FE0V1&A3&B1&D2&S0<cr>
07-13-1995 13:48:44.95 - Recv: <cr><lf>OK<cr><lf>
07-13-1995 13:48:44.95 - Interpreted response: Ok
07-13-1995 13:48:44.95 - Send:
ATS7=60S19=0L0M1&M4&K1&H1&R2&I0B1X4<cr>
07-13-1995 13:48:45.13 - Recv: <cr><lf>OK<cr><lf>
07-13-1995 13:48:45.13 - Interpreted response: Ok
07-13-1995 13:48:45.13 - Dialing.
07-13-1995 13:48:45.13 - Send: ATDT;<cr>
07-13-1995 13:48:47.15 - Recv: <cr><lf>NO DIAL TONE<cr><lf>
07-13-1995 13:48:47.16 - Interpreted response: No Dialtone
07-13-1995 13:48:47.49 - Session Statistics:
07-13-1995 13:48:47.49 -                    Reads : 58 bytes
07-13-1995 13:48:47.49 -                    Writes: 66 bytes
07-13-1995 13:48:47.49 - Sportster 14400 FAX closed.
```

The log file includes all of the AT commands that were sent by Unimodem to the modem. This can be invaluable, especially to experienced modem users, in determining whether there is a problem with the way Windows and the modem are interacting. Notice that the log includes the strings returned by the modem to Windows in response to the AT commands. Notice also toward the end of the file that the modem reports to Windows that no dial tone could be detected on the line. Because the wait-for-dial-tone option was selected, Windows did not send the dial string until it detected a dial tone. Therefore, no dialing was performed and Windows reported an error. For security and privacy reasons, the log file won't record the actual digits of the phone number dialed. So, for example, the modem command string ATDT5551212 ("dial 5551212") is logged as ATDT#######.

The Options tab, shown in Figure 4-7 on the next page, is displayed only when an application calls *lineConfigDialog;* it is not displayed from the Modems applet on the Windows Control Panel. This tab contains additional settings for dialing. Two of these options control the display of a terminal screen for entering modem control commands both before and after dialing. Like the Extra Settings field in the Advanced Connection Settings dialog box, the terminal window that is displayed allows you to manually control the modem both before and after dialing. You typically do this by entering AT commands in the terminal window, and then pressing F7 to send the commands to the modem. Entering commands at the terminal window is more flexible than entering them in the Extra Settings field because you can enter the commands both before and after dialing, not just when the modem is initialized by a first application. Only sophisticated users will want to use the terminal screens, however.

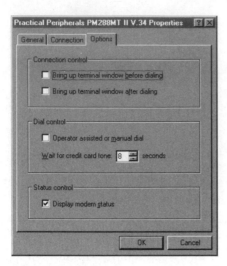

Figure 4-7. *The Options tab of the Properties dialog box for a Practical Peripherals modem.*

Another setting on the Options tab is for manual dialing. Manual dialing is useful when you are unable to dial the number automatically. When the manual dial setting is selected, Windows will prompt you with a message box that asks you to lift the receiver and dial the number manually. You dial and then listen for the screeching of the modem on the other end, which indicates that it is time for the local modem to connect. You then click the Connect button in the message box, and Windows tells the local modem to negotiate a connection with the remote modem. You should hang up the phone while the modems negotiate to avoid introducing noise onto the line.

The last setting on the Options tab is for status control. Selecting this setting displays the status of the connection in a status window.

Notice that all of the configuration changes made using *lineConfigDialog* are made to the Windows telephony drivers. No structure or information of any kind is returned to the application by the function. The settings stay in effect for as long as the application is running and does not call *lineShutDown*. Once the application calls *lineShutDown,* the settings revert to those set using the Modems applet. To make the options more permanent, or to make them apply to all applications in the system that call *lineConfigDialog,* change the settings in the Modems applet.

When an application changes the modem settings directly, it should use the MODEMDEVCAPS structure to determine which settings a modem does and does not support. Using *lineConfigDialog,* Windows will do this verification for you. For example, if you try to enter an inactivity timeout greater than the maximum allowed, Windows limits the value to the maximum allowed. These settings are reflected in the MODEMSETTINGS structure.

Another function, similar to *lineConfigDialog*, is *lineConfigDialogEdit*. *lineConfigDialogEdit* displays an identical dialog box, but it does not actually change the settings of the modem and the port. Rather, the new settings selected in the dialog box are returned to the calling application in a VARSTRING structure. This function is good for displaying initial settings to the user that are different from the system defaults. The syntax for the *lineConfigDialogEdit* function is shown below.

```
LONG lineConfigDialogEdit(DWORD dwDeviceID, HWND hwndOwner,
                          LPCSTR lpszDeviceClass,
                          LPVOID const lpDeviceConfigIn,
                          DWORD dwSize,
                          LPVARSTRING lpDeviceConfigOut);
```

The *lpDeviceConfigIn* parameter points to a VARSTRING structure that holds initial settings displayed by the dialog box. The *dwSize* parameter specifies the size of this initial information. The *lpDeviceConfigOut* parameter is a VARSTRING parameter in which the final settings in the dialog box are returned. For modems attached to COM ports, the device-specific portion of VARSTRING has the format of a DEVCFG structure, as shown on page 128.

Retrieving the Modem Icon

An application can retrieve an icon from Windows for the line device. A handle to the icon is retrieved using the function *lineGetIcon,* as shown below.

```
lineGetIcon (dwLine, lpszDataType, &hIcon)
```

The first parameter is the integer identifying the line. The second parameter specifies the media device associated with the line. With Unimodem, the associated media device is always a serial port. You can leave this parameter NULL or set it to COMM or comm/datamodem. In all three cases, a handle to a telephone icon is returned to the calling application. Drivers other than Unimodem might return icons that are different from the standard yellow telephone. Your application can use the icon to represent its minimized window using *SetClassLong,* as shown below.

```
HICON hIcon;

lineGetIcon (0, NULL, &hIcon);
SetClassLong (hWnd, GCL_HICON, hIcon);
```

The icon can also be displayed by the calling application using *DrawIcon*, as shown below.

```
hDC = GetDC (hWnd);
DrawIcon (hDC,
         100,          /* x coord of icon on client area */
         100,          /* y coord of icon on client area */
         hIcon);
ReleaseDC (hWnd, hDC);
```

Your application should not attempt to release the resources associated with the icon handle. Windows owns the icon and will free the resources when they are no longer required.

Opening a Line

More than any other step in the communications process, opening a line affects what communications functions an application can perform. An application can open a line to handle incoming calls, monitor calls, make outbound calls, or any combination of the three.

To open a line, an application calls *lineOpen,* as shown below. *lineOpen* returns a handle to the line device, which can be used to access many other telephony functions. This line handle was used in the call to *lineGetID* to retrieve the modem handle to use with the Win32c functions.

```
lineOpen (hTAPI, dwDeviceID, &hLine, dwVersionToUse,
         dwExtensionVersion, dwInstanceData, dwPrivileges,
         dwMediaModes, lpCallParams)
```

The first parameter, *hTAPI,* is the API usage handle. The second parameter, *dwDeviceID,* is the integer that identifies which line device to open. This integer should identify a line device that is compatible with the type of data the application handles and can be located by calling *lineGetDevCaps* for each supported line and checking the *dwMediaModes* member of the LINEDEVCAPS structure. The third parameter, *hLine,* is where Windows returns the handle to the line device. This parameter should be a pointer to a variable of the type HLINE. The fourth parameter, *dwVersionToUse,* is the negotiated API version. The fifth parameter, *dwExtensionVersion,* is the negotiated extension version. The extension version should be set to 0 when Unimodem is the installed telephony driver. The sixth parameter, *dwInstanceData,* is opaque application instance data that Windows passes to the application callback function defined in the call to *lineInitialize.*

The parameters you should pay the most attention to are *dwPrivileges* and *dwMediaModes*. *dwPrivileges* specifies how the application wants to handle calls on the line. If an application wants to answer incoming calls, *dwPrivileges* should include the flag LINECALLPRIVILEGE_OWNER. With this flag, Windows gives the application the opportunity to answer incoming calls as well as the opportunity to make outbound calls. A flag of LINECALLPRIVILEGE_MONITOR tells Windows to notify the application of all inbound and outbound calls that are handled by *other* applications. The application will receive messages from Windows indicating the status of all calls on the line, both inbound and outbound. However, the application will not be permitted to make or answer calls. This flag is best suited for applications that perform call logging but don't actually need to make or answer calls. The flag LINECALLPRIVILEGE_NONE tells Windows that the application is only interested in making outbound calls, and not in answering calls. It is possible to combine two of the flags when an application wants to answer incoming calls and also monitor incoming calls when it cannot answer them. In this case the application should specify LINECALLPRIVILEGE_OWNER | LINECALLPRIVILEGE_MONITOR. It is possible for an application to request to answer incoming calls but not actually get to do so. This could happen, for instance, if two applications are running and both are interested in answering incoming calls. When a call arrives, only one of the applications can answer it—the application with a higher priority for that kind of call. You'll learn how to prioritize calls later in this chapter. For now, just be aware that if an application specifies only LINECALLPRIVILEGE-_OWNER and not LINECALLPRIVILEGE_MONITOR, it might never get to answer a call or even be aware that an incoming call has arrived.

When an application attempts to open the line with LINECALLPRIVI-LEGE_OWNER, Windows checks to see whether another application has already opened the line with owner privileges. If no other application has opened the line, Windows configures the modem to automatically answer incoming calls on behalf of the opening application. Depending on the model of your modem, you might see various lights flashing and lighting up when the modem is opened with owner privileges. You will not see this happen when the modem is opened with LINECALLPRIVILEGE_MONITOR or LINECALL-PRIVILEGE_NONE. When the modem is opened with either of these last two privilege modes, Windows does not configure the modem to automatically answer incoming calls because the application has indicated that it does not want to answer incoming calls.

You will also notice that when you open the line with LINECALLPRIVILEGE-_MONITOR or LINECALLPRIVILEGE_NONE, you cannot retrieve a modem handle using *lineGetID*. Although *lineGetID* returns successfully, the modem handle it returns will be NULL. *lineGetID* will still return the device string that identifies the modem, and the application can call *CreateFile* to open the modem using this string. (Note: The modem string must be prefixed with information that lets *CreateFile* know that it's opening a device, not a file. In the case of modems, the string must be prefixed with the characters \\.\ to designate a modem string.) Or the application can wait until after an outbound call is established, and at that time call *lineGetID* to retrieve the modem handle.

The *dwMediaModes* parameter of *lineOpen* specifies which types of calls the application wants to answer or monitor. For example, specifying LINEMEDIA-MODE_DATAMODEM with owner call privileges tells Windows that the application wants to answer analog modem calls. Unimodem supports only LINEMEDIAMODE_DATAMODEM when an application specifies owner privileges. An application cannot attempt to answer fax calls by specifying LINEMEDIAMODE_G3FAX with owner privileges; the MAPI drivers have owner privileges over all incoming fax calls. Nor can an application attempt to answer incoming human voice calls (*dwMediaMode* set to LINEMEDIAMODE-_INTERACTIVEVOICE). There is no reason for applications to answer interactive voice calls; by definition, these are answered by humans. Therefore, an application cannot specify LINEMEDIAMODE_INTERACTIVEVOICE with owner privileges when it opens the line. The call to *lineOpen* will return an error if an unsupported media mode is specified, even if the unsupported mode is specified in combination with a supported media mode. The media mode setting LINEMEDIAMODE_UNKNOWN, when specified with owner privileges, tells Windows that the application wants to answer and control inbound calls whose media mode is unknown or cannot be determined. However, Unimodem does not support LINEMEDIAMODE_UNKNOWN; an application must be explicit about the kind of calls it wants to answer and control when calling *lineOpen*.

An application can, however, specify any media mode when opening a line with LINECALLPRIVILEGE_MONITOR or LINECALLPRIVILEGE_NONE. It is therefore possible to monitor inbound fax calls and to make outbound fax calls and outbound interactive voice calls. To make an outbound interactive voice call, the application should dial the number for you, and when the party on the other end of the call picks up, you lift the receiver of the telephone and begin talking. The modem speaker should be turned on so that you can hear the party pick up.

The last parameter to *lineOpen, lpCallParams,* tells Windows to select a line for the application based on specified criteria. *lpCallParams* points to a structure of type LINECALLPARAMS, as shown below.

```
typedef struct linecallparams_tag {    // Defaults:
    DWORD    dwTotalSize;               // --------

    DWORD    dwBearerMode;              // voice
```

```
    DWORD       dwMinRate;                   // (3.1kHz)
    DWORD       dwMaxRate;                   // (3.1kHz)
    DWORD       dwMediaMode;                 // interactive voice

    DWORD       dwCallParamFlags;            // 0
    DWORD       dwAddressMode;               // addressID
    DWORD       dwAddressID;                 // (any available)

    LINEDIALPARAMS   DialParams;             // (0, 0, 0, 0)

    DWORD       dwOrigAddressSize;           // 0
    DWORD       dwOrigAddressOffset;
    DWORD       dwDisplayableAddressSize;    // 0
    DWORD       dwDisplayableAddressOffset;

    DWORD       dwCalledPartySize;           // 0
    DWORD       dwCalledPartyOffset;

    DWORD       dwCommentSize;               // 0
    DWORD       dwCommentOffset;

    DWORD       dwUserUserInfoSize;          // 0
    DWORD       dwUserUserInfoOffset;

    DWORD       dwHighLevelCompSize;         // 0
    DWORD       dwHighLevelCompOffset;

    DWORD       dwLowLevelCompSize;          // 0
    DWORD       dwLowLevelCompOffset;

    DWORD       dwDevSpecificSize;           // 0
    DWORD       dwDevSpecificOffset;
} LINECALLPARAMS, FAR *LPLINECALLPARAMS;
```

lineOpen does not use all of the members of LINECALLPARAMS, so most of the members can be ignored. *lineOpen* is interested only in the following members:

> DWORD   dwTotalSize;
>
> DWORD   dwBearerMode;
>
> DWORD   dwMinRate;
>
> DWORD   dwMaxRate;
>
> DWORD   dwMediaMode;
>
> DWORD   dwAddressMode;
>
> DWORD   dwCallParamFlags;

lineOpen considers the settings made by the application for all of these members together, and it tries to locate a line that is compatible with the settings.

The first member, *dwTotalSize,* tells Windows how much memory is available for returning information. LINECALLPARAMS is a variable-sized structure, so there might be times when Windows returns extra information appended to the end of the structure. Calling *lineOpen* is not one of those times. The LINECALLPARAMS structure does not need to contain extra information when calling *lineOpen,* so *dwTotalSize* can be set to sizeof(LINECALLPARAMS). The second member, *dwBearerMode,* specifies the bearer mode of the line to open. We first encountered the bearer mode setting for a line in the LINEDEVCAPS structure. The bearer mode specifies the general class of data transfer that the line supports. Unimodem line devices support human voice-class data, i.e. LINEBEARERMODE_VOICE. Lines that support this bearer mode support analog modem data and analog fax data. Both the bearer mode and the total size must be specified, or Windows returns an error.

The third and fourth members, *dwMinRate* and *dwMaxRate,* specify the information bandwidth requirements of the line to open. Unimodem does not interpret these members. However, other Windows telephony drivers might interpret them, so you should be aware of them. Information bandwidth is not the same as baud rate, although the concepts are related. For a POTS line, both *dwMinRate* and *dwMaxRate* should be set to 3100.

The member *dwMediaMode* specifies the media modes that the line must support. You must specify the media mode in the *dwMediaModes* parameter of *lineOpen,* even when the media mode is also specified in LINECALLPARAMS. Otherwise, *lineOpen* reports an error. If owner privileges are not requested, Windows ignores the media mode parameters entirely.

The *dwAddressMode* member specifies the addressing mode that the line should support. An application should set *dwAddressMode* to one of the address modes supported by the line and enumerated in the *dwAddressModes* member of LINEDEVCAPS. Unimodem requires that this member be set to LINEADDRESSMODE_ADDRESSID. Unimodem also accepts a value of 0 for this member because LINEADDRESSMODE_ADDRESSID is the default.

The member *dwCallParamFlags* specifies flags that control the behavior of the modem when making calls. The only flag interpreted by Unimodem is LINECALLPARAMFLAGS_IDLE, which if set tells Windows to dial the call without waiting for a dial tone. This is more commonly known as *blind dialing,* and is most useful for making calls on lines that do not produce dial tones. Normally, analog lines immediately produce a dial tone when the phone is taken off the hook for dialing. If the LINECALLPARAMFLAGS_IDLE flag is not set, Windows returns an error if it does not detect a dial tone a few moments after the phone is taken off the hook.

Windows ignores the *lpCallParams* parameter of *lineOpen* entirely unless owner privileges are specified and the *dwDeviceID* parameter is set to the special value LINEMAPPER. With Unimodem, when *dwDeviceID* is set to LINEMAPPER, *lineOpen* does not configure the modem to automatically answer incoming calls, even when owner privileges are specified. Nor will an application be able to retrieve a modem handle using *lineGetID* when the line is opened with LINEMAPPER. Instead, the application must call *lineGetID* to retrieve the integer ID for the line, and then call *lineOpen* again to open the line with owner privileges. The following example demonstrates this.

```
/* Locate a line that supports answer of analog modem calls */
hLineApp=hApp;
dwDeviceID=LINEMAPPER;
lphLine=&hLine;
dwAPIVersion=dwAPIVersion;
dwExtVersion=0;
dwCallbackInstance=0;
dwPrivileges=LINECALLPRIVILEGE_OWNER;
dwMediaModes=LINEMEDIAMODE_DATAMODEM;
lpCallParams=&CallParams;
CallParams.dwTotalSize = sizeof(LINECALLPARAMS);
CallParams.dwBearerMode=LINEBEARERMODE_VOICE;
CallParams.dwMinRate=0;
CallParams.dwMaxRate=0;
CallParams.dwMediaMode=LINEMEDIAMODE_DATAMODEM;
CallParams.dwAddressMode = LINEADDRESSMODE_ADDRESSID;
lResult =  lineOpen (hLineApp, dwDeviceID, lphLine, dwAPIVersion,
                     dwExtVersion, dwCallbackInstance, dwPrivileges,
                     dwMediaModes, lpCallParams);
/* Get the line device ID corresponding to the line handle returned
   by lineOpen */
dwAddressID = 0;
hCall = NULL;
dwSelect = LINECALLSELECT_LINE;
LPVARSTRING lpDeviceID = (LPVARSTRING)
                         calloc(1, sizeof(VARSTRING)+8);
lpszDeviceClass = "tapi/line";
lpDeviceID->dwTotalSize = sizeof(VARSTRING) + 8;
lResult = lineGetID (hLine, dwAddressID, hCall, dwSelect,
                     lpDeviceID, lpszDeviceClass);
memcpy(&dwLine, (void *)
       ((BYTE *)lpDeviceID+lpDeviceID->StringOffset),
       lpDeviceID->StringSize);
/* Opens logical line device specified by dwLine to answer analog
   modem calls, and to make calls of any type */
```

(continued)

```
hLineApp=hTAPI;
dwDeviceID=dwLine;
lphLine=&hLine;
dwAPIVersion=dwVersionToUse;
dwExtVersion=0;
dwCallbackInstance=0;
dwPrivileges=LINECALLPRIVILEGE_OWNER;
dwMediaModes=LINEMEDIAMODE_DATAMODEM;
lpCallParams=NULL;
lResult = lineOpen (hLineApp, dwDeviceID, lphLine, dwAPIVersion,
                    dwExtVersion, dwCallbackInstance, dwPrivileges,
                    dwMediaModes, lpCallParams);
free (lpDeviceID);
```

This example takes advantage of knowledge about the size of the line device ID when allocating the VARSTRING structure. The line device ID will always be a DWORD value exactly four bytes long. Thus, the example allocates VARSTRING to contain just a few extra bytes—as opposed to allocating exactly sizeof(VARSTRING) bytes and calling *lineGetID* twice, once to determine how much extra memory is required, a second time to retrieve the line ID. The example allocates eight extra bytes, which is more than enough for the four-byte line handle. It allocates the extra bytes in case Windows does not align the device ID exactly at the end of the structure. The device class is set to tapi/line, which tells Windows to return a line device ID compatible with TAPI. Because LINECALLSELECT_LINE is specified in *dwSelect,* the fourth parameter of *lineGetID,* the line device ID corresponds to the line handle passed in the first parameter.

The format of the returned line device ID is STRINGFORMAT_BINARY. The example uses memcpy to copy the line device ID into a local variable.

```
memcpy(&dwLine,(void *)
      ((BYTE *)lpDeviceID+lpDeviceID->StringOffset),
       lpDeviceID->StringSize);
```

The offset of the line device ID, measured in bytes from the beginning of the VARSTRING structure, is given by the *StringOffset* member of VARSTRING. The size of the ID is specified by the *StringSize* member. Once the device ID is copied to the local variable, the example calls *lineOpen* again to open the line with owner privileges for answering incoming analog modem calls. On this second call to *lineOpen,* Windows configures the modem to automatically answer incoming calls.

There are right and wrong ways to open a line device. The following examples show some of the right ways and some of the common mistakes. The first section in the example is a call to the *lineOpen* function. Each of the following sections demonstrate possible settings for the parameters in the *lineOpen* call.

```
/*****************************/
/* syntax of call to lineOpen */
/*****************************/

lResult =  lineOpen (hLineApp, dwDeviceID, lphLine, dwAPIVersion,
                     dwExtVersion, dwCallbackInstance, dwPrivileges,
                     dwMediaModes, lpCallParams);

/***********************************************/
/* Open logical line device 0 to answer analog  */
/*   modem calls, and to make calls of any type */
/***********************************************/

HLINEAPP hLineApp=hTAPI;
DWORD dwDeviceID=0;
LPHLINE lphLine=&hLine;
DWORD dwAPIVersion=dwVersionToUse;
DWORD dwExtVersion=0;
DWORD dwCallbackInstance=0;
DWORD dwPrivileges=LINECALLPRIVILEGE_OWNER;
DWORD dwMediaModes=LINEMEDIAMODE_DATAMODEM;
LPLINECALLPARAMS const lpCallParams=NULL;

/****************************************************/
/* Open logical line device 0 to answer analog      */
/*   modem calls, and to make any type of call       */
/*   supported by the line. Analog modem calls       */
/*   answered by another application will be         */
/*   monitored.                                      */
/****************************************************/

HLINEAPP hLineApp=hApp;
DWORD dwDeviceID=0;
LPHLINE lphLine=&hLine;
DWORD dwAPIVersion=dwAPIVersion;
DWORD dwExtVersion=0;
DWORD dwCallbackInstance=0;
DWORD dwPrivileges=
      LINECALLPRIVILEGE_OWNER+LINECALLPRIVILEGE_MONITOR;
DWORD dwMediaModes=LINEMEDIAMODE_DATAMODEM;
LPLINECALLPARAMS const lpCallParams=NULL;
```

(continued)

```
/***************************************************/
/* Open logical line device 0 to make any type of */
/*   calls supported by the line. The media mode   */
/*   parameter is not interpreted.                 */
/***************************************************/

HLINEAPP hLineApp=hApp;
DWORD dwDeviceID=0;
LPHLINE lphLine=&hLine;
DWORD dwAPIVersion=dwAPIVersion;
DWORD dwExtVersion=0;
DWORD dwCallbackInstance=0;
DWORD dwPrivileges=LINECALLPRIVILEGE_NONE;
DWORD dwMediaModes=LINEMEDIAMODE_DATAMODEM;
LPLINECALLPARAMS const lpCallParams=NULL;


/***************************************************/
/* Open logical line device 0 to answer analog */
/*   modem and analog fax calls.                */
/*   ERROR:                                     */
/*   Unimodem returns an error indicating that */
/*   analog fax calls cannot be answered by     */
/*   the application.                           */
/***************************************************/

HLINEAPP hLineApp=hApp;
DWORD dwDeviceID=0;
LPHLINE lphLine=&hLine;
DWORD dwAPIVersion=dwAPIVersion;
DWORD dwExtVersion=0;
DWORD dwCallbackInstance=0;
DWORD dwPrivileges=LINECALLPRIVILEGE_OWNER;
DWORD dwMediaModes=LINEMEDIAMODE_DATAMODEM|LINEMEDIAMODE_G3FAX;
LPLINECALLPARAMS const lpCallParams=NULL;


/*********************************************/
/* Open logical line device 0 to answer    */
/*   interactive voice calls.              */
/*   ERROR:                                */
/*   Unimodem returns an error indicating  */
/*   that interactive voice calls cannot   */
/*   be answered by the application.       */
/*********************************************/
```

```
HLINEAPP hLineApp=hApp;
DWORD dwDeviceID=0;
LPHLINE lphLine=&hLine;
DWORD dwAPIVersion=dwAPIVersion;
DWORD dwExtVersion=0;
DWORD dwCallbackInstance=0;
DWORD dwPrivileges=LINECALLPRIVILEGE_OWNER;
DWORD dwMediaModes=LINEMEDIAMODE_INTERACTIVEVOICE;
LPLINECALLPARAMS const lpCallParams=NULL;

/***********************************************/
/* Locate a line device that supports the      */
/*    answering of analog modem calls. Addresses */
/*    on the line are represented by a small    */
/*    integer. The line is not actually opened  */
/*    to answer analog modem calls. Rather, the */
/*    application must get the line device ID    */
/*    using lineGetID and call lineOpen a second */
/*    time with the device ID.                  */
/***********************************************/

HLINEAPP hLineApp=hApp;
DWORD dwDeviceID=LINEMAPPER;
LPHLINE lphLine=&hLine;
DWORD dwAPIVersion=dwAPIVersion;
DWORD dwExtVersion=0;
DWORD dwCallbackInstance=0;
DWORD dwPrivileges=LINECALLPRIVILEGE_OWNER;
DWORD dwMediaModes=LINEMEDIAMODE_DATAMODEM;
LINECALLPARAMS CallParams;
LPLINECALLPARAMS const lpCallParams=&CallParams;
CallParams.dwTotalSize = sizeof(LINECALLPARAMS);
CallParams.dwBearerMode=LINEBEARERMODE_VOICE;
CallParams.dwMinRate=0;
CallParams.dwMaxRate=0;
CallParams.dwMediaMode=LINEMEDIAMODE_DATAMODEM;
CallParams.dwAddressMode = LINEADDRESSMODE_ADDRESSID;

/*********************************************/
/* ERROR:                                    */
/*    Must specify media mode parameter, even */
/*    when using LINEMAPPER.                 */
/*********************************************/
```

(continued)

```
HLINEAPP hLineApp=hApp;
DWORD dwDeviceID=LINEMAPPER;
LPHLINE lphLine=&hLine;
DWORD dwAPIVersion=dwAPIVersion;
DWORD dwExtVersion=0;
DWORD dwCallbackInstance=0;
DWORD dwPrivileges=LINECALLPRIVILEGE_OWNER;
DWORD dwMediaModes=0;
LINECALLPARAMS CallParams;
LPLINECALLPARAMS const lpCallParams=&CallParams;
CallParams.dwTotalSize = sizeof(LINECALLPARAMS);
CallParams.dwBearerMode=LINEBEARERMODE_VOICE;
CallParams.dwMinRate=0;
CallParams.dwMaxRate=0;
CallParams.dwMediaMode=LINEMEDIAMODE_DATAMODEM;
CallParams.dwAddressMode = LINEADDRESSMODE_ADDRESSID;


/*********************************************/
/* Open the line to monitor analog fax calls  */
/*   that are answered by another application. */
/*********************************************/

HLINEAPP hLineApp=hApp;
DWORD dwDeviceID=0;
LPHLINE lphLine=&hLine;
DWORD dwAPIVersion=dwAPIVersion;
DWORD dwExtVersion=0;
DWORD dwCallbackInstance=0;
DWORD dwPrivileges=LINECALLPRIVILEGE_MONITOR;
DWORD dwMediaModes=LINEMEDIAMODE_G3FAX;
LPLINECALLPARAMS const lpCallParams=NULL;


/*******************************************/
/* Open the line to make interactive voice */
/*   calls.                                */
/*******************************************/

HLINEAPP hLineApp=hApp;
DWORD dwDeviceID=0;
LPHLINE lphLine=&hLine;
DWORD dwAPIVersion=dwAPIVersion;
DWORD dwExtVersion=0;
DWORD dwCallbackInstance=0;
DWORD dwPrivileges=LINECALLPRIVILEGE_NONE;
DWORD dwMediaModes=LINEMEDIAMODE_INTERACTIVEVOICE;
LPLINECALLPARAMS const lpCallParams=NULL;
```

```
/***********************************************/
/* Return handle of a line to make analog modem */
/*   calls. The call parameters are ignored.    */
/***********************************************/

HLINEAPP hLineApp=hApp;
DWORD dwDeviceID=LINEMAPPER;
LPHLINE lphLine=&hLine;
DWORD dwAPIVersion=dwAPIVersion;
DWORD dwExtVersion=0;
DWORD dwCallbackInstance=0;
DWORD dwPrivileges=LINECALLPRIVILEGE_NONE;
DWORD dwMediaModes=LINEMEDIAMODE_DATAMODEM;
LINECALLPARAMS CallParams;
LPLINECALLPARAMS const lpCallParams=&CallParams;
CallParams.dwBearerMode=LINEBEARERMODE_VOICE;
CallParams.dwMinRate=0;              // (3.1kHz)
CallParams.dwMaxRate=0;              // (3.1kHz)
CallParams.dwMediaMode=LINEMEDIAMODE_INTERACTIVEVOICE;
CallParams.dwAddressMode = 0; //LINEADDRESSMODE_ADDRESSID;
CallParams.dwTotalSize=sizeof(LINECALLPARAMS);
```

More on *lineGetID*

You now know how to use *lineGetID* to get a modem handle that is compatible with the Win32 Communications API. In this case, *lineGetID* is called with a device class of comm/datamodem. You can also use *lineGetID* to retrieve a logical line device ID corresponding to a line handle returned by *lineOpen* by setting the device class parameter to tapi/line. Other device classes can be used with *lineOpen* to retrieve handles and line device IDs for other situations. Specifying a device class of comm returns the name of the modem attached to the COMM port associated with the line device. A modem handle is not returned when the comm device class is specified; to get a modem handle you must specify comm/datamodem, and the line must be open with owner privileges. The format of the returned modem name is STRINGFORMAT_ASCII, and the name is located at *dwStringOffset* bytes from the start of the VARSTRING structure. Specifying a device class of ndis returns an eight-byte NDIS device identifier with a format of STRINGFORMAT_BINARY. The format of the NDIS identifier associated with the line is as follows:

```
typedef struct tag_NDISLine {
    HANDLE  hDevice;          // ndis connection identifier
    CHAR    szDeviceType[1]; // name of device
} NDISLine;
```

The *hDevice* member is the identifier to pass to an NDIS MAC, such as the asynchronous MAC for dial-up networking, to associate a network connection with the call/modem connection. *The szDeviceType* member is a null-terminated ASCII string specifying the name of the device associated with the identifier.

Telephony drivers that support real-time audio data (whose media mode is LINEMEDIAMODE_AUTOMATEDVOICE) might also support the device classes wave/in, wave/out, mci/wave, and mci/midi. The initial release of Unimodem does not support these device classes, although wave/in and wave/out are available with versions of Unimodem that support voice modems. Specifying the device class wave, if supported, returns a device ID that can be used with the Windows Multimedia Extensions WAVE API to play and record audio information in real time over the phone line. Similarly, mci/wave returns a handle to use with the Multimedia Extensions Media Control Interface (MCI) to play and record live audio over the phone line. The device class mci/midi returns a handle to use with MCI for playing MIDI files over the phone line.

When an application calls *lineGetID* to retrieve the ID for a device class, it will also want to call *lineGetDevConfig,* as shown below, to retrieve additional configuration information about the device class.

```
lineGetDevConfig (dwLine, vs, lpszDeviceClass)
```

The first parameter, *dwLine,* is the integer that identifies the line device (the line ID). The second parameter, *vs,* is a VARSTRING structure, which is used in the same way that it was used in the call to *lineGetID.* The last parameter, *lpszDeviceClass,* is the device class to retrieve information for. The name of the device class is the same as for the call to *lineGetID.* For example, if *lineGetID* is called with a device class of comm/datamodem, comm/datamodem should also be the device class used to call *lineGetDevConfig.*

Windows appends configuration information to the end of the VARSTRING structure. When the device class is comm/datamodem, the configuration information has the following format:

```
typedef struct  tagDEVCFG  {
    DWORD       dwSize;
    DWORD       dwVersion;
    WORD        fwOptions;
    WORD        wWaitBong;
    COMMCONFIG  commconfig;
} DEVCFG, *PDEVCFG;
```

The *dwSize* member of the DEVCFG structure contains the total number of bytes required to return all of the configuration information about the COM port. *dwVersion* is the version number of the DEVCFG structure. When Unimodem is used, this version number is set to MDMCFG_VERSION. *fwOptions* contains options flags corresponding to the settings on the Options tab of the dialog box that is displayed by calling *lineConfigDialog*. These flags are a combination of values:

TERMINAL_PRE	Display a terminal screen before dialing.
TERMINAL_POST	Display a terminal screen after dialing.
MANUAL_DIAL	Prompt for manual dialing.
LAUNCH_LIGHTS	Display the modem tray icon.

The *wWaitBong* member specifies the number of seconds (rounded to the nearest two-tenths of a second) that the wait-for-billing-tone character ($) will cause dialing to pause before timing out. This member is meaningless if wait-for-billing-tone is not supported by the line. The last member, *commconfig*, contains a COMMCONFIG structure for the COM port. (See Chapter 3 for more details).

You can change the settings for the media device by changing the members of DEVCFG and then calling *lineSetDevConfig*, as shown below.

```
lineSetDevConfig (dwDeviceID, vs, dwSize, lpszDeviceClass)
```

The parameters of *lineSetDevConfig* are the same as the parameters of *lineGetDevConfig*, except that *lineSetDevConfig* has an extra parameter, *dwSize*. This parameter is set to the total size of the VARSTRING container, *vs*, so that Windows knows how much useful information is available in VARSTRING.

In general, the format of the information returned by *lineGetDevConfig* is not defined by Microsoft, comm/datamodem devices being the one exception. In cases where the format of the configuration is undefined, *lineGetDevConfig* and *lineSetDevConfig* are still useful. They can be used to read and later restore the configuration of the media device. An application should restore the state of any media device to the state it was in before the application used it. This way, a second application can use the device after the first application is done, without performing a reconfiguration. Consider the following scenario:

1. Application 1 configures media device X but does not use it right away.

2. Application 2 calls *lineGetDevConfig* to retrieve the configuration of media device X. The retrieved configuration is the configuration set by Application 1.

3. Application 2 reconfigures the device and uses it to transfer data.

4. Application 2 finishes using the device to transfer data and calls *lineSetDevConfig* to restore the configuration read earlier with *lineGetDevConfig*.

5. Application 1 uses the device to transfer data. The configuration set earlier by Application 1 has been restored by Application 2, so Application 1 does not have to reconfigure the device. More important, Application 1 will not try to transfer data with the device configured improperly for Application 2.

The above scenario demonstrates why an application should call *lineGetDevConfig* before using a media device to transfer information, and then call *lineSetDevConfig* after transferring the data. Doing this prevents applications from overwriting one another's configurations.

Calls also require different configurations depending on the destinations. For example, calls to a particular online service might require that the COM port be configured for 9600 baud, 8 data bits, and one stop bit. You can use *lineGetDevConfig* to read the COM port settings for a particular destination so that those settings can be put into place automatically the next time that destination is called. For example, after you configure the COM port using a call to *CommConfigDialog,* an application can call *lineGetDevConfig* to retrieve the configuration of the port. This configuration can be saved in a database (for example, in a phone directory) along with the address of the destination to call. The next time you want to call that destination, you can simply open the address book and select the destination from there. You can retrieve the configuration information for the COM port from the phone book along with the address of the destination. The application can use *lineSetDevConfig* to implement the COM port settings for that destination. Notice that the application never has to know the exact format of the configuration data; it calls *lineGetDevConfig* to read the configuration information as a block, and the application calls *lineSetDevConfig* to restore the configuration settings as a block.

Exploring Addresses

Logical line devices can have one or more addresses, which are typically identified by a phone number or by an integer value. When making, answering, or monitoring calls, an application must select an address for each call. Windows provides information to the application about addresses on a line device. This information allows the application to use the address in a variety of ways that will be discussed in this section.

Address Capabilities

To discover more details about an address, an application should call the function *lineGetAddressCaps,* as shown below.

```
lineGetAddressCaps(hTAPI, dwLine, dwAddress, dwVersionToUse,
            dwExtension, lpAddressCaps)
```

The first parameter, *hTAPI,* is the TAPI handle returned by *lineInitialize.* The second and third parameters, *dwLine* and *dwAddress,* are integer IDs that identify the line device and address. The fourth parameter, *dwVersionToUse,* is the negotiated API version returned by *lineNegotiateAPIVersion.* The fifth parameter, *dwExtension,* is the API extension ID returned by *lineNegotiateExtension-Version.* When using Unimodem, both *dwLine* and *dwAddress* must be set to 0, because Unimodem supports only a single line and a single address per line, and ID values in TAPI are always based at 0. Unimodem does not support API extensions, so *dwExtension* should also be set to 0. The last parameter points to a LINEADDRESSCAPS structure, which has the following format:

```
typedef struct lineaddresscaps_tag {
    DWORD       dwTotalSize;
    DWORD       dwNeededSize;
    DWORD       dwUsedSize;
    DWORD       dwLineDeviceID;
    DWORD       dwAddressSize;
    DWORD       dwAddressOffset;
    DWORD       dwDevSpecificSize;
    DWORD       dwDevSpecificOffset;
    DWORD       dwAddressSharing;
    DWORD       dwAddressStates;
    DWORD       dwCallInfoStates;
    DWORD       dwCallerIDFlags;
    DWORD       dwCalledIDFlags;
    DWORD       dwConnectedIDFlags;
    DWORD       dwRedirectionIDFlags;
    DWORD       dwRedirectingIDFlags;
    DWORD       dwCallStates;
    DWORD       dwDialToneModes;
    DWORD       dwBusyModes;
    DWORD       dwSpecialInfo;
    DWORD       dwDisconnectModes;
    DWORD       dwMaxNumActiveCalls;
    DWORD       dwMaxNumOnHoldCalls;
    DWORD       dwMaxNumOnHoldPendingCalls;
    DWORD       dwMaxNumConference;
    DWORD       dwMaxNumTransConf;
    DWORD       dwAddrCapFlags;
    DWORD       dwCallFeatures;
    DWORD       dwRemoveFromConfCaps;
    DWORD       dwRemoveFromConfState;
    DWORD       dwTransferModes;
```

(continued)

```
    DWORD      dwParkModes;
    DWORD      dwForwardModes;
    DWORD      dwMaxForwardEntries;
    DWORD      dwMaxSpecificEntries;
    DWORD      dwMinFwdNumRings;
    DWORD      dwMaxFwdNumRings;
    DWORD      dwMaxCallCompletions;
    DWORD      dwCallCompletionConds;
    DWORD      dwCallCompletionModes;
    DWORD      dwNumCompletionMessages;
    DWORD      dwCompletionMsgTextEntrySize;
    DWORD      dwCompletionMsgTextSize;
    DWORD      dwCompletionMsgTextOffset;
/* TAPI for Windows 95 extension */
    DWORD      dwAddressFeatures;
} LINEADDRESSCAPS, FAR *LPLINEADDRESSCAPS;
```

The LINEADDRESSCAPS structure has many members, but we will cover only the most important ones here. Many of the members apply only to digital lines, which Unimodem does not support.

The *dwLineDeviceID* member identifies the line device with which the address is associated. This is the same line device ID that is used in the *dwLine* parameter in the call to *lineGetAddressCaps*. The *dwAddressSize* and *dwAddressOffset* members identify the size and offset of the phone number for the address. This is the number of the local address, not the number to dial. This phone number is appended to the end of LINEADDRESSCAPS. Like all variable-length strings in TAPI, the phone number should be copied under the assumption that it is not NULL terminated. The following code shows how to retrieve the phone number given *dwAddressSize* and *dwAddressOffset*.

```
memcpy (szPhoneNumber, (void *)((BYTE *)lpAddressCaps +
        lpAddressCaps->dwAddressOffset),
        lpAddressCaps->dwAddressSize);
szPhoneNumber[lpAddressCaps->dwAddressSize] = 0;
```

There is also a way to get the address ID that corresponds to a phone number. A call to the function *lineGetAddressID,* shown below, returns the address ID associated with a phone number. When Unimodem is installed, *lineGetAddressID* is not available and the function returns the error LINEERR_OPERATIONUNAVAIL. However, other telephony drivers (such as UnimodemV) might implement *lineGetAddressID*.

```
lineGetAddressID(hLine, &dwAddress, LINEADDRESSMODE_DIALABLEADDR,
                 szAddress, dwSize)
```

The first parameter of *lineGetAddessID, hLine,* is the handle to the open line device. The second parameter, *dwAddress,* points to the variable where the address ID is returned. The third parameter is a flag that you must set to LINEADDRESSMODE_DIALABLEADDR. Any other value causes the function to return an error. This flag tells Windows that the fourth parameter, *szAddress,* contains the phone number of the address. The last parameter, *dwSize,* indicates the length of the phone number, so you should set it to *strlen(szAddress).* If Windows finds an address to match the phone number, the address ID is returned in *dwAddress.* Otherwise, the function returns LINEERR_INVALADDRESS.

An application should never need the phone number of the address, except perhaps for displaying to users. It should never attempt to call this phone number, since this is like dialing to call yourself. *lineGetAddressID* is not available with Unimodem because Unimodem does not store the phone number of the address, so both *dwAddressSize* and *dwAddressOffset* are 0 when you use Unimodem.

Some phone systems allow multiple phones to share an address. For example, in a large business, calls to the boss' phone cause the secretary's phone to ring. (This is known as *call coverage*). The *dwAddressSharing* member of LINEADDRESSCAPS specifies whether an address is shared among multiple phones. In the case of the boss and the secretary, this member has the LINEADDRESSSHARING_BRIDGEDEXCL flag set. This indicates that the address is bridged (shared by multiple parties) and exclusive (available to only one party at a time). Address sharing is common with digital office phone systems. Unimodem does not support address sharing, so *dwAddressSharing* has the LINEADDRESSSHARING_PRIVATE flag set, indicating that the address is assigned to a single line and cannot be shared.

The member *dwCallInfoStates* contains values that indicate what information Windows will provide to an application about calls on this address. Windows will send a message to the application indicating that certain state information for a call has changed. For example, with Unimodem installed, Windows can notify an application when the media mode of a call changes, or when the number of applications that want to own or monitor the call changes. When *dwCallInfoStates* contains the flag LINECALLINFOSTATE_MEDIAMODE, Windows will notify your application when the media mode of a call changes. The media mode of a call might change, for example, if a call is initially thought to be a data modem call but is later determined to be a fax call. The media mode of the call will change from LINEMEDIAMODE_DATAMODEM to LINEMEDIAMODE_G3FAX. The flags LINECALLINFOSTATE_NUMOWNERINCR, LINECALLINFOSTATE_NUMOWNERDECR, and LINECALLINFOSTATE_NUMMONITORS indicate, respectively, that Windows will notify your application when the number of applications that want to own a call increases or decreases, or when the number of applications monitoring the call changes. An application that performs call logging would be especially interested in being notified of these changes. (See the discussion of the LINECALLINFO structure later in this chapter in the section titled "Answering a Call").

The *dwCallStates* member indicates which call states Windows can report to an application for calls on the address. Tracking call states is very important for making and answering calls, so this is one of the most important members in the LINEADDRESSCAPS structure. For example, it is crucial for an application to know when a call has been connected or disconnected or is receiving a dial tone. The following list shows the call states that are available in Windows 95. A check mark in the right-hand column indicates Unimodem support.

LINECALLSTATE_IDLE	The call no longer exists.	✓
LINECALLSTATE_OFFERING	An incoming call has arrived.	✓
LINECALLSTATE_ACCEPTED	The incoming call has been accepted for answering by an application but is not yet connected.	✓
LINECALLSTATE_DIALTONE	The call is receiving a dial tone.	✓
LINECALLSTATE_DIALING	The call is being dialed.	✓
LINECALLSTATE_RINGBACK	The call is ringing.	✓
LINECALLSTATE_BUSY	The call is receiving a busy tone.	✓
LINECALLSTATE_SPECIALINFO	The call is in one of several special states, usually indicating that the destination cannot be reached.	
LINECALLSTATE_CONNECTED	The call is connected.	✓
LINECALLSTATE_PROCEEDING	Dialing is complete and the call is proceeding toward a connection.	✓
LINECALLSTATE_ONHOLD	The call is on hold.	
LINECALLSTATE_CONFERENCED	The call is a member of a conference call.	
LINECALLSTATE_ONHOLDPENDCONF	The call is on hold while waiting to be joined with a conference.	

LINECALLSTATE_DISCONNECTED	The call has been disconnected.	✓
LINECALLSTATE_UNKNOWN	The call state is currently unknown.	✓
LINECALLSTATE_ONHOLDPENDTRANSF	The call is on hold while waiting to be transferred.	

Figure 4-8 shows how an outbound call progresses through various states during its lifetime.

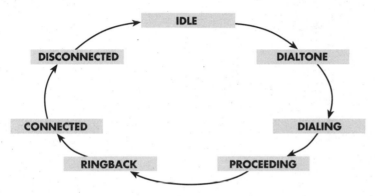

Figure 4-8. *The lifetime of an outbound call.*

In the beginning, there is no call, so the call is in the IDLE state. When the phone is taken off the hook, the call enters the DIALTONE state, indicating that a dial tone is present on the line. (If a call never reaches the DIALTONE state, something is disconnected; either the modem is disconnected from the PC, the phone line is disconnected from the modem, or the phone company has shut off your phone service!)

While the phone number is being dialed, the call is in the DIALING state. Once dialing is complete, but before the phone on the other end starts ringing, the call is in the PROCEEDING state. When the phone on the other end starts ringing, the call is in the RINGBACK state. (Or, if the other phone is busy, the call enters the BUSY state.) If the person or modem you are calling picks up the ringing phone, you cannot be certain what the call state is. If it is an interactive voice call, the call enters the CONNECTED state immediately after it is picked up. But if the call is a modem, fax, or other data call, it is not connected right away when the other party picks up the phone. With data calls, the CONNECTED state indicates that the call has been established and that data transfer can proceed. Before this can happen, the parties (both modems, for example) usually have to negotiate various data transfer parameters and protocols. This negotiation is the squawking sound that you hear when two modems connect to one another. During this negotiation phase, the state of the call might be UN-KNOWN, or it might simply remain in the RINGBACK state.

When a call fails to connect, or when it is disconnected for some reason, it becomes DISCONNECTED. A DISCONNECTED call usually transitions to the IDLE state almost immediately, indicating that the call is over.

The process is different for incoming calls, as shown in Figure 4-9.

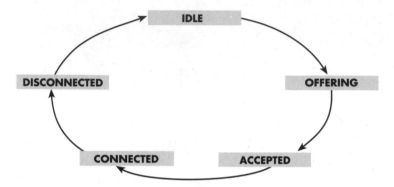

Figure 4-9. *The lifetime of an incoming call.*

For incoming calls, the first state after IDLE is typically OFFERING, which indicates that your phone is ringing. When the call is answered, the modems must negotiate the connection for transferring data. During this negotiation phase, the call is ACCEPTED but not yet CONNECTED. After negotiation, the call is CONNECTED, and data can be transferred. The call is then DISCONNECTED and returns to the IDLE state.

It is notoriously difficult for modems to reliably detect when an interactive voice call is CONNECTED. With modem and other data calls that require negotiation, detecting the CONNECTED state is easy; it is simply the state after negotiation has successfully concluded. It is also usually difficult to detect when a call is BUSY or when the remote phone is ringing (in the RINGBACK state). The BUSY and RINGBACK states are difficult to detect because of a lack of uniform standards for these states among public phone switches (especially from one country to another).

A disconnection can be very disruptive to the calling application. The more information it has about why the disconnection occurred, the more likely it can recover or reconnect successfully the next time. The *dwDisconnectModes* member of the LINEADDRESSCAPS structure contains flags that indicate how much information Windows can return about the cause of a disconnection.

LINEDISCONNECTMODE_NORMAL	This is a "normal" disconnection by the remote party. The call was disconnected normally.
LINEDISCONNECTMODE_UNKNOWN	The reason for the disconnection is unknown but might become known later.
LINEDISCONNECTMODE_REJECT	The remote party has rejected the call.
LINEDISCONNECTMODE_PICKUP	The call was picked up from elsewhere.
LINEDISCONNECTMODE_FORWARDED	The call was forwarded by the switch.
LINEDISCONNECTMODE_BUSY	The remote party's station is busy.
LINEDISCONNECTMODE_NOANSWER	The remote party's station does not answer.
LINEDISCONNECTMODE_BADADDRESS	The destination address is invalid.
LINEDISCONNECTMODE_UNREACHABLE	The remote party could not be reached.
LINEDISCONNECTMODE_CONGESTION	The network is congested.
LINEDISCONNECTMODE_INCOMPATIBLE	The remote party's station equipment is incompatible with the call.
LINEDISCONNECTMODE_UNAVAIL	The reason for the disconnection is unknown and will not become known later.
LINEDISCONNECTMODE_NODIALTONE	A dial tone was not detected.

A "normal" disconnection typically means that the remote party dropped off the line. *dwDisconnectModes* contains the flag LINEDISCONNECTMODE_ NORMAL if Windows can notify an application of a normal disconnection. A call might also become disconnected if the called party does not answer or is busy. It is something of a misnomer to say that a disconnection has occurred in these cases; after all, the call was never connected. Nevertheless, these situations are treated as disconnections. The flags LINEDISCONNECTMODE_NOANSWER and LINEDISCONNECTMODE_BUSY are set if Windows can notify an application of no answer or busy disconnections. Many times,

Windows simply will not know the reason for a disconnection. The flag LINEDISCONNECTMODE_UNAVAIL is set if Windows will report disconnections for which it cannot determine the cause.

Windows 95 with Unimodem installed supports normal, busy, no answer, and cause unavailable disconnection notifications. Many other kinds of disconnections are possible; for example, the called party might have caller ID and might reject the call. Or, the call might get forwarded away from the called party by the switch connected to the called party, causing a disconnection. Some phone systems will report a disconnection if the phone number is not in service, if all phone circuits are busy, or if your telephone equipment is not compatible with the equipment of the called party. The corresponding flags for these different disconnects are shown on the previous page. They are not supported by Unimodem.

The number of active calls that can be active on the address is specified by the member *dwMaxNumActiveCalls*. An active call is a call over which data (such as voice or modem data) can be transferred. Calls on hold are not active; data cannot be transferred over a held call. An address can typically support one simultaneously active call. When Unimodem is installed, this number is always one. The number of calls that can be on hold simultaneously is specified by the member *dwMaxNumOnHoldCalls*. Some addresses, especially addresses on digital phones, support multiple calls per address. Usually, only one call at a time can be active, but many calls can be simultaneously on hold, in some cases up to four or five at a time. However, POTS lines don't support the holding of calls (unless you have call waiting), and Unimodem does not support the holding of calls or call waiting. The *dwMaxNumOnHoldCalls* member is therefore 0 when Unimodem is installed.

The *dwAddrCapFlags* member specifies miscellaneous capabilities of the address. Most of the flags that make up this member relate to addresses on digital lines. However, several of the flags relate to addresses on lines of all types, including the most basic POTS lines. If the LINEADDRCAPFLAGS_SECURE flag is set, calls on the address can be made secure. Making a call secure means protecting the call from unwanted tones and interruptions; call-waiting tones are the most typical tones that can interrupt a call. Call-waiting tones are not a problem for voice calls, because they simply remind the person on the phone that another caller is trying to get through. But modems and fax machines don't understand these tones, and extraneous tones can destroy data when they interrupt a modem or fax data stream. Calls are typically made secure by sending a special sequence of tones to the phone switch. However, if the phone switch does not allow calls to be secure, the application cannot make it secure. When Unimodem is installed, the LINEADDRCAPFLAGS_SECURE flag is not set, indicating that calls cannot be made secure even if the phone switch allows them to be. Phone users with call waiting who make modem or fax calls run the risk that their data will be corrupted by call-waiting tones from a second caller during data transfer.

The *dwAddrCapFlags* member might also include the flag LINEADDRCAPFLAGS-_ORIGOFFHOOK. If this flag is set, the modem can automatically take the phone off the hook when making outbound calls. Virtually all analog modems can do this for outbound data calls, but this capability alone will not result in the flag being set. Rather, the modem must be able to take the phone off the hook for any type of outbound call, including interactive voice calls. Few modems support this capability, so the flag is not set when using Unimodem.

Another important flag in the *dwAddrCapFlags* member is LINEADDRCAP-FLAGS_DIALED. This flag is set if the address supports the dialing of outbound calls. If the flag is not set, outbound calls cannot be dialed on the address. This is not the same as saying that outbound calls cannot be made on the address. For example, it is possible that merely picking up the phone, without dialing, will cause a connection to be made to another party (as in old war movies). In other words, the address could be a hot line that is "hard wired" to one particular party. If the flag is not set, it might mean that the address does not support outbound calls at all—it can only answer inbound calls. This flag is set when Unimodem is installed.

Another important flag is LINEADDRCAPFLAGS_PARTIALDIAL. If this flag is set, the address supports the partial dialing of calls. When partial dialing is supported, it is not necessary to dial the entire phone number at once. Rather, the phone number can be dialed in stages. Unimodem supports partial dialing; it's one of the most useful telephony features, especially because Unimodem does not support digit generation. (The recently released Unimodem voice extensions support digit generation.) More on this later.

Probably the most interesting member in LINEADDRESSCAPS is the one called *dwCallFeatures*. This member contains flags that describe which TAPI functions are available for calls on the address. Possible values for the flags in this member are shown below.

LINECALLFEATURE_ACCEPT	*lineAccept*
LINECALLFEATURE_ADDTOCONF	*lineAddToConference*
LINECALLFEATURE_ANSWER	*lineAnswer*
LINECALLFEATURE_BLINDTRANSFER	*lineBlindTransfer*
LINECALLFEATURE_COMPLETECALL	*lineCompleteCall*
LINECALLFEATURE_COMPLETETRANSF	*lineCompleteTransfer*
LINECALLFEATURE_DIAL	*lineDial*
LINECALLFEATURE_DROP	*lineDrop*
LINECALLFEATURE_GATHERDIGITS	*lineGatherDigits*

LINECALLFEATURE_GENERATEDIGITS	*lineGenerateDigits*
LINECALLFEATURE_GENERATETONE	*lineGenerateTone*
LINECALLFEATURE_HOLD	*lineHold*
LINECALLFEATURE_MONITORDIGITS	*lineMonitorDigits*
LINECALLFEATURE_MONITORMEDIA	*lineMonitorMedia*
LINECALLFEATURE_MONITORTONES	*lineMonitorTones*
LINECALLFEATURE_PARK	*linePark*
LINECALLFEATURE_PREPAREADDCONF	*linePrepareAddToConference*
LINECALLFEATURE_REDIRECT	*lineRedirect*
LINECALLFEATURE_RELEASEUSERUSER	*lineReleaseUserUserInfo*
LINECALLFEATURE_REMOVEFROMCONF	*lineRemoveFromConference*
LINECALLFEATURE_SECURECALL	*lineSecureCall*
LINECALLFEATURE_SENDUSERUSER	*lineSendUserUserInfo*
LINECALLFEATURE_SETCALLPARAMS	*lineSetCallParams*
LINECALLFEATURE_SETMEDIACONTROL	*lineSetMediaControl*
LINECALLFEATURE_SETTERMINAL	*lineSetTerminal*
LINECALLFEATURE_SETUPCONF	*lineSetupConference*
LINECALLFEATURE_SETUPTRANSFER	*lineSetupTransfer*
LINECALLFEATURE_SWAPHOLD	*lineSwapHold*
LINECALLFEATURE_UNHOLD	*lineUnHold*

Notice that the list of functions above does not include any of the TAPI functions we have discussed so far in this chapter. That is because the functions in the list are only for setting up and controlling calls, which we haven't discussed how to do yet. Unimodem supports only a small subset of these functions. The call setup and control functions in the list that are supported by Unimodem are *lineAccept* (LINECALLFEATURE_ACCEPT), *lineAnswer* (LINECALLFEATURE_ANSWER), *lineDial* (LINECALLFEATURE_DIAL), *lineDrop* (LINECALLFEATURE_DROP), *lineMonitorMedia* (LINECALLFEATURE_MONITORMEDIA), and *lineSetCallParams* (LINECALLFEATURE_SETCALLPARAMS). The functions *lineGenerateDigits* (LINECALLFEATURE_GENERATEDIGITS) and *lineMonitorDigits* (LINECALLFEATURE_MONITORDIGITS) are supported by UnimodemV. The purpose of some of these functions will become clear in the later sections of this chapter on making and answering calls.

Messages

During the call to *lineInitialize,* an application passes Windows a pointer to a callback function to which Windows sends messages about lines and addresses. When a line message is sent to the application callback function, the *dwMessage* parameter of the callback function is set to LINE_LINEDEV-STATE. The *dwParam1* parameter to the callback identifies the particular line state message. By default, Windows sends only one message to an application relating to lines or addresses; this message (in *dwParam1*) is LINEDEVSTATE_REINIT. An application that uses the line device in any way, even if only to monitor the line for calls, must trap and process the LINE_LINEDEVSTATE/LINEDEVSTATE_REINIT message. Windows sends this message when you have made serious configuration changes to the telephony system using the Windows Control Panel while an application is running. Remember that *lineInitialize* returns LINEERR_REINIT for as long as TAPI is not available to the application. It returns this error if you have not finished installing and removing telephony drivers or if other applications that use TAPI have not shut down their usage of TAPI. That is why it is so important for an application to trap LINEDEVSTATE_REINIT and shut down usage of TAPI, because failing to do so can interfere with the functioning of other applications that are also using TAPI.

Windows also reports the insertion of a PCMCIA modem into the computer or its removal from the computer. When a PCMCIA modem is removed, an application receives the LINEDEVSTATE_OUTOFSERVICE message, which indicates a physical disconnection from the phone line. When the PCMCIA modem is re-inserted, the application receives the LINEDEVSTATE_INSERVICE message, indicating a reconnection to the phone line. The application can also receive LINEDEVSTATE_CONNECTED and LINEDEVSTATE_DISCONNECTED messages when a PCMCIA modem is inserted or removed. For analog modems, these last two flags mean the same thing as LINEDEVSTATE_INSERVICE and LINEDEVSTATE_OUTOFSERVICE, respectively, and should be processed in the same manner.

Line messages

The line messages shown on pages 142–43 can be reported to an application by Windows. Only a subset of these messages will actually be reported, depending on the capabilities of the telephony driver that is installed.

LINEDEVSTATE_OTHER	Device-status items other than those specified in the rest of this list have changed. The application should check the current line status structure to determine which items have changed.
LINEDEVSTATE_RINGING	The switch tells the line to alert the user.
LINEDEVSTATE_CONNECTED	The line was previously disconnected and is now connected to TAPI.
LINEDEVSTATE_DISCONNECTED	This line was previously connected and is now disconnected from TAPI.
LINEDEVSTATE_MSGWAITON	The "message waiting" indicator is turned on.
LINEDEVSTATE_MSGWAITOFF	The "message waiting" indicator is turned off.
LINEDEVSTATE_INSERVICE	The line is connected to TAPI. This happens when TAPI is first activated or when the line wire is physically plugged in and in service at the switch while TAPI is active.
LINEDEVSTATE_OUTOFSERVICE	The line is out of service at the switch or physically disconnected. TAPI cannot be used to operate on the line device.
LINEDEVSTATE_MAINTENANCE	Maintenance is being performed on the line at the switch. TAPI cannot be used to operate on the line device.
LINEDEVSTATE_OPEN	The line has been opened by another application.
LINEDEVSTATE_CLOSE	The line has been closed by another application.
LINEDEVSTATE_NUMCALLS	The number of calls on the line device has changed.
LINEDEVSTATE_NUMCOMPLETIONS	The number of outstanding call completions on the line device has changed.

LINEDEVSTATE_TERMINALS	The terminal settings have changed. This may happen, for example, if multiple line devices share terminals among them (for example, two lines sharing a phone terminal).
LINEDEVSTATE_ROAMMODE	The roam mode of the line device has changed (cellular).
LINEDEVSTATE_BATTERY	The battery level has changed significantly (cellular).
LINEDEVSTATE_SIGNAL	The signal level has changed significantly (cellular).
LINEDEVSTATE_DEVSPECIFIC	The line's device-specific information has changed.
LINEDEVSTATE_REINIT	Items have changed in the configuration of line devices. To become aware of these changes (such as the appearance of new line devices) the application should reinitialize its use of TAPI.
LINEDEVSTATE_LOCK	The locked status of the line device has changed. (For more information, refer to the description of the LINEDEVSTATUSFLAGS_LOCKED bit in the LINEDEVSTATUSFLAGS_ constants.)
LINEDEVSTATE_CAPSCHANGE	One or more of the members in the LINEDEVCAPS structure for the address have changed.
LINEDEVSTATE_CONFIGCHANGE	The configuration of the media devices associated with the line device has changed.
LINEDEVSTATE_TRANSLATECHANGE	One or more members of the LINETRANSLATECAPS structure have changed.
LINEDEVSTATE_COMPLCANCEL	Completion ID has been externally canceled and is no longer valid.
LINEDEVSTATE_REMOVED	The device is being removed from the system by the service provider.

Different telephony drivers report different line status events. An application can determine which line status events the installed driver can report by examining the *dwLineStates* member of the LINEDEVCAPS structure. This member contains flags that are set if the event can be reported, and are not set otherwise. For example, Unimodem will send status messages when an incoming call appears on the line (LINEDEVSTATE_RINGING), when the line is opened or closed by another application (LINEDEVSTATE_OPEN and LINEDEVSTATE-_CLOSE), and of course LINEDEVSTATE_REINIT (discussed earlier in this section). Unimodem also supports the LINEDEVSTATE_CONNECTED, LINEDEVSTATE-_DISCONNECTED, LINEDEVSTATE_INSERVICE, LINEDEVSTATE_OUTOF-SERVICE, LINEDEVSTATE_TRANSLATECHANGE, and LINEDEVSTATE_ REMOVED messages.

When an application receives a LINE_LINEDEVSTATE message, it should call *lineGetLineDevStatus,* as shown below. *lineGetLineDevStatus* returns important information about the status of the line.

```
lineGetLineDevStatus (hLine, &linestatus)
```

The first parameter, *hLine,* is a handle to the line device. The second parameter points to a LINEDEVSTATUS structure, shown below, that contains information about the current status of the line device. Often, the LINE_LINEDEVSTATE message is sent as the result of changes in one or more members of LINEDEVSTATUS. For instance, the LINE_LINEDEVSTATE/LINEDEVSTATE_OTHER message indicates a change in the line's status that is not identified by one of the preset LINEDEVSTATE_ constants. The only way for the application to discover the status change is to call *lineGetLineDevStatus* and check the members of LINEDEVSTATUS to determine what changed.

```
typedef struct linedevstatus_tag {
    DWORD      dwTotalSize;
    DWORD      dwNeededSize;
    DWORD      dwUsedSize;
    DWORD      dwNumOpens;
    DWORD      dwOpenMediaModes;
    DWORD      dwNumActiveCalls;
    DWORD      dwNumOnHoldCalls;
    DWORD      dwNumOnHoldPendCalls;
    DWORD      dwLineFeatures;
    DWORD      dwNumCallCompletions;
    DWORD      dwRingMode;
    DWORD      dwSignalLevel;
    DWORD      dwBatteryLevel;
    DWORD      dwRoamMode;
    DWORD      dwDevStatusFlags;
    DWORD      dwTerminalModesSize;
```

```
    DWORD    dwTerminalModesOffset;
    DWORD    dwDevSpecificSize;
    DWORD    dwDevSpecificOffset;
} LINEDEVSTATUS, FAR *LPLINEDEVSTATUS;
```

The *dwNumOpens* member of LINEDEVSTATUS specifies how many times *lineOpen* has been called on the line by all applications. An application that monitors the line should check this member in response to the LINE_LINEDEVSTATE/LINEDEVSTATE_OPEN and LINE_LINEDEVSTATE/LINE-DEVSTATE_CLOSE messages. Be careful: This member does not specify the number of applications that opened the line. Rather, it specifies the total number of times the line was opened. A single application can open the line multiple times; for example, the Exchange Server opens the line twice, so if Exchange is running along with another application that opens the line once, *dwNumOpens* is set to 3.

The *dwOpenMediaModes* member specifies the different media modes for which the line has been opened. This can be one of the most useful members for an application to check, since the media mode for which the line is opened determines the types of calls that can be made or answered. This member contains LINEMEDIAMODE_ flags. (See the discussion of the LINEDEVCAPS structure in the section titled "Exploring Lines" earlier in this chapter for a list of media mode flags.) If a flag is set, the line is opened for the corresponding media mode. An application should check this member in response to the LINE_LINEDEVSTATE/LINEDEVSTATE_OPEN message. Note that calling *lineOpen* with "monitor" or "none" privileges will not cause a change in the open media modes.

The *dwNumActiveCalls* member specifies how many active (as opposed to held or idle) calls exist on the line. For Unimodem, this member is always 0 (no calls) or 1 (one call). An application should check this member in response to the LINE_LINEDEVSTATE/LINEDEVSTATE_NUMCALLS message.

Applications that make calls should check the *dwLineFeatures* member for the LINEFEATURE_MAKECALL flag before attempting to place a call. If this flag is not set, the application cannot make calls on the line.

Address messages

In addition to notifying an application of changes in the status of a line, Windows can also notify it of changes to the state of an address. Address state changes are sent with the LINE_ADDRESSSTATE message to the application callback function. When the callback receives this message, the *dwParam1* parameter identifies the address to which the message applies (always 0 when

Unimodem is used), and the *dwParam2* parameter identifies the particular address state change as one of the following values:

LINEADDRESSSTATE_OTHER	Address-status items other than those listed below have changed. The application should check the current address status to determine which items have changed.
LINEADDRESSSTATE_DEVSPECIFIC	The device-specific item of the address status has changed.
LINEADDRESSSTATE_INUSEZERO	The address has changed to idle. (It is in use by zero stations.)
LINEADDRESSSTATE_INUSEONE	The address has changed from idle or from being used by many bridged stations to being used by only one station.
LINEADDRESSSTATE_INUSEMANY	The monitored or bridged address has changed from being used by one station to being used by more than one station.
LINEADDRESSSTATE_NUMCALLS	The number of calls on the address has changed due to an event such as a new inbound call, an outbound call on the address, or a call changing its hold status.
LINEADDRESSSTATE_FORWARD	The forwarding status of the address has changed, including the number of rings for determining a no-answer condition. The application should check the address status to determine details about the address's current forwarding status.
LINEADDRESSSTATE_TERMINALS	The terminal settings for the address have changed.

When a LINE_ADDRESSSTATE message is received, an application should call *lineGetLineAddressStatus,* as shown below. *lineGetLineAddressStatus* returns important information about the status of the address.

```
lineGetLineAddressStatus (hLine, dwAddress, &linestatus)
```

The first parameter, *hLine,* is a handle to the line device. The second parameter is the address ID; when the LINE_ADDRESSSTATE message is received, an application can pass *dwParam1* from the callback straight through to this parameter.

The third parameter points to a LINEADDRESSSTATUS structure, shown below, that contains information about the current status of the address. Often, the LINE_ADDRESSSTATE message is sent as the values change in one or more members of LINEADDRESSSTATUS.

```
typedef struct lineaddressstatus_tag {
    DWORD    dwTotalSize;
    DWORD    dwNeededSize;
    DWORD    dwUsedSize;
    DWORD    dwNumInUse;
    DWORD    dwNumActiveCalls;
    DWORD    dwNumOnHoldCalls;
    DWORD    dwNumOnHoldPendCalls;
    DWORD    dwAddressFeatures;
    DWORD    dwNumRingsNoAnswer;
    DWORD    dwForwardNumEntries;
    DWORD    dwForwardSize;
    DWORD    dwForwardOffset;
    DWORD    dwTerminalModesSize;
    DWORD    dwTerminalModesOffset;
    DWORD    dwDevSpecificSize;
    DWORD    dwDevSpecificOffset;
} LINEADDRESSSTATUS, FAR *LPLINEADDRESSSTATUS;
```

The *dwNumInUse* member specifies how many phones are currently using the address. In office environments, it is possible for multiple phones to connect, or bridge, with the same address. For example, a secretary's phone might have a bridged connection with the phones of several people who the secretary supports. The secretary's phone is said to be bridged to each of those addresses. When a call comes in for one of these people, the secretary's phone also rings. Unimodem does not support line bridging; *dwNumInUse* is 0 if the address is not being used, and 1 if it is being used; *dwNumInUse* is never greater than 1. In this case, the LINE_ADDRESSSTATE/LINEADDRESSSTATE_INUSEZERO message is sent when the address transitions from being used by one phone to not being used, and the LINE_ADDRESSSTATE/LINEADDRESSSTATE_INUSEONE message is sent when the address transitions from not being in use to being in use by one phone.

dwNumActiveCalls specifies the number of active calls on the address. This member serves the same purpose as the *dwNumActiveCalls* member in LINEDEVSTATUS, except that it is specific to the address, whereas the member in LINEDEVSTATUS specifies the sum total of all active calls on all addresses on the line. With Unimodem, this member is always either 0 (no active calls) or 1 (active call on the address).

The *dwAddressFeatures* member specifies which features are available on the address in its current state. An application that makes outbound calls should check this member to ensure that the LINEADDRFEATURE_MAKECALL flag is set. If this flag is not set, outbound calls cannot be made from the address in its current state.

The *dwNumRingsNoAnswer* member specifies how many times a call can ring before it is considered a no-answer. This member is only meaningful if the address supports the LINECALLSTATE_RINGING call state, because if the address does not support this call state, the address cannot detect ring tones and hence cannot determine how many rings have occurred.

Status messages

By default, Windows does not send an application any line or address status messages except the LINE_LINEDEVSTATUS/LINEDEVSTATUS_REINIT message. An application can specify notification of additional messages using the function *lineSetStatusMessages,* as shown below.

```
lineSetStatusMessages (hLine, dwLineMessages, dwAddressMessages)
```

The first parameter, *hLine,* is the line handle. The second parameter, *dwLineMessages,* is a mask of LINEDEVSTATE_ flags, each flag corresponding to a LINE_LINEDEVSTATE message for which the application wants to be notified. The third parameter, *dwAddressMessages,* is a mask of LINEADDRESSSTATE_ flags, each flag corresponding to a LINE_ADDRESSSTATE message for which the application wants to be notified.

An application can determine the line and address messages for which it will receive notification by calling *lineGetStatusMessages,* as shown below.

```
lineGetStatusMessages(hLine, &dwLineMessages, &dwAddressMessages)
```

The first parameter, *hLine,* is the line handle. The second and third parameters point to DWORD variables returning bitmasks of flags. Each flag corresponds to a line or an address status message for which the application will receive notification.

Canonical and Dialable Addresses

Windows 95 defines a universal format for the storage of all phone numbers (addresses), called the *canonical format* (or international format). This format enables Windows to determine precisely what country, area code, and local number an address refers to. In other words, a canonical address uniquely identifies a particular party anywhere in the world.

The format of a canonical address is strictly defined. A canonical address must begin with the + character followed by one or more digits identifying the country (the country code), the area code, and then the local number. In some cases, the area code can be omitted (such as in a small country with no area codes). If the area code is included, it must be contained within parentheses. The following is an example of a valid canonical address for Santa Clara, California.

+1 (408) 5553456

Notice that the country code and area code are separated by a single space, and that the area code and local number are also separated by a single space. No spaces are embedded in the digits of the local number. In the example, the leading 1 is the country code of the United States. Every country has a unique country code. (For example, Spain is 34.) International callers must first dial an international calling sequence plus 1 in order to reach numbers inside the United States. (Note: The country code for the United States is 1, but this is not the same as the 1 you must dial from within the United States to make a domestic long-distance call.)

Even though a canonical address uniquely identifies a party anywhere in the world, the actual number you dial might vary from the canonical form. Take the above-mentioned example from Santa Clara. To call that number from a private home in Portland, Oregon, you would dial

1 408 5553456

This is basically the same as the canonical form, less the + prefix. The number is dialed as a long-distance number within the United States, so a 1 and the area code are required to prefix the local number. In this case we got lucky: The country code of the United States happens to match the long-distance calling prefix for numbers within the United States, so the canonical address looks very similar to the actual address we would dial to make the call.

Now consider what happens when the same number is dialed from within a hotel room in Portland instead of a private address. Now the caller must dial

8 1 408 5553456

The prefix 8 allows the caller to access the long-distance phone network from within the hotel. In dialing parlance, the 8 is the long-distance dialing prefix for the hotel. If the caller wants to use a credit card to avoid the hotel mark-up on long-distance calls, the number to dial becomes

8 0 408 5553456

The 0 is the prefix for accessing the calling-card system. When this prefix is included, the caller will be prompted to enter a calling card number before the call goes through.

Finally, suppose that the same number is dialed from a hotel room within Santa Clara itself. The number becomes:

9 5553456

The country code and the area code are gone because the call is now a local call. The prefix 9 is appended to the number to access the external (local) phone network from within the hotel.

A dialable address can also include control characters such as *T* for tone dialing, *W* to wait for a dial tone, and so on. Clearly, a single canonical address can correspond to many dialable addresses, depending on the location from which the address is dialed and whether or not a calling card is used to make the call. What is required, then, is a way to convert from the universal canonical format for a phone number to the dialable number corresponding to the particular location and calling card (if any) used by the caller. Windows provides three ways to convert between a canonical number and a dialable number. First, it provides an application with enough information to perform the conversion itself. Second, it provides a function, *lineTranslateAddress,* to automatically convert between the formats, based on the current location and calling card settings. Third, it provides a function, *lineTranslateDialog,* to allow you to interactively convert between the formats; you can change location settings and calling card information at the same time to accurately reflect the current situation. These changes are reflected, interactively, in the dialable number, so you can instantly see the effects of your configuration changes.

Conversion information

The function *lineGetTranslateCaps,* whose syntax is shown below, returns information about your currently selected location and calling card. An application can use this information to convert a canonical address to a dialable address, or it can simply display this information to you. The latter is the more likely use of the function because Windows provides functions for converting canonical addresses to dialable addresses; an application will probably not bother to duplicate this functionality.

```
LONG WINAPI lineGetTranslateCaps(
    HLINEAPP hTAPI,
    DWORD dwVersionToUse,
    LPLINETRANSLATECAPS lpTranslateCaps)
```

The first parameter, *hTAPI,* is the TAPI handle. The second parameter, *dwVersionToUse,* is the negotiated API version. The last parameter points to a structure of type LINETRANSLATECAPS. This structure has the following format:

```
typedef struct linetranslatecaps_tag {
    DWORD dwTotalSize;
    DWORD dwNeededSize;
    DWORD dwUsedSize;
    DWORD dwNumLocations;
    DWORD dwLocationListSize;
```

```
    DWORD dwLocationListOffset;
    DWORD dwCurrentLocationID;
    DWORD dwNumCards;
    DWORD dwCardListSize;
    DWORD dwCardListOffset;
    DWORD dwCurrentPreferredCardID;
} LINETRANSLATECAPS, FAR *LPLINETRANSLATECAPS;
```

Appended to the end of the LINETRANSLATECAPS structure is a list of locations and calling cards that you have configured. Locations and calling cards are typically configured from the Windows Control Panel, using the Modems applet. To configure a location or calling card, you open the Modems applet and click on the Dialing Properties button. The Dialing Properties dialog box appears, as shown in Figure 4-10, indicating the currently configured location, the dialing rules for that location, and what, if any, calling card to use.

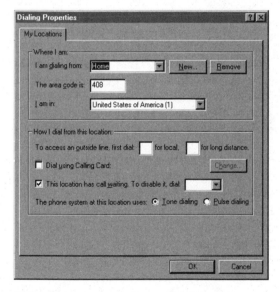

Figure 4-10. *The Dialing Properties dialog box accessed from the Modems applet.*

The dialog box contains a combo box titled "I am dialing from," which displays the currently selected location. You can select a location from the list box or add a new location by clicking the New button. If you select an existing location, all of the dialing properties for that location are displayed in the fields of the dialog box. If you enter the name of a new location, you should also enter the dialing properties for that location and save the properties with the new settings by clicking OK. Dialing properties include the area code and the country for the location. You select the country from an extensive list of countries.

You cannot add a new country; if a new country suddenly comes into existence, it is up to Microsoft to add (and remove) countries. (And you thought the U.S. government was powerful.)

Other dialing properties include prefixes to access an outside line, such as 9 for local calls and 8 for long-distance calls. If you select the "Dial using Calling Card" check box, the calling card information is included in dialable numbers when the numbers are converted from canonical format. In fact, calling card information is included even when the number to dial is local; in other words, all calls made from that location will use the calling card. This can save you the trouble of carrying change in your pockets to pay for local calls from, say, public phones (assuming you can somehow connect your PC to the public phone line). However, it might cost you a little more because your long-distance company will be involved in what would have been a local call. For this reason, you might want to configure two sets of dialing properties for each location—one using your calling card, one not. You can change the calling card to use for the location by clicking the Change button, which is enabled only after you select the "Dial using Calling Card" check box. A dialog box appears, in which you select an existing calling card or enter the name of a calling card that is not in the list. Click the Advanced button to configure the local, long-distance, and international dialing rules for the new calling card. Here are examples of calling card dialing rules:

Local   G

Long distance   102881FG

International   10288011EFG

The first five digits, 10288, are the prefix for accessing the AT&T telephone network. The digits 011 indicate an international call. The letter E is a placeholder for the country code, the letter F is a placeholder for the area code, and the letter G is a placeholder for the local number. Windows substitutes one or more digits for each letter when it dials the number. This substitution of digits for letters make up the *dialing rules* that apply to calls using that calling card. A letter H is used as a placeholder for the calling card number. Notice that no letter H appears in the examples above. That is because this particular "calling card" is not a calling card at all; rather, it is a set of rules for direct dialing over the AT&T network. Calling cards are simply collections of dialing rules, which may or may not correspond to the rules for physical calling cards. Another dialing rule you can specify in this dialog box is !, which indicates that the phone hookswitch should be connected for ½ second and then released. This dialing rule is useful for switching between calls on a line that supports call waiting.

In the field called "This location has call waiting," you can enter the digits that can be dialed to disable call waiting. This important property is frequently overlooked. Often, the phone company provides a special prefix that prevents call-waiting calls from intruding on an existing call. In other words, if you make a call using a certain prefix, you won't hear the call-waiting tone when another call tries to get through. The caller will simply hear a busy tone. If you make modem and fax calls from a location that has call waiting, it is very important that you use the special prefix so that Windows will make the call secure. (Even if the feature flags indicate that calls cannot be secured, this is a "back door" for screening them using the dialing properties.)

Finally, you can specify whether the location uses tone or pulse dialing. Almost every location in the United States uses tone dialing, but many other countries still use the older pulse dialing technology.

The location information returned by *lineGetTranslateCaps* reflects the location properties set in the Dialing Properties dialog box. The *dwNumLocations* member of LINETRANSLATECAPS defines the number of locations that you configured. There is always at least one location, the default location, even if you have not configured any location information. For each location, a LINELOCATIONENTRY structure is appended to the LINETRANSLATECAPS structure. The format of LINELOCATIONENTRY is as follows:

```
typedef struct linelocationentry_tag {
    DWORD dwPermanentLocationID;
    DWORD dwLocationNameSize;
    DWORD dwLocationNameOffset;
    DWORD dwCountryCode;
    DWORD dwCityCodeSize;
    DWORD dwCityCodeOffset,
    DWORD dwPreferredCardID;
    DWORD dwLocalAccessCodeSize;
    DWORD dwLocalAccessCodeOffset;
    DWORD dwLongDistanceAccessCodeSize;
    DWORD dwLongDistanceAccessCodeOffset;
    DWORD dwTollPrefixListSize;
    DWORD dwTollPrefixListOffset;
    DWORD dwCountryID;
    DWORD dwOptions;
    DWORD dwCancelCallWaitingSize;
    DWORD dwCancelCallWaitingOffset;
} LINELOCATIONENTRY, FAR *LPLINELOCATIONENTRY;
```

The first member, *dwPermanentLocationID,* is a unique identifier for the location. This can be any number, and it is not necessarily the same as the position of the location in the location list. An application should check the *dwCurrentLocationID* member of LINETRANSLATECAPS and compare it to the *dwPermanentLocationID* member of each LINELOCATIONENTRY structure in the list to locate the entry for the currently selected location. The name of the location is defined in size-offset form, using the *dwLocationNameSize* and *dwLocationNameOffset* members. Note that the offset is relative to the LINETRANSLATECAPS structure, not the LINELOCATIONENTRY structure. This is true for all size-offset members in LINELOCATIONENTRY.

The country code for the location is defined by the *dwCountryCode* member. The area code (also known as the city code) is defined by *dwCityCodeSize* and *dwCityCodeOffset*. If a credit card is used with the location, *dwPreferredCardID* is a small integer that identifies the credit card and that can be used to locate additional information about the credit card, as you will see below. The location can be a business, building, or hotel that requires local and long-distance access codes to dial an outside number. These access codes are defined in size-offset format by the *dwLocalAccessCodeSize, dwLocalAccessCodeOffset, dwLongDistanceAccessCodeSize,* and *dwLongDistanceAccessCodeOffset* members.

To change the current location, an application can call *lineSetCurrentLocation*, as shown below.

```
LONG WINAPI lineSetCurrentLocation(
    HLINEAPP hTAPI,
    DWORD dwLocation)
```

The first parameter, *hTAPI,* is the TAPI handle. *dwLocation* is the permanent location ID for the location you want to make into the current location. This parameter should be the *dwPermanentLocationID* member of one of the LINELOCATIONENTRY structures, not the index of the structure in the location list.

The next two members of LINELOCATIONENTRY, *dwTollPrefixListSize* and *dwTollPrefixListOffset,* identify the toll list to use for the location. Toll lists are necessary because in many parts of the United States, dialing a call within the same area code as the location can incur long-distance charges. This is why it is often handy to dial even "local" calls using a calling card. In most of North America, long-distance calls within the same area code must be preceded by a 1, just as long-distance calls to other area codes are. Whether a "local" number is treated as long distance depends on the first three digits of the number. For example, from a particular location in a particular area code, all phone numbers beginning with 727, 836, and 534 might be treated as long-distance numbers. Calls to numbers like 727 5555 would have to be preceded by a 1. (The area code might also be required.)

Windows lets you specify which "local" areas are to be treated as long distance for a particular location, using what are known as *toll lists*. A toll list is a string of one or more three-digit prefixes, separated by commas, specifying the areas to receive long-distance treatment. For the example above, the toll list would be 727, 836, 534. When converting from canonical to dialable format, Windows treats any phone number whose local part begins with any one of these three digits as a long-distance number. It typically attaches 1 and the area code to any such number when converting to the dialable format.

In many areas, attaching a 1 to the phone number still does not result in a complete call. Often the area code needs to be attached even if it is the same as the one you are dialing from. In the example above, if the area code is 408, the canonical phone number is converted to 1 408 727 5555. The only way in Windows 95 to change this option to include the area code is to edit the telephon.ini file. In the Locations section of telephon.ini, find the location to which you have attached the toll list. The argument prior to the toll list in the positional arguments list is the *insertareacode* argument. Setting *insertareacode* to 0 suppresses the area code when dialing long distance to a number whose prefix is in the toll list. Setting *insertareacode* to 1 (the default) includes the area code. (This is one of the rare instances when you should directly modify telephon.ini.)

The toll list for a location can be modified by calling the function *lineSetTollList,* as shown below.

```
lineSetTollList (hTAPI, dwLine, lpAddress, dwOption)
```

The first parameter, *hTAPI,* is the TAPI handle. The second parameter, *dwLine,* is the line device ID. The third parameter is the phone number, in canonical format, from which to extract the toll prefix. Windows simply extracts the first three digits from the local portion of the number and adds them to the toll list for the location. Note, however, that Windows does this only for addresses in certain countries, typically only countries in North America (which have the country code 1). For other countries, Windows does not modify the toll list. The last parameter, *dwOption,* tells Windows whether to add the prefix to the toll list or remove it from the list. If the option is LINETOLLLISTOPTION_ADD, the prefix is extracted from the address and added to the toll list for the location. Otherwise, if the option is LINETOLLLISTOPTION_ REMOVE, Windows searches the location's toll list for the first three digits of the address and removes them from the toll list.

Getting back to the LINELOCATIONENTRY structure, the *dwCountryID* member is an index that can be used to retrieve more detailed information about the country to which the address belongs. This is not the same as the country code in the *dwCountryCode* member of the same structure. Rather, it is an identifier that can be used with the *lineGetCountry* function, as shown below.

```
lineGetCountry(dwCountryID, dwAPIVersion, lpLineCountryList)
```

The first parameter, *dwCountryID,* is the value of the *dwCountryID* member of LINELOCATIONENTRY. The second parameter, *dwAPIVersion,* is the API version to use. This is not necessarily the negotiated version, but rather the highest version supported by the application. The last parameter points to a structure of type LINECOUNTRYLIST, as shown below.

```
typedef struct linecountrylist_tag {
    DWORD dwTotalSize;
    DWORD dwNeededSize;
    DWORD dwUsedSize;
    DWORD dwNumCountries;
    DWORD dwCountryListSize;
    DWORD dwCountryListOffset;
} LINECOUNTRYLIST, FAR *LPLINECOUNTRYLIST;
```

The *dwNumCountries* member specifies the number of countries in the list. This is always 1 unless the *dwCountryID* parameter is set to 0, in which case the function returns information on every country that Windows knows about, which is many, many KBs of information. The country list size and offset members point to one or more LINECOUNTRYENTRY structures (shown below), each of which contains details about a particular country. When the *dwCountryID* parameter is not 0, a single structure is returned with details about the country specified by *dwCountryID*.

```
typedef struct linecountryentry_tag {
    DWORD dwCountryID;
    DWORD dwCountryCode;
    DWORD dwNextCountryID;
    DWORD dwCountryNameSize;
    DWORD dwCountryNameOffset;
    DWORD dwSameAreaRuleSize;
    DWORD dwSameAreaRuleOffset;
    DWORD dwLongDistanceRuleSize;
    DWORD dwLongDistanceRuleOffset;
    DWORD dwInternationalRuleSize;
    DWORD dwInternationalRuleOffset;
} LINECOUNTRYENTRY, FAR *LPLINECOUNTRYENTRY;
```

The members *dwCountryID* and *dwCountryCode* specify the ID and country code for the country. When information on more than one country is returned, the *dwNextCountryID* member specifies which country is next in the list. The name of the country is specified in size-offset form by the members *dwCountryNameSize* and *dwCountryNameOffset*. The local, long-distance, and international dialing rules are specified by the size members (and corresponding offset members) of *dwSameAreaRuleSize*, *dwLongDistanceRuleSize*, and *dwInternationalRuleSize*. Note that these members might be empty—that is, the dialing rules might be NULL, in which case the size is 1 and the offset is some nonzero number, indicating a string comprised of a single NULL character.

Once again getting back to the LINELOCATIONENTRY structure, the *dwOptions* member specifies certain miscellaneous options for the location. The only option currently defined by Microsoft is LINELOCATIONOPTION- _PULSEDIAL. This option is set if pulse dialing is selected as one of the dialing properties for the location. If the location has a digit sequence for disabling call-waiting tones, that digit sequence is defined (as a string) by the *dwCancelCallWaitingSize* and *dwCancelCallWaitingOffset* members.

Referring back to the LINETRANSLATECAPS structure, there are a few members left to cover. The *dwNumCards* member specifies how many calling cards are available for use on the line. Information on each available calling card is appended to the end of LINETRANSLATECAPS, just as information on the available locations is also appended. The *dwCardListOffset* member specifies the offset from the beginning of LINETRANSLATECAPS where the list begins. The *dwCurrentPreferredCardID* member specifies which of the cards in the list is the one currently selected for use when dialing. The first card in the list is always called None (Direct Dial) and is selected when no calling card is used. The ID of this card is 0, so if *dwCurrentPreferedCardID* is 0, no calling card is selected for use when dialing. Each entry in the list of cards has the format of a LINECARDENTRY structure, shown below.

```
typedef struct linecardentry_tag {
    DWORD dwPermanentCardID;
    DWORD dwCardNameSize;
    DWORD dwCardNameOffset;
    DWORD dwCardNumberDigits;
    DWORD dwSameAreaRuleSize;
    DWORD dwSameAreaRuleOffset;
    DWORD dwLongDistanceRuleSize;
    DWORD dwLongDistanceRuleOffset;
    DWORD dwInternationalRuleSize;
    DWORD dwInternationalRuleOffset;
    DWORD dwOptions;
} LINECARDENTRY, FAR *LPLINECARDENTRY;
```

The *dwPermanentCardID* member uniquely identifies the card. This member is not the index of the card in the list. The application should compare *dwPreferredCardID* to the *dwPermanentCardID* member of each card in the list. A match indicates that the card is the one currently selected for dialing. The name of the card is specified in size-offset form by the *dwCardNameSize* and *dwCardNameOffset* members. Although for security reasons the actual digits of the calling card are not returned, the number of digits in the calling card number is returned, in the member *dwCardNumberDigits*. An application can use this information to insert filler bytes into a text control (usually one * for every digit) to represent the number for the card. The rules to use with the card for local, long-distance, and international dialing are returned as strings, in size-offset form, in the *dwSameAreaRuleSize, dwSameAreaRuleOffset, dwLong-DistanceRuleSize, dwLongDistanceRuleOffset, dwInternationalRuleSize,* and *dwInternationalRuleOffset* members. Remember, all offsets are from the beginning of the LINETRANSLATECAPS structure.

Finally, the *dwOptions* member of LINECARDENTRY returns miscellaneous options that are in effect for the card. A value of LINECARDOPTION_PREDEFINED indicates that the card is predefined by Microsoft and shipped with Windows. Predefined cards cannot be removed using the Control Panel; they can only be "hidden"—not displayed from the Control Panel.

Automatic conversion

That's a lot of information on canonical and dialable addresses, but you will need every bit of it if you want to write your own code for converting a canonical address to a dialable address. Fortunately, there are a couple of built-in Windows functions that will do the conversion for you. The first of these functions is *lineTranslateAddress,* whose syntax is shown below.

```
LONG lineTranslateAddress(
    HLINEAPP hTAPI,
    DWORD dwLine,
    DWORD dwVersionToUse,
    LPCSTR lpszAddressIn,
    DWORD dwCard,
    DWORD dwTranslateOptions,
    LPLINETRANSLATEOUTPUT lpTranslateOutput)
```

The first parameter, *hTAPI,* is the TAPI handle. The second parameter, *dwLine,* identifies the line device. The third parameter, *dwVersionToUse,* is the negotiated API version. The fourth parameter, *lpszAddressIn,* is the address in canonical format to be converted to dialable format. The address can be in noncanonical format, but if it is the function won't do much translation and the calling application will have much work left to do to convert the address to dialable format. Remember, canonical format means: +, country code, space, area code in parentheses, space, and then the local part of the address. Any mistakes in the canonical format can lead to truly bizarre errors, such as the function returning LINEERR_INIFILECORRUPT. This is a scary error, because it implies a corrupted configuration. You can get this error, for example, by passing a number like +5551234 or +(908) 5551234. So be careful that the address you supply is in correct canonical format.

The *dwCard* parameter specifies the calling card to use during the address translation. *lineTranslateAddress* always uses the currently selected calling card during the translation, but this parameter lets you override the selected calling card and select some other card. The *dwCard* parameter is ignored unless the *dwTranslateOptions* parameter is set to LINETRANSLATEOPTIONS-_CARDOVERRIDE.

The last parameter, *lpTranslateOutput,* points to a LINETRANSLATEOUTPUT structure. This structure has the following format:

```
typedef struct linetranslateoutput_tag {
    DWORD dwTotalSize;
    DWORD dwNeededSize;
    DWORD dwUsedSize;
    DWORD dwDialableStringSize;
    DWORD dwDialableStringOffset;
    DWORD dwDisplayableStringSize;
    DWORD dwDisplayableStringOffset;
    DWORD dwCurrentCountry;
    DWORD dwDestCountry;
    DWORD dwTranslateResults;
} LINETRANSLATEOUTPUT, FAR *LPLINETRANSLATEOUTPUT;
```

The members *dwDialableStringSize* and *dwDialableStringOffset* specify the result of converting the canonical address to a dialable address. The results can be quite dramatic. For example, consider how the canonical address +1 (408) 5552345 is converted to a number that is dialable from a hotel room in Santa Clara. First, the country code is removed, since the user's current location is within the same country as the number to dial. Then the area code is removed, since the location is within the area code. *lineTranslateAddress* checks that the first three digits of the local part of the number are not in the toll prefix list for the number. If 555 is in the toll prefix list, 1 and probably the area code are prefixed to the dialable number to make it a long-distance number. To gain access to an outside line from the hotel room, 9 (or whatever local dialing prefix is specified in the Dialing Properties dialog box) is prefixed to the dialable number. If tone dialing is configured for the location, *T* is prefixed to the dialable address. Assuming that 555 is not in the toll list, the dialable number returned is T 9 5552345. *lineTranslateAddress* even inserts the spaces, just to make the number look good. This string should not be displayed to users because it could contain private information such as calling card numbers.

The *dwDisplayableStringSize* and *dwDisplayableStringOffset* members define an address that resembles the dialable address, but without the confusing control characters—no *T* for tone dialing, no *W* to wait for a dial tone, no $ to wait for a billing tone (a bong). This is called the *displayable address*—that is, the dialable address in a format suitable for displaying to users. If a calling card is used, the calling card access code is replaced in the displayable address with the name of the calling card.

The country code for the currently selected location is returned in the member *dwCurrentCountry*. The country code of the number to dial is extracted from the canonical address and returned in the member *dwDestCountry*. Finally, the *dwTranslateResults* member contains flags that indicate the decisions that *lineTranslateAddress* made during conversion of the address to dialable form. This member can consist of one or more of the following flags:

LINETRANSLATERESULT_CANONICAL	The input address is in valid canonical format.
LINETRANSLATERESULT_INTERNATIONAL	The call is an international call.
LINETRANSLATERESULT_LONGDISTANCE	The call is a long-distance call.
LINETRANSLATERESULT_LOCAL	The call is a local call.
LINETRANSLATERESULT_INTOLLLIST	The local call is dialed as long distance because the country has toll calling and the local number prefix appears in the toll list for the selected location.
LINETRANSLATERESULT_NOTINTOLLLIST	The local prefix does not appear in the toll list for the selected location.
LINETRANSLATERESULT_DIALBILLING	The returned address contains a $.
LINETRANSLATERESULT_DIALQUIET	The returned address contains a @.
LINETRANSLATERESULT_DIALDIALTONE	The returned address contains a *W*.
LINETRANSLATERESULT_DIALPROMPT	The returned address contains a ?.

If LINETRANSLATERESULT_CANONICAL is not set, the input address was not in canonical format, and the conversion was almost certainly unsuccessful. When this flag is not set, it is usually as good as an error message. The flags LINETRANSLATERESULT_LOCAL, LINETRANSLATERESULT_LONGDISTANCE, and LINETRANSLATERESULT_INTERNATIONAL indicate whether the input address was for a local, long-distance, or international call. For local calls, the flags LINETRANSLATERESULT_INTOLLLIST and LINETRANSLATERESULT_NOT-INTOLLLIST indicate whether the local number's prefix is in the toll list for the location. If neither of these flags is set, it means the input address specifies a country that does not support local toll numbers. The other flags specify whether special control characters like wait-for-dial-tone and wait-for-quiet are present in the dialable format of the address.

Interactive conversion

lineTranslateAddress is a powerful function, but it does have one major drawback: It is not interactive. When you call *lineTranslateAddress,* the canonical address you specify as input gets converted to a dialable address, which is returned as the output. To make this conversion, the function examines the current dialing properties, so the properties in effect when the function is called are applied to the conversion. Unfortunately, users tend to forget to update the Dialing Properties dialog box as they travel from location to location, so the function is vulnerable to using incorrect information when making the conversion. An interactive conversion function would solve these problems by allowing the user to make changes to the dialing properties while observing the effect of those changes on the conversion of a canonical phone number to dialable format. That is what *lineTranslateDialog* does. The syntax for *lineTranslateDialog* is shown below.

```
LONG lineTranslateDialog(
    HLINEAPP hTAPI,
    DWORD dwLine,
    DWORD dwVersionToUse,
    HWND hwndOwner,
    LPCSTR lpszAddressIn)
```

The first parameter, *hTAPI,* is the TAPI handle. *dwLine* is the line device ID and *dwVersionToUse* is the negotiated API version. The fourth parameter, *hwndOwner,* is a handle to the application window. This window handle is a big clue that the function displays a modal dialog box of some kind (as if the name *lineTranslateDialog* were not enough of a clue). The last parameter is a phone number in canonical format.

lineTranslateDialog displays a dialog box, shown in Figure 4-11 on the next page, that is identical in most respects to the Dialing Properties dialog box. The main difference is that with *lineTranslateDialog,* the dialable address corresponding to the input canonical address is displayed at the bottom of the dialog box. You can interactively modify the dialing properties and immediately see the effect on the dialable address. For example, you can change locations, add new locations, change the area code or country of origin, change the dialing prefixes to reach an outside line, disable call waiting, and select the use of pulse or tone dialing. You can even select a calling card. The resulting changes to the dialable address are displayed immediately.

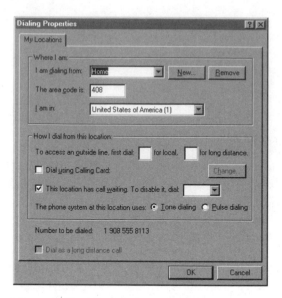

Figure 4-11. *The Dialing Properties dialog box accessed from the* lineTranslateDialog *function.*

The function does not return the dialable address. However, the new dialing properties take effect. After *lineTranslateDialog* finishes, the application should call *lineTranslateAddress* to retrieve the dialable address corresponding to the canonical address. The dialable address returned by *lineTranslate-Address* will look exactly like the one displayed by *lineTranslateDialog*.

A Skeleton Telephony Application

This chapter has presented a great deal of information on the Telephony API. To help you understand how it all ties together, this section presents a skeleton telephony application that initializes the telephony environment, reads configuration information, and in general prepares for communications. This application, called COMDIAL, consists of two source files, COMDIAL.C and MYTAPI_.C. COMDIAL.C contains the main window function and ancillary functions for managing terminal capabilities (like the Windows HyperTerminal accessory program). MYTAPI_.C contains the communications functionality. It might be useful to follow along in the code as we discuss some of the different functions.

The heart of COMDIAL (if a skeleton can have a heart) is a structure called MYTAPI, defined in COMDIAL.H, which serves as a central repository for various handles, IDs, pointers, and flags. In particular, the MYTAPI structure holds the TAPI handle, the negotiated version number, the line and address IDs that the application will use, the handle to the open line, the handle to the modem, the modem name, and an assortment of pointers and flags. The pointers reference configuration information that is returned by TAPI, such as the LINEDEVCAPS structure *(mytapi.pLinedevcaps)* and the ADDRESSCAPS structure *(mytapi.pLineaddresscaps)*. The flags indicate whether the pointers are valid. For example, if the flag *mytapi.bLinedevcapsalloced* is TRUE, the pointer *mytapi.pLinedevcaps* points to allocated memory containing a LINEDEVCAPS structure. (The use of the pointers and flags will become clearer as the discussion of the code progresses.)

Many of the functions in MYTAPI_.C are simply wrappers for various TAPI functions. The function *telephonyGetModemCaps* (shown in the code listing) is a good example. Its purpose is to allocate memory for the COMMPROP and MODEMDEVCAPS structures, and then to retrieve these structures from Windows so that the application has a local copy to work with. The function first checks whether the memory for the structures has already been allocated by a previous call to the function. It does this by checking the member flag *bCommpropalloced* of the structure MYTAPI. MYTAPI contains one flag for each piece of allocated memory; the flags have names that closely correspond to the names of the pointers with which they are associated. For example, the *pCommprop* pointer member in MYTAPI points to a COMMPROP structure with a MODEMDEVCAPS structure appended. The *bCommpropalloced* flag indicates whether memory for this structure has been allocated by the application. In general, the name of the flag is formed by appending the suffix *alloced* to the name of the pointer, and by changing the *p* pointer prefix to a *b*.

The function *telephonyGetModemCaps* then allocates memory for the COMMPROP and MODEMDEVCAPS structures. It initially allocates enough memory for both structures, i.e. *sizeof(COMMPROP) + sizeof(MODEMDEVCAPS)*. However, it does not allocate any extra space for the additional information that Windows might append to the MODEMDEVCAPS structure. *telephonyGetModemCaps* then calls *GetCommProperties* to retrieve the information from Windows. The function then checks the required size of the MODEMDEVCAPS structure to determine how much space is required for the extra information appended to the structure. The function reallocates the memory for the information to the new size, and calls *GetCommProperties* again. The pointer *mytapi.pModemcaps* is set to point to the MODEMDEVCAPS structure appended to the COMMPROP structure. If all goes well, the function sets the flag *mytapi.bCommpropalloced* to indicate that a local copy of the structures is now in memory.

Notice that the call to *GetCommProperties* requires the modem handle, *mytapi.hComm*. This implies that the *telephonyGetModemCaps* function cannot be called until the application retrieves the modem handle by calling *lineGetID*, which in turn cannot be called until the line handle is known through a call to *lineOpen*. So the order in which the functions are called is important.

With minor differences, the *telephonyGetModemSettings* function works in a similar manner to retrieve the COMMCONFIG and MODEMSETTINGS structures. The main difference is the call to *GetCommConfig*, which retrieves the COMMCONFIG structure and the appended MODEMSETTINGS structure and explicitly returns the required size for all available information in the parameter *dwsize*. There is no need to check the members of the returned structures for the required size; *GetCommConfig* returns it explicitly.

The function *mylineGetDevConfig* is a wrapper for *lineGetDevConfig,* and *mylineGetDevCaps* is a wrapper for *lineGetDevCaps.* An application can call both of these functions before the line is opened, since they use the line device ID and not the line handle to retrieve the information. *mylineGetLineDevStatus* and *mylineGetAddressStatus* are wrappers for the *lineGetLineDevStatus* and *lineGetAddressStatus* functions, respectively. These functions require a handle to an open line, so they can be called only after the line is opened.

The function *mylineGetID* should look familiar. It is simply a wrapper function for *lineGetID,* which we discussed earlier in the chapter. The line must be open when this function is called. The function sets the flag *mytapi.bGotcommhandle* to indicate that the modem handle has been retrieved.

The function *telephonySettings* is a wrapper for the *lineConfigDialogEdit* function. Once you have selected new modem settings using *lineConfigDialogEdit,* the wrapper function calls *lineSetDevConfig* to make the settings active and then calls *mylineGetDevConfig* to retrieve the updated modem device settings. Notice that this function uses the "lazy" approach of allocating far more memory than it will likely need when calling *lineConfigDialogEdit* the first time. This prevents the unpleasant possibility that the dialog box will have to be displayed twice.

Three functions in MYTAPI_.C are what you might call "megafunctions." That is, they call multiple wrapper functions or otherwise perform a composite of actions. The first of the megafunctions is *telephonyCaps*. It retrieves from Windows the LINEADDRESSCAPS structure and the LINETRANSLATECAPS structure, and it also calls the wrapper functions for *lineGetLineDevStatus* and *lineGetAddressStatus*. The grouping of functionality in *telephonyCaps,* as in all the megafunctions, is mostly for convenience. No strict laws of design govern the grouping of the functions. In this case, we designed the megafunction to show how a telephony application is implemented—not necessarily the best way to group functionality. Notice that in retrieving the LINEADDRESSCAPS structure, a loop is employed to check each address supported by the line device until the loop finds an address that supports the answering of calls. If no address is found that supports the answering of calls, the function fails because the skeleton application will be used to both make and answer calls. The following check is made to ensure that the address supports answering calls:

```
if (!(mytapi.pLineaddresscaps->dwCallFeatures &
    LINECALLFEATURE_ANSWER)) {
    i++;
    continue;
}
```

The loop is an unnecessary precaution when Unimodem is installed, because the line will typically support only one address and that address will be able to answer calls. But this is good practice if you want the code to be portable to other telephony drivers without problems.

Another megafunction is *telephonyInitialize,* which initializes the application for using Windows telephony. First it calls *lineInitialize,* checking for the LINE-ERR_REINIT return value. If *lineInitialize* succeeds, the flag *mytapi.bInitialized* is set to TRUE to indicate that the line is successfully initialized. If TAPI is reinitializing, the function sleeps for 5 seconds and then tries again. The use of *Sleep* versus a *PeekMessage* loop is a design choice; you can use either one.

The function next calls *lineNegotiateAPIVersion* for each supported line device. When it locates a line device that supports the same API version as the application, it calls the wrapper function for *lineGetDevCaps. telephonyInitialize* then checks the device capabilities of the line to ensure that data modem calls are supported, because analog modem data is the type of data that the application will process. The application doesn't use any API extensions, so it does not attempt to negotiate an extended API version. When a line is found that supports data modem calls, the function retrieves and saves the current modem device settings so that it can restore them when it terminates. Everything in *telephonyInitialize* is accomplished before the line is opened, so the megafunction does not require a line handle.

The third megafunction, *telephonyOpen,* opens the line selected in *telephony-Initialize* with owner privileges. The function then calls *myDrawTAPIIcon,* which is simply a wrapper function for *lineGetIcon.* This function retrieves the

Modems icon from Windows and makes it the application icon. Next, *telephonyOpen* calls *telephonyCaps,* which we just discussed. It then calls *lineSetStatusMessages* to enable the application to receive all line and address messages that are supported by the installed telephony driver. After that, the function retrieves the modem handle using *mylineGetID.* Finally, the COMM-PROP, MODEMDEVCAPS, COMMCONFIG, and MODEMSETTINGS structures are retrieved by calling *telephonyGetModemCaps* and *telephonyGetModem-Settings.*

If an error occurs at any time during *telephonyInitialize* and *telephonyOpen,* a *goto* is executed to the target *done.* This results in a call to the function *telephonyShutdown,* which is the converse of *telephonyInitialize* and *telephony-Open*—it undoes whatever the functions have done since the error occurred. During each stage of *telephonyInitialize* and *telephonyOpen,* flags are set indicating whether the line has been initialized and opened, which structures have been allocated, and so on. *telephonyShutdown* checks these flags and cleans up. If the *mytapi.bLineopen* flag is set, *telephonyShutdown* calls *lineClose* on the open line handle to close the line. If the flag *mytapi.bOlddevconfigalloced* is set, *telephonyShutdown* calls *lineSetDevConfig* to restore the state of the serial device to what it was before the application started using it. If the flag *mytapi.bReading* is set, *telephonyShutdown* calls *GetExitCodeThread* to find out if the thread is still active; if it is, *CloseHandle* is called on the handle to the thread. If the flag *mytapi.bGotcommhandle* is set, *CloseHandle* is called on the modem handle to ensure that the handle is free for other applications to use. If *mytapi.bInitialized* is set, *lineShutdown* is called on the TAPI handle to shut down the use of Windows telephony. Finally, any allocated memory is freed and the flags are all reset for next time.

The skeleton application also includes an extensive callback function for the line, called *LineCallBackProc.* This function is set in the call to *lineInitialize* as the callback for Windows to use. Most of the callback is empty "boilerplate" for the various messages that Windows might send, which individual applications built on the skeleton can process as they wish. In some cases, where the processing of a message is done in a more or less standard way, we have filled in some code. For example, when the LINE_ADDRESSSTATE message is received, the callback function calls *mylineGetAddressStatus* to retrieve the LINE-ADDRESSSTATUS structure, which holds the updated status information. Similarly, for the LINE_LINEDEVSTATE message, the callback calls *mylineGetLineDev-Status* to retrieve the updated LINEDEVSTATUS structure. How the application processes the updated line or address status is left to individual implementations, with one exception: If the LINE_LINEDEVSTATE message has a subtype of LINEDEVSTATE_REINIT, the application should be programmed to shut down its use of telephony by calling *telephonyShutdown,* as previously discussed, and then call *telephonyInitialize* to reinitialize. The function *telephonyInitialize,* you'll recall, contains a loop that calls *lineInitialize* every 5 seconds for as long as Windows telephony is reinitializing. You can break the loop at any time if you want to give up and try again later.

You'll see how to fill in other messages in the callback later in this chapter as the skeleton is fleshed out to make and answer calls. Some messages will never be fleshed out, either because Unimodem does not currently use them or because their implementation is application-specific.

There's not a whole lot to say about the source file COMDIAL.C. It contains the main window procedure for the application, plus a whole bunch of code for managing the display window so the window will act like an interactive terminal. Virtually all of this terminal code is copied directly from the sample terminal application included with the Windows 95 SDK. The main window procedure manages the application menu, which contains options to configure the modem (Modem/Configure), make calls (Modem/Make Call), answer calls (Modem/Answer Call), and disconnect calls (Modem/Disconnect). We'll discuss the options for making and answering calls later on. The Modem/Configure option calls *telephonyInitialize* if the current occurrence of the application has not yet initialized Windows telephony; it enables the Modem/Make Call, Modem/Answer Call, and Modem/Disconnect options once everything is initialized. It then calls *telephonySettings* to display a dialog box for entering new telephony settings. The Modem/Disconnect option calls *lineDrop* (a function we'll explain later), and then it calls *telephonyShutdown.* The application also calls *telephonyShutdown* when you exit. As you'll see in a moment, calling *telephonyShutdown* has the side effect of disconnecting any connected calls, although it is not the preferred method of doing so.

Once the skeleton application is in place, you can add code for making and answering calls. That is the subject of the next section, "Making Phone Calls."

Following are the code listings for the skeleton programs MYTAPI_.C and COMDIAL.C. We omitted some of the functions because they aren't relevant to our communications discussion. You can see the omitted functions as well as all the other code for these programs by installing the programs from the companion disk onto your hard drive and viewing them on your PC.

```
#include "comdial.h"
#include "resource.h"


MYTAPI mytapi;
extern HWND hTTYWnd;

/////////////////////////////////////////////////////////////////////
//    telephonyInitialize - megafunction to retrieve all
//        configuration information needed for telephony, plus
//        initialize TAPI and open the line.
/////////////////////////////////////////////////////////////////////
int telephonyInitialize(HWND hWnd, HINSTANCE hInst)
{
    LONG lrc;
    int i;
    LINEEXTENSIONID extensions;

    // initialize application use of TAPI
    while (lineInitialize(&mytapi.hTAPI, hInst,
                mytapi.CallbackProc =
            (LINECALLBACK)MakeProcInstance
            ((FARPROC)LineCallBackProc, hInst),
            "TAPIProcess", &mytapi.dwNumLines) ==
            LINEERR_REINIT) {
        Sleep (5);                 // sleep for five seconds
        if (MessageBox(hWnd, "Telephony system is \
                    reinitializing - Click Cancel to abort",
                    "Error", MB_RETRYCANCEL) ==IDCANCEL)
                goto done;
    } // end while (TAPI reinitializing)

    // bool indicates lineInitialize called successfully
    mytapi.bInitialized = TRUE;

    // check every logical line for one that support modem data
    for (i=0; (unsigned)i<mytapi.dwNumLines; i++) {

            // negotiate version of TAPI to use
            lrc = lineNegotiateAPIVersion(mytapi.hTAPI, i,
                    WIN95TAPIVERSION, WIN95TAPIVERSION,
                    &mytapi.dwVersionToUse, &extensions);
            if (lrc)
                continue;
```

```
            // get line device caps
            lrc = mylineGetDevCaps ();
            if (lrc)
                goto done;

            // check that the line supports modems
            if (mytapi.pLinedevcaps->dwMediaModes &
                LINEMEDIAMODE_DATAMODEM) {
                mytapi.dwLine = i;
                break;
            }

        }

    // get current configuration of serial comm device
    lrc = mylineGetOldDevConfig();
    if (lrc)
        goto done;
    lrc = mylineGetDevConfig();
    if (lrc)
        goto done;

    return 0;

done:
    // error!  clean up and return error code

    telephonyShutdown();

    return lrc;

}

int telephonyOpen(HWND hWnd, HINSTANCE hInst)
{
    LONG lrc;

    // open the line device
    lrc = lineOpen(mytapi.hTAPI, mytapi.dwLine, &mytapi.hLine,
                    mytapi.dwVersionToUse, 0, 0,
                    LINECALLPRIVILEGE_OWNER, LINEMEDIAMODE_DATAMODEM,
                    NULL);
    if (lrc)
        goto done;
```

(continued)

```
    // bool indicates lineOpen called successfully
    mytapi.bLineopen = TRUE;

    // get the telephony icon and make it ours
    myDrawTAPIIcon(hWnd);

    // get other telephony configuration info
    lrc = telephonyCaps();
    if (lrc)
        goto done;

    // receive all possible status messages for the
    // line device and address
    lineSetStatusMessages(mytapi.hLine,
        mytapi.pLinedevcaps->dwLineStates,
        mytapi.pLineaddresscaps->dwAddressStates);

    // get modem capabilities
    lrc = telephonyGetModemCaps();
    if (lrc)
        goto done;

    // get current modem settings
    lrc = telephonyGetModemSettings();
    if (lrc)
        goto done;

    // success

    return 0;

done:
    // error!  clean up and return error code

    telephonyShutdown();

    return lrc;

} // end procedure (telephony initialize)
```

```
/////////////////////////////////////////////////////////////
//     telephonyGetModemCaps - get COMMPROP and MODEMDEVCAPS
//          structures
/////////////////////////////////////////////////////////////
LONG telephonyGetModemCaps()
{
    DWORD dwsize = sizeof(COMMPROP)+sizeof(MODEMDEVCAPS);
    LONG lrc;

    // if space already allocated for structure, free it up
    if (mytapi.bCommpropalloced) {
        free (mytapi.pCommprop);
        mytapi.bCommpropalloced = FALSE;
    }

    // allocate memory for structure
    mytapi.pCommprop = (COMMPROP *) calloc (1, dwsize);
    if (!mytapi.pCommprop)
        return -1;
    mytapi.bCommpropalloced = TRUE;
    // set structure size
    mytapi.pCommprop->wPacketLength = (WORD)dwsize;


    // get modem handle for use with serial comm api
    // NOTE: WE GET THE HANDLE, USE IT, THEN CLOSE IT AGAIN RIGHT
    // AWAY SO THAT THE MODEM IS NOT RESERVED BY OUR APPLICATION
    lrc = mylineGetID();
    if (lrc) {
        free (mytapi.pCommprop);
        mytapi.bCommpropalloced = FALSE;
        return -1;
    }
    // get information into structure
    lrc = GetCommProperties(mytapi.hComm, mytapi.pCommprop);

    // Close the modem handle
    CloseHandle (mytapi.hComm);
    mytapi.bGotcommhandle = FALSE;
```

(continued)

```
        // bomb out if error
        if (!lrc)  {
            free (mytapi.pCommprop);
            mytapi.bCommpropalloced = FALSE;
            return -1;
        }

        // reallocate and try again
        mytapi.pModemcaps = (MODEMDEVCAPS *)
                          mytapi.pCommprop->wcProvChar;
        dwsize = mytapi.pModemcaps->dwRequiredSize + sizeof(COMMPROP);
        free (mytapi.pCommprop);
        mytapi.bCommpropalloced = FALSE;
        mytapi.pCommprop = (COMMPROP *) calloc (1, dwsize);
        if (!mytapi.pCommprop)
            return -1;
        mytapi.bCommpropalloced = TRUE;
        mytapi.pCommprop->wPacketLength = (WORD)dwsize;

        // get modem handle for use with serial comm api
        // NOTE: WE GET THE HANDLE, USE IT, THEN CLOSE IT AGAIN RIGHT
        // AWAY SO THAT THE MODEM IS NOT RESERVED BY OUR APPLICATION
        lrc =  mylineGetID();
        if (lrc) {
            free (mytapi.pCommprop);
            mytapi.bCommpropalloced = FALSE;
            return -1;
        }
        // try again
        lrc = GetCommProperties(mytapi.hComm, mytapi.pCommprop);

        // Close the modem handle
        CloseHandle (mytapi.hComm);
        mytapi.bGotcommhandle = FALSE;

        if (!lrc)  {
            free (mytapi.pCommprop);
            mytapi.bCommpropalloced = FALSE;
            return -1;
        }
        mytapi.pModemcaps = (MODEMDEVCAPS *)
                          mytapi.pCommprop->wcProvChar;

        return 0;


} // end procedure (telephonyGetModemCaps)
```

```
///////////////////////////////////////////////////////////////
//     telephonyGetModemSettings - get COMMCONFIG and MODEMSETTINGS
//          structures
///////////////////////////////////////////////////////////////
LONG telephonyGetModemSettings()
{
    DWORD dwsize = sizeof(COMMCONFIG)+sizeof(MODEMSETTINGS);
    LONG lrc;

    do {

        // if space already allocated for structure, free it up
        if (mytapi.bCommconfigalloced) {
            free (mytapi.pCommconfig);
            mytapi.bCommconfigalloced = FALSE;
        }

        // allocate memory for structure
        mytapi.pCommconfig = (COMMCONFIG *) calloc (1, dwsize);
        if (!mytapi.pCommconfig)
            return -1;
        mytapi.bCommconfigalloced = TRUE;
        // set structure size
        mytapi.pCommconfig->dwSize = dwsize;

        // get modem handle for use with serial comm api
        // NOTE: WE GET THE HANDLE, USE IT, THEN CLOSE IT AGAIN
        // RIGHT AWAY SO THAT THE MODEM IS NOT RESERVED BY OUR
        // APPLICATION
        lrc = mylineGetID();
        if (lrc) {
            free (mytapi.pCommconfig);
            mytapi.bCommconfigalloced = FALSE;
            return -1;
        }
        // get information into structure
        lrc = GetCommConfig(mytapi.hComm, mytapi.pCommconfig,
                            &dwsize);

        // Close the modem handle
        CloseHandle (mytapi.hComm);
        mytapi.bGotcommhandle = FALSE;
```

(continued)

```
        // bomb out if error
        if (!lrc) {
            free (mytapi.pCommconfig);
            mytapi.bCommconfigalloced = FALSE;
            return -1;
        }

        mytapi.pModemsettings = (MODEMSETTINGS *)
            mytapi.pCommconfig->wcProviderData;
        // try again
        if (mytapi.pCommconfig->dwSize < dwsize) {
            continue;
        }

        break;
    } while (TRUE);

    return 0;

} // end procedure (telephonyGetModemSettings)

//////////////////////////////////////////////////////////////////
//    myDrawTAPIIcon - get telephony icon and make it ours
//////////////////////////////////////////////////////////////////
void myDrawTAPIIcon(HWND hwnd)
{
    HICON hIcon;

    // get handle to telephony icon
    lineGetIcon (mytapi.dwLine, NULL, &hIcon);
    // make the icon ours
    SetClassLong (hwnd, GCL_HICON, (LONG)hIcon);

}

//////////////////////////////////////////////////////////////////
//    mylineGetDevConfig - get configuration of serial device
//////////////////////////////////////////////////////////////////
LONG mylineGetDevConfig()
{
    LONG lrc;
    DWORD dwSize;
```

```
    // if space already allocated for structure, free it up
    if (mytapi.bDevconfigalloced) {
        free (mytapi.pDevconfig);
        mytapi.bDevconfigalloced = FALSE;
    }

    // allocate memory for structure
    mytapi.pDevconfig = (VARSTRING *) calloc (1, sizeof(VARSTRING));
    if (!mytapi.pDevconfig)
        return -1;
    mytapi.bDevconfigalloced = TRUE;

    // set structure size
    mytapi.pDevconfig->dwTotalSize = sizeof(VARSTRING);

    do {
            // get information into structure
            lrc = lineGetDevConfig(mytapi.dwLine,
                mytapi.pDevconfig,
                "comm/datamodem");
            // bomb out if error
            if (lrc)  {
                free (mytapi.pDevconfig);
                mytapi.bDevconfigalloced = FALSE;
                return lrc;
            }
            // reallocate and try again
            if (mytapi.pDevconfig->dwTotalSize
                < mytapi.pDevconfig->dwNeededSize) {
                    dwSize = mytapi.pDevconfig->dwNeededSize;
                    free (mytapi.pDevconfig);
                    mytapi.bDevconfigalloced = FALSE;
                    mytapi.pDevconfig = (VARSTRING *)
                                        calloc(1, dwSize);
                    if (!mytapi.pDevconfig)
                        return -1;
                    mytapi.bDevconfigalloced = TRUE;
                    mytapi.pDevconfig->dwTotalSize = dwSize;
                    continue;
            } /* end if (need more space) */
            break; /* success  */
    } while (TRUE);

    return lrc;

}
```

(continued)

```
///////////////////////////////////////////////////////////
//    mylineGetOldDevConfig - get configuration of serial device for
//    later restore when program terminates
///////////////////////////////////////////////////////////
LONG mylineGetOldDevConfig()
{
    LONG lrc;
    DWORD dwSize;


    // if space already allocated for structure, free it up
    if (mytapi.bOlddevconfigalloced) {
        free (mytapi.pOlddevconfig);
        mytapi.bOlddevconfigalloced = FALSE;
    }

    // allocate memory for structure
    mytapi.pOlddevconfig = (VARSTRING *)
                            calloc (1, sizeof(VARSTRING));
    if (!mytapi.pOlddevconfig)
        return -1;
    mytapi.bOlddevconfigalloced = TRUE;

    // set structure size
    mytapi.pOlddevconfig->dwTotalSize = sizeof(VARSTRING);

    do {
            // get information into structure
            lrc = lineGetDevConfig(mytapi.dwLine,
                mytapi.pOlddevconfig,
                "comm/datamodem");
            // bomb out if error
            if (lrc)  {
                free (mytapi.pOlddevconfig);
                mytapi.bOlddevconfigalloced = FALSE;
                return lrc;
            }
            // reallocate and try again
            if (mytapi.pOlddevconfig->dwTotalSize
                < mytapi.pOlddevconfig->dwNeededSize) {
                    dwSize = mytapi.pOlddevconfig->dwNeededSize;
                    free (mytapi.pOlddevconfig);
                    mytapi.bOlddevconfigalloced = FALSE;
                    mytapi.pOlddevconfig = (VARSTRING *)
                                            calloc(1, dwSize);
                    if (!mytapi.pOlddevconfig)
                        return -1;
```

```
                    mytapi.bOlddevconfigalloced = TRUE;
                    mytapi.pOlddevconfig->dwTotalSize = dwSize;
                    continue;
            } /* end if (need more space) */
            break; /* success  */
    } while (TRUE);

    return lrc;

}
/////////////////////////////////////////////////////////////////
//    mylineGetID - get modem handle
/////////////////////////////////////////////////////////////////
LONG mylineGetID ()
{
    CommID FAR *cid;
    VARSTRING  *vs;
    LONG lrc;
    DWORD dwSize;

        mytapi.bGotcommhandle = FALSE;

        // allocate memory for structure
        vs = (VARSTRING *) calloc (1, sizeof(VARSTRING));
        // set structure size
        vs->dwTotalSize = sizeof(VARSTRING);

        do {
                // get information into structure
                lrc = lineGetID(mytapi.hLine, 0L, NULL,
                            LINECALLSELECT_LINE, vs,
                            "comm/datamodem");
                // bomb out if error
                if (lrc) {
                    free (vs);
                    return -1;
                }
                // reallocate and try again
                if (vs->dwTotalSize < vs->dwNeededSize) {
                        dwSize = vs->dwNeededSize;
                        free (vs);
                        vs = (VARSTRING *) calloc(1, dwSize);
                        vs->dwTotalSize = dwSize;
                        continue;
                } /* end if (need more space) */
                break; /* success  */
        } while (TRUE);
```

(continued)

```
            // copy modem handle and modem name from structure
            cid = (CommID FAR *) ((LPSTR)vs + vs->dwStringOffset);
            lstrcpy (mytapi.szModemName, &cid->szDeviceName[0]);
            // save modem handle
            mytapi.hComm = cid->hComm;
            // done with structure; free it
            free (vs);

            // set flag to indicate modem handle has been retrieved
            mytapi.bGotcommhandle = TRUE;

            return 0;

} /* end function (GetCommHandle) */
/////////////////////////////////////////////////////////////////////
//     mylineGetCallID - get modem handle associated with call
/////////////////////////////////////////////////////////////////////
LONG mylineGetCallID ()
{
    CommID FAR *cid;
    VARSTRING  *vs;
    LONG lrc;
    DWORD dwSize;

        mytapi.bGotcommhandle = FALSE;

        // allocate memory for structure
        vs = (VARSTRING *) calloc (1, sizeof(VARSTRING));
        // set structure size
        vs->dwTotalSize = sizeof(VARSTRING);

        do {
                // get information into structure
                lrc = lineGetID(NULL, 0L, mytapi.hCall,
                            LINECALLSELECT_CALL, vs,
                            "comm/datamodem");
                // bomb out if error
                if (lrc)  {
                    free (vs);
                    return -1;
                }
```

```
                        // reallocate and try again
                        if (vs->dwTotalSize < vs->dwNeededSize) {
                                dwSize = vs->dwNeededSize;
                                free (vs);
                                vs = (VARSTRING *) calloc(1, dwSize);
                                vs->dwTotalSize = dwSize;
                                continue;
                        } /* end if (need more space) */
                        break; /* success  */
                } while (TRUE);

                // copy modem handle and modem name from structure
                cid = (CommID FAR *) ((LPSTR)vs + vs->dwStringOffset);
                lstrcpy (mytapi.szModemName, &cid->szDeviceName[0]);
                // save modem handle
                mytapi.hComm = cid->hComm;
                // done with structure; free it
                free (vs);

                // set flag to indicate modem handle has been retrieved
                mytapi.bGotcommhandle = TRUE;

                return 0;

} /* end function (GetCommHandle) */

//////////////////////////////////////////////////////////////////////
//      mylineGetDevCaps - get LINEDEVCAPS structure
//////////////////////////////////////////////////////////////////////
LONG mylineGetDevCaps()
{
        LONG lrc;
        DWORD dwsize;

        // if space already allocated for structure, free it up
        if (mytapi.bLinedevcapsalloced) {
                free (mytapi.pLinedevcaps);
                mytapi.bLinedevcapsalloced = FALSE;
        }
```

(continued)

```
        // allocate memory for structure
        mytapi.pLinedevcaps = (LINEDEVCAPS *)
                             calloc(1, sizeof(LINEDEVCAPS));
        if (!mytapi.pLinedevcaps)
            return LINEERR_NOMEM;
        mytapi.bLinedevcapsalloced = TRUE;
        // set structure size
        mytapi.pLinedevcaps->dwTotalSize = sizeof(LINEDEVCAPS);
        do {
            // get information into structure
            lrc = lineGetDevCaps(mytapi.hTAPI, mytapi.dwLine,
                            mytapi.dwVersionToUse,
                            0, mytapi.pLinedevcaps);
            // bomb out if error
            if (lrc) {
                free (mytapi.pLinedevcaps);
                mytapi.bLinedevcapsalloced = FALSE;
                return lrc;
            }
            dwsize = mytapi.pLinedevcaps->dwNeededSize;
            // reallocate and try again
            if (mytapi.pLinedevcaps->dwTotalSize < dwsize) {
                free (mytapi.pLinedevcaps);
                mytapi.bLinedevcapsalloced = FALSE;
                mytapi.pLinedevcaps = (LINEDEVCAPS *) calloc(1, dwsize);
                if (!mytapi.pLinedevcaps)
                    return LINEERR_NOMEM;
                mytapi.bLinedevcapsalloced = TRUE;
                mytapi.pLinedevcaps->dwTotalSize = dwsize;
                continue;
            }
            break;
        } while (TRUE);

        return lrc;
}


//////////////////////////////////////////////////////////////////
//    telephonyCaps - megafunction to get LINEADDRESSCAPS,
//        LINETRANSLATECAPS, LINEDEVSTATUS, and LINEADDRESSSTATUS
//        structures.
//////////////////////////////////////////////////////////////////
```

```
LONG telephonyCaps()
{
    LONG lrc;
    DWORD dwsize;
    int i;

    // if space already allocated for structure, free it up
    if (mytapi.bLineaddresscapsalloced) {
        free (mytapi.pLineaddresscaps);
        mytapi.bLineaddresscapsalloced = FALSE;
    }

    // allocate memory for structure
    mytapi.pLineaddresscaps = (LINEADDRESSCAPS *)
                                calloc(1, sizeof(LINEADDRESSCAPS));
    if (!mytapi.pLineaddresscaps)
        return LINEERR_NOMEM;
    mytapi.bLineaddresscapsalloced = TRUE;
    // set structure size
    mytapi.pLineaddresscaps->dwTotalSize = sizeof(LINEADDRESSCAPS);

    // check each address supported by the line device for one
    // that allows calls to be answered
    i = 0;
    do {
        // get information into structure
        lrc = lineGetAddressCaps(mytapi.hTAPI, mytapi.dwLine, i,
                    mytapi.dwVersionToUse,
                    0, mytapi.pLineaddresscaps);
        // bomb out if error
        if (lrc) {
            free (mytapi.pLineaddresscaps);
            mytapi.bLineaddresscapsalloced = FALSE;
            return lrc;
        }

        // make sure address can answer calls
        if (!(mytapi.pLineaddresscaps->dwCallFeatures &
            LINECALLFEATURE_ANSWER)){
            i++;
            continue;
        }
```

(continued)

```
    // reallocate and try again
    dwsize = mytapi.pLineaddresscaps->dwNeededSize;
    if (mytapi.pLineaddresscaps->dwTotalSize < dwsize) {
        free (mytapi.pLineaddresscaps);
        mytapi.bLineaddresscapsalloced = FALSE;
        mytapi.pLineaddresscaps = (LINEADDRESSCAPS *)
                                    calloc(1, dwsize);
        if (!mytapi.pLineaddresscaps)
            return LINEERR_NOMEM;
        mytapi.bLineaddresscapsalloced = TRUE;
        mytapi.pLineaddresscaps->dwTotalSize = dwsize;
        continue;
    }
    break;
} while ((unsigned)i < mytapi.pLinedevcaps->dwNumAddresses);

// if no address was found to answer calls, bomb out
if ((unsigned)i == mytapi.pLinedevcaps->dwNumAddresses) {
    free (mytapi.pLineaddresscaps);
    mytapi.bLineaddresscapsalloced = FALSE;
    return -1;
}

// set address id to use
mytapi.dwAddress = i;


// now get address translate caps

// if space already allocated for structure, free it up
if (mytapi.bLinetranslatecapsalloced) {
    free (mytapi.pLinetranslatecaps);
    mytapi.bLinetranslatecapsalloced = FALSE;
}

// allocate memory for structure
mytapi.pLinetranslatecaps =
    (LINETRANSLATECAPS *) calloc(1, sizeof(LINETRANSLATECAPS));
if (!mytapi.pLinetranslatecaps)
    return LINEERR_NOMEM;
mytapi.bLinetranslatecapsalloced = TRUE;
// set structure size
mytapi.pLinetranslatecaps->dwTotalSize =
    sizeof(LINETRANSLATECAPS);
```

```
do {
    // get information into structure
    lrc = lineGetTranslateCaps(mytapi.hTAPI,
                               mytapi.dwVersionToUse,
                               mytapi.pLinetranslatecaps);
    // bomb out if error
    if (lrc) {
        free (mytapi.pLinetranslatecaps);
        mytapi.bLinetranslatecapsalloced = FALSE;
        return lrc;
    }

    // reallocate and try again
    dwsize = mytapi.pLinetranslatecaps->dwNeededSize;
    if (mytapi.pLinetranslatecaps->dwTotalSize < dwsize) {
        free (mytapi.pLinetranslatecaps);
        mytapi.bLinetranslatecapsalloced = FALSE;
        mytapi.pLinetranslatecaps = (LINETRANSLATECAPS *)
                                    calloc(1, dwsize);
        if (!mytapi.pLinetranslatecaps)
            return LINEERR_NOMEM;
        mytapi.bLinetranslatecapsalloced = TRUE;
        mytapi.pLinetranslatecaps->dwTotalSize = dwsize;
        continue;
    }
    break;
} while (TRUE);


// get line device status
lrc = mylineGetLineDevStatus();
if (lrc)
    return lrc;

// get address status
lrc = mylineGetAddressStatus();
if (lrc)
    return lrc;

return lrc;


}
```

(continued)

```
//////////////////////////////////////////////////////////////////
//    mylineGetAddressStatus - get LINEADDRESSSTATUS structure
//////////////////////////////////////////////////////////////////
LONG mylineGetAddressStatus()
{
    LONG lrc;
    DWORD dwsize;

    // if space already allocated for structure, free it up
    if (mytapi.bLineaddressstatusalloced) {
        free (mytapi.pLineaddressstatus);
        mytapi.bLineaddressstatusalloced = FALSE;
    }

    // allocate memory for structure
    mytapi.pLineaddressstatus =
        (LINEADDRESSSTATUS *) calloc(1, sizeof(LINEADDRESSSTATUS));
    if (!mytapi.pLineaddressstatus)
        return LINEERR_NOMEM;
    mytapi.bLineaddressstatusalloced = TRUE;
    // set structure size
    mytapi.pLineaddressstatus->dwTotalSize =
        sizeof(LINEADDRESSSTATUS);

    do {
        // get information into structure
        lrc = lineGetAddressStatus(mytapi.hLine, mytapi.dwAddress,
                mytapi.pLineaddressstatus);
        // bomb out if error
        if (lrc) {
            free (mytapi.pLineaddressstatus);
            mytapi.bLineaddressstatusalloced = FALSE;
            return lrc;
        }

        // reallocate and try again
        dwsize = mytapi.pLineaddressstatus->dwNeededSize;
        if (mytapi.pLineaddressstatus->dwTotalSize < dwsize) {
            free (mytapi.pLineaddressstatus);
            mytapi.bLineaddressstatusalloced = FALSE;
            mytapi.pLineaddressstatus =
                (LINEADDRESSSTATUS *) calloc(1, dwsize);
            if (!mytapi.pLineaddressstatus)
                return LINEERR_NOMEM;
```

```
            mytapi.bLineaddressstatusalloced = TRUE;
            mytapi.pLineaddressstatus->dwTotalSize = dwsize;
            continue;
        }
        break;
    } while (TRUE);

    return lrc;


}


///////////////////////////////////////////////////////////////////
//    mylineGetLineDevStatus - get LINEDEVSTATUS structure
///////////////////////////////////////////////////////////////////
LONG mylineGetLineDevStatus()
{
    LONG lrc;
    DWORD dwsize;

    // if space already allocated for structure, free it up
    if (mytapi.bLinedevstatusalloced) {
        free (mytapi.pLinedevstatus);
        mytapi.bLinedevstatusalloced = FALSE;
    }

    // allocate memory for structure
    mytapi.pLinedevstatus =
        (LINEDEVSTATUS *) calloc(1, sizeof(LINEDEVSTATUS));
    if (!mytapi.pLinedevstatus)
        return LINEERR_NOMEM;
    mytapi.bLinedevstatusalloced = TRUE;
    // set structure size
    mytapi.pLinedevstatus->dwTotalSize = sizeof(LINEDEVSTATUS);

    do {
        // get information into structure
        lrc = lineGetLineDevStatus(mytapi.hLine,
                                mytapi.pLinedevstatus);
        // bomb out if error
        if (lrc) {
            free (mytapi.pLinedevstatus);
            mytapi.bLinedevstatusalloced = FALSE;
            return lrc;
        }
```

(continued)

```
            // reallocate and try again
            dwsize = mytapi.pLinedevstatus->dwNeededSize;
            if (mytapi.pLinedevstatus->dwTotalSize < dwsize) {
                free (mytapi.pLinedevstatus);
                mytapi.bLinedevstatusalloced = FALSE;
                mytapi.pLinedevstatus =
                    (LINEDEVSTATUS *) calloc(1, dwsize);
                if (!mytapi.pLinedevstatus)
                    return LINEERR_NOMEM;
                mytapi.bLinedevstatusalloced = TRUE;
                mytapi.pLinedevstatus->dwTotalSize = dwsize;
                continue;
            }
            break;
    } while (TRUE);

    return lrc;
}


////////////////////////////////////////////////////////////////
//    mylineGetCallStatus - get LINECALLSTATUS structure
////////////////////////////////////////////////////////////////
LONG mylineGetCallStatus()
{
    LONG lrc;
    DWORD dwsize;

    // if space already allocated for structure, free it up
    if (mytapi.bLinecallstatusalloced) {
        free (mytapi.pLinecallstatus);
        mytapi.bLinecallstatusalloced = FALSE;
    }

    // allocate memory for structure
    mytapi.pLinecallstatus = (LINECALLSTATUS *)
                            calloc(1, sizeof(LINECALLSTATUS));
    if (!mytapi.pLinecallstatus)
        return LINEERR_NOMEM;
    mytapi.bLinecallstatusalloced = TRUE;
    // set structure size
    mytapi.pLinecallstatus->dwTotalSize = sizeof(LINECALLSTATUS);

    do {
        // get information into structure
        lrc = lineGetCallStatus(mytapi.hCall,
                            mytapi.pLinecallstatus);
```

```
        // bomb out if error
        if (lrc) {
            free (mytapi.pLinecallstatus);
            mytapi.bLinecallstatusalloced = FALSE;
            return lrc;
        }

        // reallocate and try again
        dwsize = mytapi.pLinecallstatus->dwNeededSize;
        if (mytapi.pLinecallstatus->dwTotalSize < dwsize) {
            free (mytapi.pLinecallstatus);
            mytapi.bLinecallstatusalloced = FALSE;
            mytapi.pLinecallstatus =
                (LINECALLSTATUS *) calloc(1, dwsize);
            if (!mytapi.pLinecallstatus)
                return LINEERR_NOMEM;
            mytapi.bLinecallstatusalloced = TRUE;
            mytapi.pLinecallstatus->dwTotalSize = dwsize;
            continue;
        }
        break;
    } while (TRUE);

    return lrc;
}


//////////////////////////////////////////////////////////////////
//      mylineGetCallInfo - get LINECALLINFO structure
//////////////////////////////////////////////////////////////////
LONG mylineGetCallInfo()
{
    LONG lrc;
    DWORD dwsize;

    // if space already allocated for structure, free it up
    if (mytapi.bLinecallinfoalloced) {
        free (mytapi.pLinecallinfo);
        mytapi.bLinecallinfoalloced = FALSE;
    }
```

(continued)

```
// allocate memory for structure
mytapi.pLinecallinfo =
    (LINECALLINFO *) calloc(1, sizeof(LINECALLINFO));
if (!mytapi.pLinecallinfo)
    return LINEERR_NOMEM;
mytapi.bLinecallinfoalloced = TRUE;
// set structure size
mytapi.pLinecallinfo->dwTotalSize = sizeof(LINECALLINFO);

do {
    // get information into structure
    lrc = lineGetCallInfo(mytapi.hCall, mytapi.pLinecallinfo);
    // bomb out if error
    if (lrc) {
        free (mytapi.pLinecallinfo);
        mytapi.bLinecallinfoalloced = FALSE;
        return lrc;
    }

    // reallocate and try again
    dwsize = mytapi.pLinecallinfo->dwNeededSize;
    if (mytapi.pLinecallinfo->dwTotalSize < dwsize) {
        free (mytapi.pLinecallinfo);
        mytapi.bLinecallinfoalloced = FALSE;
        mytapi.pLinecallinfo =
            (LINECALLINFO *) calloc(1, dwsize);
        if (!mytapi.pLinecallinfo)
            return LINEERR_NOMEM;
        mytapi.bLinecallinfoalloced = TRUE;
        mytapi.pLinecallinfo->dwTotalSize = dwsize;
        continue;
    }
    break;
} while (TRUE);

return lrc;
}
```

```
/////////////////////////////////////////////////////////////////
//    telephonyShutdown - megafunction to close line, shut down
//        telephony, close modem handle, restore serial device
//        configuration, and free up various allocated structures.
/////////////////////////////////////////////////////////////////
void telephonyShutdown()
{
    DWORD id;

    // close line if open
    if (mytapi.bLineopen)
        lineClose(mytapi.hLine);
    // restore serial device configuration
    if (mytapi.bOlddevconfigalloced)
        lineSetDevConfig (mytapi.dwLine,
                        (LPVOID)((LPBYTE)mytapi.pOlddevconfig +
                        mytapi.pOlddevconfig>dwStringOffset),
                        mytapi.pOlddevconfig->dwStringSize,
                        "comm/datamodem");
    // shutdown the read thread if it is running
    if (mytapi.bReading) {
        /* kill the read thread */
        mytapi.bReading = FALSE;
        /* wait for thread to die... */
        while (GetExitCodeThread(mytapi.hThread, &id)) {
            if (id == STILL_ACTIVE)
                continue;
            else
                break;
        } /* end while (no error reading thread exit code) */
        CloseHandle (mytapi.hThread);
    }
    // close modem handle if open
    if (mytapi.bGotcommhandle)
        CloseHandle (mytapi.hComm);
    // shutdown tapi if initialized
    if (mytapi.bInitialized)
        lineShutdown(mytapi.hTAPI);
```

(continued)

```
        // free up various structures if allocated
        if (mytapi.bLinedevcapsalloced)
            free (mytapi.pLinedevcaps);
        if (mytapi.bLineaddresscapsalloced)
            free (mytapi.pLineaddresscaps);
        if (mytapi.bLinetranslatecapsalloced)
            free (mytapi.pLinetranslatecaps);
        if (mytapi.bLinedevstatusalloced)
            free (mytapi.pLinedevstatus);
        if (mytapi.bLineaddressstatusalloced)
            free (mytapi.pLineaddressstatus);
        if (mytapi.bDevconfigalloced)
            free (mytapi.pDevconfig);
        if (mytapi.bOlddevconfigalloced)
            free (mytapi.pOlddevconfig);
        if (mytapi.bCommpropalloced)
            free (mytapi.pCommprop);
        if (mytapi.bCommconfigalloced)
            free (mytapi.pCommconfig);
        if (mytapi.bLinecallinfoalloced)
            free(mytapi.pLinecallinfo);
        if (mytapi.bLinecallstatusalloced)
            free(mytapi.pLinecallstatus);

        // set flags to indicate that the structures are no longer
        // allocated
        mytapi.bLinedevcapsalloced = FALSE;
        mytapi.bLineaddresscapsalloced = FALSE;
        mytapi.bLinetranslatecapsalloced = FALSE;
        mytapi.bLinedevstatusalloced = FALSE;
        mytapi.bLineaddressstatusalloced = FALSE;
        mytapi.bDevconfigalloced = FALSE;
        mytapi.bGotcommhandle = FALSE;
        mytapi.bCommpropalloced = FALSE;
        mytapi.bCommconfigalloced = FALSE;
        mytapi.bLineopen = FALSE;
        mytapi.bInitialized = FALSE;
        mytapi.bLinecallinfoalloced = FALSE;
        mytapi.bLinecallstatusalloced = FALSE;
        mytapi.bReading = FALSE;
        mytapi.bWaitForCall = FALSE;

    } // end function (telephonyShutdown)
```

```
///////////////////////////////////////////////////////////
//    telephonySettings - change telephony settings
///////////////////////////////////////////////////////////
LONG telephonySettings(HWND hwnd)
{
    LONG lrc;
    LPVARSTRING vs =
        calloc(1, mytapi.pDevconfig->dwTotalSize + 15000);

    // update our local settings structure
    lrc = mylineGetDevConfig();
    if (lrc)
        return lrc;

    vs->dwTotalSize = mytapi.pDevconfig->dwTotalSize + 15000;
    // display dialog to change telephony settings
    lrc = lineConfigDialogEdit(mytapi.dwLine, hwnd,
                            "comm/datamodem",
                            (LPVOID)((LPBYTE)mytapi.pDevconfig +
                            mytapi.pDevconfig->dwStringOffset),
                            mytapi.pDevconfig->dwStringSize,
                            vs);
    if (lrc) {
        free (vs);
        return lrc;
    }

    // make new settings active
    lrc = lineSetDevConfig (mytapi.dwLine, (LPVOID)((LPBYTE)vs +
                            vs->dwStringOffset),
                            vs->dwStringSize, "comm/datamodem");
    if (lrc) {
        free (vs);
        return lrc;
    }

    free (vs);

    // update our local settings structure
    lrc = mylineGetDevConfig();

    return lrc;
}
```

(continued)

```
///////////////////////////////////////////////////////////////
//    LineCallBackProc - message function for TAPI events
///////////////////////////////////////////////////////////////
/* callback function */
void FAR PASCAL LineCallBackProc(DWORD dwDevice,
          DWORD dwMessage,DWORD dwInstance,DWORD dwParam1,
          DWORD dwParam2,DWORD dwParam3)
{
    HMENU hMenu;
    DWORD id;
    LONG lrc;

    switch (dwMessage) {
        case LINE_ADDRESSSTATE:

            mylineGetAddressStatus();

            // update menus
            hMenu = GetMenu(hTTYWnd);
            if (mytapi.pLineaddressstatus->dwAddressFeatures &
                LINEADDRFEATURE_MAKECALL)
                EnableMenuItem(hMenu, IDM_MAKECALL,
                            MF_ENABLED | MF_BYCOMMAND) ;
            else
                EnableMenuItem(hMenu, IDM_MAKECALL,
                            MF_GRAYED | MF_DISABLED |
                            MF_BYCOMMAND ) ;

            switch (dwParam2) {
                case LINEADDRESSSTATE_OTHER:
                    break;
                case LINEADDRESSSTATE_DEVSPECIFIC:
                    break;
                case LINEADDRESSSTATE_INUSEZERO:
                    break;
                case LINEADDRESSSTATE_INUSEONE:
                    break;
                case LINEADDRESSSTATE_INUSEMANY:
                    break;
                case LINEADDRESSSTATE_NUMCALLS:
                    break;
                case LINEADDRESSSTATE_FORWARD:
                    break;
                case LINEADDRESSSTATE_TERMINALS:
                    break;
                default:
                    break;
```

```
        } //end switch
        break;
case LINE_CALLINFO:

        mylineGetCallInfo();
        switch (dwParam1) {
            case LINECALLINFOSTATE_OTHER:
                break;
            case LINECALLINFOSTATE_DEVSPECIFIC:
                break;
            case LINECALLINFOSTATE_BEARERMODE:
                break;
            case LINECALLINFOSTATE_RATE:
                break;
            case LINECALLINFOSTATE_MEDIAMODE:
                break;
            case LINECALLINFOSTATE_APPSPECIFIC:
                break;
            case LINECALLINFOSTATE_CALLID:
                break;
            case LINECALLINFOSTATE_RELATEDCALLID:
                break;
            case LINECALLINFOSTATE_ORIGIN:
                break;
            case LINECALLINFOSTATE_REASON:
                break;
            case LINECALLINFOSTATE_COMPLETIONID:
                break;
            case LINECALLINFOSTATE_NUMOWNERINCR:
                break;
            case LINECALLINFOSTATE_NUMOWNERDECR:
                break;
            case LINECALLINFOSTATE_NUMMONITORS:
                break;
            case LINECALLINFOSTATE_TRUNK:
                break;
            case LINECALLINFOSTATE_CALLERID:
                break;
            case LINECALLINFOSTATE_CALLEDID:
                break;
            case LINECALLINFOSTATE_CONNECTEDID:
                break;
            case LINECALLINFOSTATE_REDIRECTIONID:
                break;
            case LINECALLINFOSTATE_REDIRECTINGID:
                break;
```

(continued)

```
            case LINECALLINFOSTATE_DISPLAY:
                break;
            case LINECALLINFOSTATE_USERUSERINFO:
                break;
            case LINECALLINFOSTATE_HIGHLEVELCOMP:
                break;
            case LINECALLINFOSTATE_LOWLEVELCOMP:
                break;
            case LINECALLINFOSTATE_CHARGINGINFO:
                break;
            case LINECALLINFOSTATE_TERMINAL:
                break;
            case LINECALLINFOSTATE_DIALPARAMS:
                break;
            case LINECALLINFOSTATE_MONITORMODES:
                break;
            default:
                break;
        } //end switch
        break;
    case LINE_CALLSTATE:

        switch (dwParam3) {
            case LINECALLPRIVILEGE_MONITOR:

                break;
            case LINECALLPRIVILEGE_OWNER:

                // save call handle
                mytapi.hCall = (HCALL)dwDevice;

                // update local call information
                mylineGetCallStatus();
                mylineGetCallInfo();

                // update menus
                hMenu = GetMenu(hTTYWnd);
                // drop call
                if (mytapi.pLinecallstatus->dwCallFeatures &
                    LINECALLFEATURE_DROP)
                    EnableMenuItem( hMenu, IDM_DISCONNECT,
                                MF_ENABLED |MF_BYCOMMAND ) ;
```

```
        else
            EnableMenuItem(hMenu, IDM_DISCONNECT,
                            MF_GRAYED |
                            MF_DISABLED | MF_BYCOMMAND);
        // answer call
        if (mytapi.pLinecallstatus->dwCallFeatures &
            LINECALLFEATURE_ANSWER)
            EnableMenuItem(hMenu, IDM_ANSWER,
                            MF_ENABLED | MF_BYCOMMAND);
        else
            EnableMenuItem(hMenu, IDM_ANSWER, MF_GRAYED|
                            MF_DISABLED | MF_BYCOMMAND) ;


        break;
    default:
        break;
} //end switch
switch (dwParam1) {
    case LINECALLSTATE_IDLE:

        // deallocate call resources
        lineDeallocateCall (mytapi.hCall);

        // re-enable make call
        // update menus
        hMenu = GetMenu(hTTYWnd);
        if (mytapi.pLineaddressstatus->dwAddressFeatures &
            LINEADDRFEATURE_MAKECALL)
            EnableMenuItem(hMenu, IDM_MAKECALL,
                            MF_ENABLED | MF_BYCOMMAND);
        else
            EnableMenuItem(hMenu, IDM_MAKECALL,
                            MF_GRAYED | MF_DISABLED |
                            MF_BYCOMMAND ) ;

        break;
    case LINECALLSTATE_OFFERING:
```

(continued)

```
                        if (mytapi.bWaitForCall) {
                            // answer incoming calls
                            lrc =  lineAnswer(mytapi.hCall,NULL,0);
                            if (!(lrc >0 )) {
                                ProcessTAPIError(lrc);
                                myMessageBox("Error answering call");
                            }
                        }

                break;
            case LINECALLSTATE_ACCEPTED:


                break;
            case LINECALLSTATE_DIALTONE:


                switch (dwParam2) {
                    case LINEDIALTONEMODE_NORMAL:


                        break;
                    case LINEDIALTONEMODE_SPECIAL:


                        break;
                    case LINEDIALTONEMODE_INTERNAL:


                        break;
                    case LINEDIALTONEMODE_EXTERNAL:


                        break;
                    case LINEDIALTONEMODE_UNKNOWN:


                        break;
                    case LINEDIALTONEMODE_UNAVAIL:


                        break;
                    default:
                        break;
                } //end switch
                break;
```

```
        case LINECALLSTATE_DIALING:


    break;
case LINECALLSTATE_RINGBACK:


    break;
case LINECALLSTATE_BUSY:


    switch (dwParam2) {
        case LINEBUSYMODE_STATION:


            break;
        case LINEBUSYMODE_TRUNK:


            break;
        case LINEBUSYMODE_UNKNOWN:


            break;
        case LINEBUSYMODE_UNAVAIL:


            break;
        default:
            break;
    } //end switch
    break;
case LINECALLSTATE_SPECIALINFO:


    switch (dwParam2) {
        case LINESPECIALINFO_NOCIRCUIT:


            break;
        case LINESPECIALINFO_CUSTIRREG:


            break;
```

(continued)

```
            case LINESPECIALINFO_REORDER:


                break;
            case LINESPECIALINFO_UNKNOWN:


                break;
            case LINESPECIALINFO_UNAVAIL:


                break;
            default:
                break;
        } //end switch
        break;
    case LINECALLSTATE_CONNECTED:

        /* create the thread for reading bytes */
        mytapi.bReading = TRUE;
        if ((mytapi.hThread=CreateThread
                (NULL, /*def security */
                0, /* def stack size */
                (LPTHREAD_START_ROUTINE)ReadThread,
                NULL, /* param to pass to thread */
                0, &id)) ==
                INVALID_HANDLE_VALUE) {
            /* handle error */
            MessageBox
                (NULL, "Error creating READ thread",
                 "",MB_OK);
            break;
        } /* end if (error creating read thread) */

        break;
    case LINECALLSTATE_PROCEEDING:


        break;
    case LINECALLSTATE_ONHOLD:


        break;
    case LINECALLSTATE_CONFERENCED:


        break;
```

```
case LINECALLSTATE_ONHOLDPENDCONF:


    break;
case LINECALLSTATE_DISCONNECTED:


    /* kill the read thread */
    if (mytapi.bReading) {
        mytapi.bReading = FALSE;
        /* wait for thread to die... */
        while
            (GetExitCodeThread(mytapi.hThread, &id)) {
            if (id == STILL_ACTIVE)
                continue;
            else
                break;
        } /* end while
            (no error reading thread exit code) */
        CloseHandle (mytapi.hThread);
    }

    switch (dwParam2) {
        case LINEDISCONNECTMODE_NORMAL:


            break;
        case LINEDISCONNECTMODE_UNKNOWN:


            break;
        case LINEDISCONNECTMODE_REJECT:


            break;
        case LINEDISCONNECTMODE_PICKUP:


            break;
        case LINEDISCONNECTMODE_FORWARDED:


            break;
```

(continued)

```
                    case LINEDISCONNECTMODE_BUSY:


                        break;
                    case LINEDISCONNECTMODE_NOANSWER:


                        break;
                    case LINEDISCONNECTMODE_BADADDRESS:


                        break;
                    case LINEDISCONNECTMODE_UNREACHABLE:


                        break;
                    case LINEDISCONNECTMODE_CONGESTION:


                        break;
                    case LINEDISCONNECTMODE_INCOMPATIBLE:


                        break;
                    case LINEDISCONNECTMODE_UNAVAIL:


                        break;
                    default:
                        break;
                } //end switch
                break;
            case LINECALLSTATE_UNKNOWN:


                break;
            default:
                break;
        } //end switch
        break;
    case LINE_CLOSE:


        break;
```

```
case LINE_DEVSPECIFIC:


    break;
case LINE_DEVSPECIFICFEATURE:


    break;
case LINE_GATHERDIGITS:


    switch (dwParam1) {
        case LINEGATHERTERM_BUFFERFULL:


            break;
        case LINEGATHERTERM_TERMDIGIT:


            break;
        case LINEGATHERTERM_FIRSTTIMEOUT:


            break;
        case LINEGATHERTERM_INTERTIMEOUT:


            break;
        case LINEGATHERTERM_CANCEL:


            break;
        default:
            break;
    } //end switch
    break;
case LINE_GENERATE:


    switch (dwParam1) {
        case LINEGENERATETERM_DONE:


            break;
```

(continued)

```
                    case LINEGENERATETERM_CANCEL:


                        break;
                default:
                        break;
            } //end switch
        break;
case LINE_LINEDEVSTATE:

        mylineGetLineDevStatus();

        // update menus
        hMenu = GetMenu(hTTYWnd);
        if (mytapi.pLinedevstatus->dwLineFeatures &
            LINEFEATURE_MAKECALL)
            EnableMenuItem(hMenu, IDM_MAKECALL,
                            MF_ENABLED | MF_BYCOMMAND) ;
        else
            EnableMenuItem(hMenu, IDM_MAKECALL, MF_GRAYED |
                            MF_DISABLED | MF_BYCOMMAND) ;


        switch (dwParam1) {
            case LINEDEVSTATE_OTHER:


                break;
            case LINEDEVSTATE_RINGING:


                break;
            case LINEDEVSTATE_CONNECTED:

                break;
            case LINEDEVSTATE_DISCONNECTED:

                break;
            case LINEDEVSTATE_MSGWAITON:

                break;
            case LINEDEVSTATE_MSGWAITOFF:

                break;
            case LINEDEVSTATE_NUMCOMPLETIONS:

                break;
```

```
        case LINEDEVSTATE_INSERVICE:

            break;
        case LINEDEVSTATE_OUTOFSERVICE:

            break;
        case LINEDEVSTATE_MAINTENANCE:

            break;
        case LINEDEVSTATE_OPEN:

            break;
        case LINEDEVSTATE_CLOSE:

            break;
        case LINEDEVSTATE_NUMCALLS:

            break;
        case LINEDEVSTATE_TERMINALS:

            break;
        case LINEDEVSTATE_ROAMMODE:

            break;
        case LINEDEVSTATE_BATTERY:

            break;
        case LINEDEVSTATE_SIGNAL:

            break;
        case LINEDEVSTATE_DEVSPECIFIC:

            break;
        case LINEDEVSTATE_REINIT:

            break;
        case LINEDEVSTATE_LOCK:

            break;
        default:
            break;
    } //end switch
    break;
```

(continued)

```
            case LINE_MONITORDIGITS:

                switch (dwParam2) {
                    case LINEDIGITMODE_PULSE:

                        break;
                    case LINEDIGITMODE_DTMF:

                        break;
                    case LINEDIGITMODE_DTMFEND:

                        break;
                    default:
                        break;
                } //end switch
                break;
            case LINE_MONITORMEDIA:

                switch (dwParam1) {
                    case LINEMEDIAMODE_INTERACTIVEVOICE:

                        break;
                    case LINEMEDIAMODE_AUTOMATEDVOICE:

                        break;
                    case LINEMEDIAMODE_DATAMODEM:

                        break;
                    case LINEMEDIAMODE_G3FAX:

                        break;
                    case LINEMEDIAMODE_TDD:

                        break;
                    case LINEMEDIAMODE_G4FAX:

                        break;
                    case LINEMEDIAMODE_DIGITALDATA:

                        break;
                    case LINEMEDIAMODE_TELETEX:

                        break;
                    default:
                        break;
                } //end switch
                break;
            case LINE_MONITORTONE:
```

```
        break;
case LINE_REPLY:

        switch (dwParam2) {
            case LINEERR_ALLOCATED:

                myMessageBox(" LINEERR_ALLOCATED");
                break;
            case LINEERR_BADDEVICEID:

                myMessageBox(" LINEERR_BADDEVICEID");
                break;
            case LINEERR_BEARERMODEUNAVAIL:

                myMessageBox(" LINEERR_BEARERMODEUNAVAIL");
                break;
            case LINEERR_CALLUNAVAIL:

                myMessageBox(" LINEERR_CALLUNAVAIL");
                break;
            case LINEERR_COMPLETIONOVERRUN:

                myMessageBox(" LINEERR_COMPLETIONOVERRUN");
                break;
        case LINEERR_CONFERENCEFULL:

            myMessageBox(" LINEERR_CONFERENCEFULL");
                break;
            case LINEERR_DIALBILLING:

                myMessageBox(" LINEERR_DIALBILLING");
                break;
            case LINEERR_DIALDIALTONE:

                myMessageBox(" LINEERR_DIALDIALTONE");
                break;
            case LINEERR_DIALPROMPT:

                myMessageBox(" LINEERR_DIALPROMPT");
                break;
            case LINEERR_DIALQUIET:

                myMessageBox(" LINEERR_DIALQUIET");
                break;
```

(continued)

```
            case LINEERR_INCOMPATIBLEAPIVERSION:

                myMessageBox(" LINEERR_INCOMPATIBLEAPIVERSION");
                break;
            case LINEERR_INCOMPATIBLEEXTVERSION:

                myMessageBox(" LINEERR_INCOMPATIBLEEXTVERSION");
                break;
            case LINEERR_INIFILECORRUPT:

                myMessageBox(" LINEERR_INIFILECORRUPT");
                break;
            case LINEERR_INUSE:

                myMessageBox(" LINEERR_INUSE");
                break;
            case LINEERR_INVALADDRESS:

                myMessageBox(" LINEERR_INVALADDRESS");
                break;
            case LINEERR_INVALADDRESSID:

                myMessageBox(" LINEERR_INVALADDRESSID");
                break;
            case LINEERR_INVALADDRESSMODE:

                myMessageBox(" LINEERR_INVALADDRESSMODE");
                break;
            case LINEERR_INVALADDRESSSTATE:

                myMessageBox(" LINEERR_INVALADDRESSSTATE");
                break;
            case LINEERR_INVALAPPHANDLE:

                myMessageBox(" LINEERR_INVALAPPHANDLE");
                break;
            case LINEERR_INVALAPPNAME:

                myMessageBox(" LINEERR_INVALAPPNAME");
                break;
            case LINEERR_INVALBEARERMODE:

                myMessageBox(" LINEERR_INVALBEARERMODE");
                break;
            case LINEERR_INVALCALLCOMPLMODE:

                myMessageBox(" LINEERR_INVALCALLCOMPLMODE");
                break;
```

```
case LINEERR_INVALCALLHANDLE:

    myMessageBox(" LINEERR_INVALCALLHANDLE");
    break;
case LINEERR_INVALCALLPARAMS:

    myMessageBox(" LINEERR_INVALCALLPARAMS");
    break;
case LINEERR_INVALCALLPRIVILEGE:

    myMessageBox(" LINEERR_INVALCALLPRIVILEGE");
    break;
case LINEERR_INVALCALLSELECT:

    myMessageBox(" LINEERR_INVALCALLSELECT");
    break;
case LINEERR_INVALCALLSTATE:

    myMessageBox(" LINEERR_INVALCALLSTATE");
    break;
case LINEERR_INVALCALLSTATELIST:

    myMessageBox(" LINEERR_INVALCALLSTATELIST");
    break;
case LINEERR_INVALCARD:

    myMessageBox(" LINEERR_INVALCARD");
    break;
case LINEERR_INVALCOMPLETIONID:

    myMessageBox(" LINEERR_INVALCOMPLETIONID");
    break;
case LINEERR_INVALCONFCALLHANDLE:

    myMessageBox(" LINEERR_INVALCONFCALLHANDLE");
    break;
case LINEERR_INVALCONSULTCALLHANDLE:

    myMessageBox(" LINEERR_INVALCONSULTCALLHANDLE");
    break;
case LINEERR_INVALCOUNTRYCODE:

    myMessageBox(" LINEERR_INVALCOUNTRYCODE");
    break;
```

(continued)

```
        case LINEERR_INVALDEVICECLASS:

            myMessageBox(" LINEERR_INVALDEVICECLASS");
            break;
        case LINEERR_INVALDEVICEHANDLE:

            myMessageBox(" LINEERR_INVALDEVICEHANDLE");
            break;
        case LINEERR_INVALDIALPARAMS:

            myMessageBox(" LINEERR_INVALDIALPARAMS");
            break;
        case LINEERR_INVALDIGITLIST:

            myMessageBox(" LINEERR_INVALDIGITLIST");
            break;
        case LINEERR_INVALDIGITMODE:

            myMessageBox(" LINEERR_INVALDIGITMODE");
            break;
        case LINEERR_INVALDIGITS:

            myMessageBox(" LINEERR_INVALDIGITS");
            break;
        case LINEERR_INVALEXTVERSION:

            myMessageBox(" LINEERR_INVALEXTVERSION");
            break;
        case LINEERR_INVALGROUPID:

            myMessageBox(" LINEERR_INVALGROUPID");
            break;
        case LINEERR_INVALLINEHANDLE:

            myMessageBox(" LINEERR_INVALLINEHANDLE");
            break;
        case LINEERR_INVALLINESTATE:

            myMessageBox(" LINEERR_INVALLINESTATE");
            break;
        case LINEERR_INVALLOCATION:

            myMessageBox(" LINEERR_INVALLOCATION");
            break;
        case LINEERR_INVALMEDIALIST:

            myMessageBox(" LINEERR_INVALMEDIALIST");
            break;
```

```
case LINEERR_INVALMEDIAMODE:

    myMessageBox(" LINEERR_INVALMEDIAMODE");
    break;
case LINEERR_INVALMESSAGEID:

    myMessageBox(" LINEERR_INVALMESSAGEID");
    break;
case LINEERR_INVALPARAM:

    myMessageBox(" LINEERR_INVALPARAM");
    break;
case LINEERR_INVALPARKID:

    myMessageBox(" LINEERR_INVALPARKID");
    break;
case LINEERR_INVALPARKMODE:

    myMessageBox(" LINEERR_INVALPARKMODE");
    break;
case LINEERR_INVALPOINTER:

    myMessageBox(" LINEERR_INVALPOINTER");
    break;
case LINEERR_INVALPRIVSELECT:

    myMessageBox(" LINEERR_INVALPRIVSELECT");
    break;
case LINEERR_INVALRATE:

    myMessageBox(" LINEERR_INVALRATE");
    break;
case LINEERR_INVALREQUESTMODE:

    myMessageBox(" LINEERR_INVALREQUESTMODE");
    break;
case LINEERR_INVALTERMINALID:

    myMessageBox(" LINEERR_INVALTERMINALID");
    break;
case LINEERR_INVALTERMINALMODE:

    myMessageBox(" LINEERR_INVALTERMINALMODE");
    break;
```

(continued)

```
        case LINEERR_INVALTIMEOUT:

            myMessageBox(" LINEERR_INVALTIMEOUT");
            break;
        case LINEERR_INVALTONE:

            myMessageBox(" LINEERR_INVALTONE");
            break;
        case LINEERR_INVALTONELIST:

            myMessageBox(" LINEERR_INVALTONELIST");
            break;
        case LINEERR_INVALTONEMODE:

            myMessageBox(" LINEERR_INVALTONEMODE");
            break;
        case LINEERR_INVALTRANSFERMODE:

            myMessageBox(" LINEERR_INVALTRANSFERMODE");
            break;
        case LINEERR_LINEMAPPERFAILED:

            myMessageBox(" LINEERR_LINEMAPPERFAILED");
            break;
        case LINEERR_NOCONFERENCE:

            myMessageBox(" LINEERR_NOCONFERENCE");
            break;
        case LINEERR_NODEVICE:

            myMessageBox(" LINEERR_NODEVICE");
            break;
        case LINEERR_NODRIVER:

            myMessageBox(" LINEERR_NODRIVER");
            break;
        case LINEERR_NOMEM:

            myMessageBox(" LINEERR_NOMEM");
            break;
        case LINEERR_NOREQUEST:

            myMessageBox(" LINEERR_NOREQUEST");
            break;
        case LINEERR_NOTOWNER:

            myMessageBox(" LINEERR_NOTOWNER");
            break;
```

```
case LINEERR_NOTREGISTERED:

    myMessageBox(" LINEERR_NOTREGISTERED");
    break;
case LINEERR_OPERATIONFAILED:

    myMessageBox(" LINEERR_OPERATIONFAILED");
    break;
case LINEERR_OPERATIONUNAVAIL:

    myMessageBox(" LINEERR_OPERATIONUNAVAIL");
    break;
case LINEERR_RATEUNAVAIL:

    myMessageBox(" LINEERR_RATEUNAVAIL");
    break;
case LINEERR_RESOURCEUNAVAIL:

    myMessageBox(" LINEERR_RESOURCEUNAVAIL");
    break;
case LINEERR_REQUESTOVERRUN:

    myMessageBox(" LINEERR_REQUESTOVERRUN");
    break;
case LINEERR_STRUCTURETOOSMALL:

    myMessageBox(" LINEERR_STRUCTURETOOSMALL");
    break;
case LINEERR_TARGETNOTFOUND:

    myMessageBox(" LINEERR_TARGETNOTFOUND");
    break;
case LINEERR_TARGETSELF:

    myMessageBox(" LINEERR_TARGETSELF");
    break;
case LINEERR_UNINITIALIZED:

    myMessageBox(" LINEERR_UNINITIALIZED");
    break;
case LINEERR_USERUSERINFOTOOBIG:

    myMessageBox(" LINEERR_USERUSERINFOTOOBIG");
    break;
```

(continued)

```
                case LINEERR_REINIT:

                    myMessageBox(" LINEERR_REINIT");
                    break;
                case LINEERR_ADDRESSBLOCKED:

                    myMessageBox(" LINEERR_ADDRESSBLOCKED");
                    break;
                case LINEERR_BILLINGREJECTED:

                    myMessageBox(" LINEERR_BILLINGREJECTED");
                    break;
                case LINEERR_INVALFEATURE:

                    myMessageBox(" LINEERR_INVALFEATURE");
                    break;
                case LINEERR_NOMULTIPLEINSTANCE:

                    myMessageBox(" LINEERR_NOMULTIPLEINSTANCE");
                    break;
                default:
                    break;
            } //end switch
            break;
        case LINE_REQUEST:

            switch (dwParam1) {
                case LINEREQUESTMODE_MAKECALL:

                    break;
                case LINEREQUESTMODE_MEDIACALL:

                    break;
                case LINEREQUESTMODE_DROP:

                    break;
                default:
                    break;
            } //end switch
            break;
        default:
            break;
    } //end switch

    return;

} /* LineCallBackProc */
```

```
//////////////////////////////////////////////////////////////////
//      ProcessTAPIError - print TAPI error message
//////////////////////////////////////////////////////////////////
void ProcessTAPIError (LONG lrc)
{
          switch (lrc) {
              case LINEERR_ALLOCATED:

                  myMessageBox(" LINEERR_ALLOCATED");
                  break;
              case LINEERR_BADDEVICEID:

                  myMessageBox(" LINEERR_BADDEVICEID");
                  break;
              case LINEERR_BEARERMODEUNAVAIL:

                  myMessageBox(" LINEERR_BEARERMODEUNAVAIL");
                  break;
              case LINEERR_CALLUNAVAIL:

                  myMessageBox(" LINEERR_CALLUNAVAIL");
                  break;
              case LINEERR_COMPLETIONOVERRUN:

                  myMessageBox(" LINEERR_COMPLETIONOVERRUN");
                  break;
              case LINEERR_CONFERENCEFULL:

                  myMessageBox(" LINEERR_CONFERENCEFULL");
                  break;
              case LINEERR_DIALBILLING:

                  myMessageBox(" LINEERR_DIALBILLING");
                  break;
              case LINEERR_DIALDIALTONE:

                  myMessageBox(" LINEERR_DIALDIALTONE");
                  break;
              case LINEERR_DIALPROMPT:

                  myMessageBox(" LINEERR_DIALPROMPT");
                  break;
              case LINEERR_DIALQUIET:

                  myMessageBox(" LINEERR_DIALQUIET");
                  break;
```

(continued)

```
        case LINEERR_INCOMPATIBLEAPIVERSION:

            myMessageBox(" LINEERR_INCOMPATIBLEAPIVERSION");
            break;
        case LINEERR_INCOMPATIBLEEXTVERSION:

            myMessageBox(" LINEERR_INCOMPATIBLEEXTVERSION");
            break;
        case LINEERR_INIFILECORRUPT:

            myMessageBox(" LINEERR_INIFILECORRUPT");
            break;
        case LINEERR_INUSE:

            myMessageBox(" LINEERR_INUSE");
            break;
        case LINEERR_INVALADDRESS:

            myMessageBox(" LINEERR_INVALADDRESS");
            break;
        case LINEERR_INVALADDRESSID:

            myMessageBox(" LINEERR_INVALADDRESSID");
            break;
        case LINEERR_INVALADDRESSMODE:

            myMessageBox(" LINEERR_INVALADDRESSMODE");
            break;
        case LINEERR_INVALADDRESSSTATE:

            myMessageBox(" LINEERR_INVALADDRESSSTATE");
            break;
        case LINEERR_INVALAPPHANDLE:

            myMessageBox(" LINEERR_INVALAPPHANDLE");
            break;
        case LINEERR_INVALAPPNAME:

            myMessageBox(" LINEERR_INVALAPPNAME");
            break;
        case LINEERR_INVALBEARERMODE:

            myMessageBox(" LINEERR_INVALBEARERMODE");
            break;
        case LINEERR_INVALCALLCOMPLMODE:

            myMessageBox(" LINEERR_INVALCALLCOMPLMODE");
            break;
```

```
case LINEERR_INVALCALLHANDLE:

    myMessageBox(" LINEERR_INVALCALLHANDLE");
    break;
case LINEERR_INVALCALLPARAMS:

    myMessageBox(" LINEERR_INVALCALLPARAMS");
    break;
case LINEERR_INVALCALLPRIVILEGE:

    myMessageBox(" LINEERR_INVALCALLPRIVILEGE");
    break;
case LINEERR_INVALCALLSELECT:

    myMessageBox(" LINEERR_INVALCALLSELECT");
    break;
case LINEERR_INVALCALLSTATE:

    myMessageBox(" LINEERR_INVALCALLSTATE");
    break;
case LINEERR_INVALCALLSTATELIST:

    myMessageBox(" LINEERR_INVALCALLSTATELIST");
    break;
case LINEERR_INVALCARD:

    myMessageBox(" LINEERR_INVALCARD");
    break;
case LINEERR_INVALCOMPLETIONID:

    myMessageBox(" LINEERR_INVALCOMPLETIONID");
    break;
case LINEERR_INVALCONFCALLHANDLE:

    myMessageBox(" LINEERR_INVALCONFCALLHANDLE");
    break;
case LINEERR_INVALCONSULTCALLHANDLE:

    myMessageBox(" LINEERR_INVALCONSULTCALLHANDLE");
    break;
case LINEERR_INVALCOUNTRYCODE:

    myMessageBox(" LINEERR_INVALCOUNTRYCODE");
    break;
```

(continued)

```
        case LINEERR_INVALDEVICECLASS:

            myMessageBox(" LINEERR_INVALDEVICECLASS");
            break;
    case LINEERR_INVALDEVICEHANDLE:

            myMessageBox(" LINEERR_INVALDEVICEHANDLE");
            break;
    case LINEERR_INVALDIALPARAMS:

            myMessageBox(" LINEERR_INVALDIALPARAMS");
            break;
    case LINEERR_INVALDIGITLIST:

            myMessageBox(" LINEERR_INVALDIGITLIST");
            break;
    case LINEERR_INVALDIGITMODE:

            myMessageBox(" LINEERR_INVALDIGITMODE");
            break;
    case LINEERR_INVALDIGITS:

            myMessageBox(" LINEERR_INVALDIGITS");
            break;
    case LINEERR_INVALEXTVERSION:

            myMessageBox(" LINEERR_INVALEXTVERSION");
            break;
    case LINEERR_INVALGROUPID:

            myMessageBox(" LINEERR_INVALGROUPID");
            break;
    case LINEERR_INVALLINEHANDLE:

            myMessageBox(" LINEERR_INVALLINEHANDLE");
            break;
    case LINEERR_INVALLINESTATE:

            myMessageBox(" LINEERR_INVALLINESTATE");
            break;
    case LINEERR_INVALLOCATION:

            myMessageBox(" LINEERR_INVALLOCATION");
            break;
    case LINEERR_INVALMEDIALIST:

            myMessageBox(" LINEERR_INVALMEDIALIST");
            break;
```

```
case LINEERR_INVALMEDIAMODE:

    myMessageBox(" LINEERR_INVALMEDIAMODE");
    break;
case LINEERR_INVALMESSAGEID:

    myMessageBox(" LINEERR_INVALMESSAGEID");
    break;
case LINEERR_INVALPARAM:

    myMessageBox(" LINEERR_INVALPARAM");
    break;
case LINEERR_INVALPARKID:

    myMessageBox(" LINEERR_INVALPARKID");
    break;
case LINEERR_INVALPARKMODE:

    myMessageBox(" LINEERR_INVALPARKMODE");
    break;
case LINEERR_INVALPOINTER:

    myMessageBox(" LINEERR_INVALPOINTER");
    break;
case LINEERR_INVALPRIVSELECT:

    myMessageBox(" LINEERR_INVALPRIVSELECT");
    break;
case LINEERR_INVALRATE:

    myMessageBox(" LINEERR_INVALRATE");
    break;
case LINEERR_INVALREQUESTMODE:

    myMessageBox(" LINEERR_INVALREQUESTMODE");
    break;
case LINEERR_INVALTERMINALID:

    myMessageBox(" LINEERR_INVALTERMINALID");
    break;
case LINEERR_INVALTERMINALMODE:

    myMessageBox(" LINEERR_INVALTERMINALMODE");
    break;
```

(continued)

```
        case LINEERR_INVALTIMEOUT:

            myMessageBox(" LINEERR_INVALTIMEOUT");
            break;
        case LINEERR_INVALTONE:

            myMessageBox(" LINEERR_INVALTONE");
            break;
        case LINEERR_INVALTONELIST:

            myMessageBox(" LINEERR_INVALTONELIST");
            break;
        case LINEERR_INVALTONEMODE:

            myMessageBox(" LINEERR_INVALTONEMODE");
            break;
        case LINEERR_INVALTRANSFERMODE:

            myMessageBox(" LINEERR_INVALTRANSFERMODE");
            break;
        case LINEERR_LINEMAPPERFAILED:

            myMessageBox(" LINEERR_LINEMAPPERFAILED");
            break;
        case LINEERR_NOCONFERENCE:

            myMessageBox(" LINEERR_NOCONFERENCE");
            break;
        case LINEERR_NODEVICE:

            myMessageBox(" LINEERR_NODEVICE");
            break;
        case LINEERR_NODRIVER:

            myMessageBox(" LINEERR_NODRIVER");
            break;
        case LINEERR_NOMEM:

            myMessageBox(" LINEERR_NOMEM");
            break;
        case LINEERR_NOREQUEST:

            myMessageBox(" LINEERR_NOREQUEST");
            break;
        case LINEERR_NOTOWNER:

            myMessageBox(" LINEERR_NOTOWNER");
            break;
```

```
case LINEERR_NOTREGISTERED:

    myMessageBox(" LINEERR_NOTREGISTERED");
    break;
case LINEERR_OPERATIONFAILED:

    myMessageBox(" LINEERR_OPERATIONFAILED");
    break;
case LINEERR_OPERATIONUNAVAIL:

    myMessageBox(" LINEERR_OPERATIONUNAVAIL");
    break;
case LINEERR_RATEUNAVAIL:

    myMessageBox(" LINEERR_RATEUNAVAIL");
    break;
case LINEERR_RESOURCEUNAVAIL:

    myMessageBox(" LINEERR_RESOURCEUNAVAIL");
    break;
case LINEERR_REQUESTOVERRUN:

    myMessageBox(" LINEERR_REQUESTOVERRUN");
    break;
case LINEERR_STRUCTURETOOSMALL:

    myMessageBox(" LINEERR_STRUCTURETOOSMALL");
    break;
case LINEERR_TARGETNOTFOUND:

    myMessageBox(" LINEERR_TARGETNOTFOUND");
    break;
case LINEERR_TARGETSELF:

    myMessageBox(" LINEERR_TARGETSELF");
    break;
case LINEERR_UNINITIALIZED:

    myMessageBox(" LINEERR_UNINITIALIZED");
    break;
case LINEERR_USERUSERINFOTOOBIG:

    myMessageBox(" LINEERR_USERUSERINFOTOOBIG");
    break;
```

(continued)

```
                    case LINEERR_REINIT:

                        myMessageBox(" LINEERR_REINIT");
                        break;
                    case LINEERR_ADDRESSBLOCKED:

                        myMessageBox(" LINEERR_ADDRESSBLOCKED");
                        break;
                    case LINEERR_BILLINGREJECTED:

                        myMessageBox(" LINEERR_BILLINGREJECTED");
                        break;
                    case LINEERR_INVALFEATURE:

                        myMessageBox(" LINEERR_INVALFEATURE");
                        break;
                    case LINEERR_NOMULTIPLEINSTANCE:

                        myMessageBox(" LINEERR_NOMULTIPLEINSTANCE");
                        break;
                    default:
                        break;
                } //end switch

}

//////////////////////////////////////////////////////////////////
//      myMessageBox - easy message box function
//////////////////////////////////////////////////////////////////
void myMessageBox (LPSTR s)
{
    MessageBox (NULL, "Error", s, MB_OK);
}


//------------------------------------------------------------------
//
//   Module: comdial.c
//
//   Purpose:
//       This sample application demonstrates communications
//       in Windows 95.
//
//   Description of functions:
//       Descriptions are contained in the function headers.
//
//------------------------------------------------------------------
//
```

```
//   Written by Charles Mirho.
//   Copyright (c) 1996 Charles Mirho. All Rights Reserved.
//
//-------------------------------------------------------------------

#include "tty.h"
#include "resource.h"
#include "comdial.h"

HINSTANCE ghInst;             //global instance handle, for now.
HWND   hTTYWnd ;              //global window handle
PTTYINFO pTTYInfo;
extern MYTAPI mytapi;
#define MAXDSZ    30        //max size of dial string parts


LRESULT CALLBACK DialDialogProc(HWND hwnd, UINT message, WPARAM
                                wParam, LPARAM lParam);
void MakeLettersIntoDigits (LPSTR dialstring);


#if !defined(_WIN32)
#include <ver.h>
#endif

// Windows NT defines APIENTRY, but 3.x doesn't
#if !defined (APIENTRY)
#define APIENTRY far pascal
#endif

// Windows 3.x uses a FARPROC for dialogs
#if !defined(_WIN32)
#define DLGPROC FARPROC
#endif

//
//    FUNCTION: WinMain(HINSTANCE, HINSTANCE, LPSTR, int)
//
//    PURPOSE: calls initialization function, processes message loop
//
```

(continued)

```c
int APIENTRY WinMain(
            HINSTANCE hInstance,
            HINSTANCE hPrevInstance,
            LPSTR lpCmdLine,
            int nCmdShow
            )
{
    MSG msg;
    HMENU hMenu;
    BOOL bOldState = FALSE;


    // Other instances of app running?
    if (!hPrevInstance) {
        // Initialize shared things
        if (!InitApplication(hInstance)) {
            return (FALSE);              // Exits if unable to initialize
        }
    }

    if (NULL == (hTTYWnd = InitInstance( hInstance, nCmdShow )))
        return ( FALSE ) ;

    ghInst = hInstance;

    hMenu = GetMenu( hTTYWnd ) ;

    EnableMenuItem( hMenu, IDM_DISCONNECT,
                    MF_GRAYED | MF_DISABLED | MF_BYCOMMAND ) ;
    EnableMenuItem( hMenu, IDM_MAKECALL,
                    MF_GRAYED | MF_DISABLED | MF_BYCOMMAND ) ;
    EnableMenuItem( hMenu, IDM_ANSWER,
                    MF_GRAYED | MF_DISABLED | MF_BYCOMMAND ) ;
    EnableMenuItem( hMenu, IDM_CONFIGUREMODEM,
                    MF_ENABLED | MF_BYCOMMAND ) ;

    CreateTTYInfo( hTTYWnd );
    if (NULL == (pTTYInfo =
            (PTTYINFO) GetWindowLong( hTTYWnd,GWL_PTTYINFO )))
        return ( FALSE ) ;

    while (GetMessage(&msg, NULL, 0, 0)) {
            if (!TranslateAccelerator (msg.hwnd, ghAccel, &msg)) {
                TranslateMessage(&msg); // Translates virtual key codes
                DispatchMessage(&msg);  // Dispatches message to window
            }
    } /* end while (not a quit message) */
```

```
        DestroyTTYInfo( hTTYWnd ) ;

    // Returns the value from PostQuitMessage
    return (msg.wParam);

    // This will prevent 'unused formal parameter' warnings
    lpCmdLine;
}

//-------------------------------------------------------------------
// BOOL NEAR InitApplication( HANDLE hInstance )
//
// Description:
//     First time initialization stuff. This registers information
//     such as window classes.
//
// Parameters:
//     HANDLE hInstance
//         Handle to this instance of the application.
//
//-------------------------------------------------------------------

BOOL NEAR InitApplication( HANDLE hInstance )
{
    WNDCLASS  wndclass ;

    // register tty window class

    wndclass.style =         0 ;
    wndclass.lpfnWndProc =   TTYWndProc ;
    wndclass.cbClsExtra =    0 ;
    wndclass.cbWndExtra =    sizeof( DWORD ) ;
    wndclass.hInstance =     hInstance ;
    wndclass.hIcon =         NULL;
    wndclass.hCursor =       LoadCursor( NULL, IDC_ARROW ) ;
    wndclass.hbrBackground = (HBRUSH) (COLOR_WINDOW + 1) ;
    wndclass.lpszMenuName =  MAKEINTRESOURCE( IDR_MENU1) ;
    wndclass.lpszClassName = gszTTYClass ;

    return( RegisterClass( &wndclass ) ) ;

} // end of InitApplication()
```

```
//------------------------------------------------------------------
//   HWND NEAR InitInstance( HANDLE hInstance, int nCmdShow )
//
//   Description:
//       Initializes instance specific information.
//
//   Parameters:
//      HANDLE hInstance
//          Handle to instance
//
//       int nCmdShow
//          How do we show the window?
//
//------------------------------------------------------------------

HWND NEAR InitInstance( HANDLE hInstance, int nCmdShow )
{
   HWND   hTTYWnd ;

   // create the TTY window
   hTTYWnd = CreateWindow( gszTTYClass, gszAppName,
                           WS_OVERLAPPEDWINDOW,
                           CW_USEDEFAULT, CW_USEDEFAULT,
                           CW_USEDEFAULT, CW_USEDEFAULT,
                           NULL, NULL, hInstance, NULL ) ;

   if (NULL == hTTYWnd)
      return ( NULL ) ;

   ShowWindow( hTTYWnd, nCmdShow ) ;
   UpdateWindow( hTTYWnd ) ;

   return ( hTTYWnd ) ;

} // end of InitInstance()

//------------------------------------------------------------------
//   LRESULT FAR PASCAL  TTYWndProc( HWND hWnd, UINT uMsg,
//                                    WPARAM wParam, LPARAM lParam )
//
//   Description:
//       This is the TTY Window Proc. This handles ALL messages
//       to the tty window.
//
//   Parameters:
//       As documented for Window procedures.
//
//------------------------------------------------------------------
```

```
LRESULT FAR PASCAL  TTYWndProc( HWND hWnd, UINT uMsg,
                                WPARAM wParam, lPARAM lParam )
{
    LONG lrc;
    HMENU hMenu;
    LONG lResult;

    switch (uMsg)
    {
        case WM_CREATE:
          mytapi.bInitialized = FALSE;
          break;

        case WM_COMMAND:
        {
            switch ((DWORD) wParam)
            {

              case IDM_DISCONNECT:

                    // disconnect any connected calls
                    lResult =  lineDrop(mytapi.hCall,NULL,0);
                    if (!(lResult>0)) {
                        ProcessTAPIError(lResult);
                        MessageBox(hWnd, "ERROR", "Error dropping call",
                                   MB_OK);
                    }
                    // need to place a wait loop here until linedrop
                    // succeeds
                    // then close the line, but do not completely shut
                    // down

                    //telephonyShutdown();
                    hMenu = GetMenu(hWnd);
                    EnableMenuItem( hMenu, IDM_DISCONNECT, MF_GRAYED |
                                    MF_DISABLED | MF_BYCOMMAND ) ;
                    EnableMenuItem( hMenu, IDM_MAKECALL, MF_GRAYED |
                                    MF_DISABLED | MF_BYCOMMAND ) ;
                    EnableMenuItem( hMenu, IDM_ANSWER, MF_GRAYED |
                                    MF_DISABLED | MF_BYCOMMAND ) ;
                    break;
```

(continued)

```
        case IDM_ANSWER:

            if (!mytapi.bLineopen) {
                if (telephonyOpen(hWnd, ghInst)) {
                    MessageBox(hWnd, "Error",
                                "Error opening line", MB_OK);
                    break;
                }
            }

            mytapi.bWaitForCall = TRUE;

            break;

        case IDM_MAKECALL: {
            char szTemp[60];
            LPLINETRANSLATEOUTPUT lto;
            LINECALLPARAMS *pCallParams;

            if (!mytapi.bLineopen) {
                if (telephonyOpen(hWnd, ghInst)) {
                    MessageBox(hWnd, "Error",
                                "Error opening line", MB_OK);
                    break;
                }
            }

            if (!(mytapi.pLineaddressstatus->dwAddressFeatures &
                LINEADDRFEATURE_MAKECALL)) {
                MessageBox(hWnd, "Error",
                            "Line/address does not support \
                            lineMakeCall", MB_OK);
                break;
            }

            if (!DialogBox (GetModuleHandle(NULL),
                MAKEINTRESOURCE(IDD_DIAL),
                hWnd, (DLGPROC)DialDialogProc))
                break;

            if (mytapi.szDialNumber[0] != '+') {
                szTemp[0] = '+';
                lstrcpy(&szTemp[1], mytapi.szDialNumber);
                lstrcpy(mytapi.szDialNumber, szTemp);
            }
```

```
lResult = lineTranslateDialog(mytapi.hTAPI,
    mytapi.dwLine, mytapi.dwVersionToUse,
    hWnd, mytapi.szDialNumber);

if (!(lResult==0)) {
    /* Process error */
    ProcessTAPIError(lResult);
    MessageBox(hWnd, "ERROR",
                "Error translating address",
                MB_OK);
    break;
}

lto = (LINETRANSLATEOUTPUT *)
    calloc(sizeof(LINETRANSLATEOUTPUT)+5000,1);
lto->dwTotalSize = sizeof(LINETRANSLATEOUTPUT)+5000;
lResult = lineTranslateAddress(mytapi.hTAPI,
    mytapi.dwLine, mytapi.dwVersionToUse,
    mytapi.szDialNumber, 0,
    0,lto);
if (!(lResult==0)) {
    /* Process error */
    ProcessTAPIError(lResult);
    MessageBox(hWnd, "ERROR",
                "Error translating address",
                MB_OK);
    free (lto);
    break;
}
else {
    memcpy (mytapi.szDialNumber,
            (LPSTR)
            ((DWORD)lto+lto->dwDialableStringOffset),
            lto->dwDialableStringSize);
    mytapi.szDialNumber[lto->dwDialableStringSize]=0;
}
free (lto);
```

(continued)

```
pCallParams = (LINECALLPARAMS *)
            calloc(sizeof(LINECALLPARAMS),1);
pCallParams->dwTotalSize = sizeof(LINECALLPARAMS);
pCallParams->dwBearerMode = LINEBEARERMODE_VOICE;
pCallParams->dwMediaMode = LINEMEDIAMODE_DATAMODEM;
pCallParams->dwCallParamFlags =
    LINECALLPARAMFLAGS_IDLE;
pCallParams->dwAddressMode =
    LINEADDRESSMODE_ADDRESSID;

lResult =  lineMakeCall(mytapi.hLine, &mytapi.hCall,
    mytapi.szDialNumber, 0, pCallParams);
if (!(lResult>0)) {
    ProcessTAPIError(lResult);
    MessageBox(hWnd, "ERROR", "Error making call",
            MB_OK);
    free (pCallParams);
    break;
}
free (pCallParams);
hMenu = GetMenu(hWnd);
EnableMenuItem( hMenu, IDM_DISCONNECT,
            MF_ENABLED | MF_BYCOMMAND ) ;

break;

}
case IDM_CONFIGUREMODEM:

    hMenu = GetMenu(hWnd);

    // if not initialized, do it now

    if (!mytapi.bInitialized) {
        if (telephonyInitialize(hWnd, ghInst)) {
            MessageBox(hWnd, "Error",
                    "Error initializing", MB_OK);
            break;
        }

        EnableMenuItem( hMenu, IDM_DISCONNECT, MF_GRAYED |
                    MF_DISABLED | MF_BYCOMMAND ) ;
        EnableMenuItem( hMenu, IDM_MAKECALL, MF_ENABLED |
                    MF_BYCOMMAND ) ;
        EnableMenuItem( hMenu, IDM_ANSWER,
                    MF_ENABLED | MF_BYCOMMAND ) ;
    }
```

```
                    // get new settings
                    lResult = telephonySettings (hWnd);
                    if (!(lResult==0)) {
                        ProcessTAPIError(lResult);
                        MessageBox(hWnd, "ERROR",
                                    "Error configuring modem", MB_OK);
                    }

                    break;


            case IDM_EXIT:
                PostMessage( hWnd, WM_CLOSE, 0, 0L ) ;
                break ;
        }
    }
    break ;

    case WM_PAINT:  {
    PAINTSTRUCT ps;
        PaintTTY( hWnd ) ;
        break ;
    }
    case WM_SIZE:
        SizeTTY( hWnd, HIWORD( lParam ), LOWORD( lParam ) ) ;
        break ;

    case WM_HSCROLL:
        ScrollTTYHorz( hWnd, (WORD) wParam, LOWORD( lParam ) ) ;
        break ;

    case WM_VSCROLL:
        ScrollTTYVert( hWnd, (WORD) wParam, LOWORD( lParam ) ) ;
        break ;

    case WM_CHAR:

            /* echo to local window if echo turned on */
              if (LOCALECHO (pTTYInfo)) {
                    WriteTTYBlock(hWnd, (LPBYTE)&wParam, 1 );
              }
```

(continued)

```
                    if (!WriteFile(mytapi.hComm, (LPBYTE)&wParam, 1, &lrc,
                              NULL)) {
                        /* handle error */
                        locProcessCommError(GetLastError ());
                    } /* end if (error reading bytes) */

                break ;

        case WM_SETFOCUS:
            SetTTYFocus( hWnd ) ;
            break ;

        case WM_KILLFOCUS:
            KillTTYFocus( hWnd ) ;
            break ;

        case WM_DESTROY:
            PostQuitMessage( 0 ) ;
            break ;

        case WM_CLOSE:
            if (IDOK != MessageBox( hWnd, "OK to close window?",
                              "TTY Sample",
                              MB_ICONQUESTION | MB_OKCANCEL ))
                break ;

            // shutdown telephony

            if (mytapi.bInitialized)
                telephonyShutdown();

        default:
            return( DefWindowProc( hWnd, uMsg, wParam, lParam ) ) ;
    }
    return 0L ;

} // end of TTYWndProc()

/****************************************************************************
    FUNCTION: DialDialogProc
****************************************************************************/
LRESULT CALLBACK DialDialogProc(HWND hwnd, UINT message,
                                WPARAM wParam, LPARAM lParam)
{
  char szBuf[MAXDSZ];
  static char szCurArea[10], szCurCountry[10];
  BOOL bForeignCountry = FALSE;
```

```
if ((message == WM_COMMAND) && (LOWORD(wParam) == IDOK)) {
  mytapi.szDialNumber[0] = '+';
  mytapi.szDialNumber[1] = 0;

  //get country code
  GetDlgItemText(hwnd, IDC_COUNTRYCODE, szBuf, MAXDSZ-1);
  MakeLettersIntoDigits (szBuf);
  strcat(mytapi.szDialNumber, szBuf);

  //get area code
  GetDlgItemText(hwnd, IDC_AREACODE, szBuf, MAXDSZ-1);
  MakeLettersIntoDigits (szBuf);
  strcat(mytapi.szDialNumber, "(");
  strcat(mytapi.szDialNumber, szBuf);
  strcat(mytapi.szDialNumber, ")");

  //get phone number
  GetDlgItemText(hwnd, IDC_PHONENUMBER, szBuf, MAXDSZ-1);
  MakeLettersIntoDigits (szBuf);
  strcat(mytapi.szDialNumber, szBuf);

  EndDialog (hwnd, TRUE);
  return TRUE;
}
if ((message == WM_COMMAND) && (LOWORD(wParam) == IDCANCEL)) {
  EndDialog (hwnd, FALSE);
  return TRUE;
}
if (message == WM_INITDIALOG) {
  //get current country and area
  tapiGetLocationInfo (szCurCountry, szCurArea);
  // initialize dialog fields
  SetDlgItemText(hwnd, IDC_COUNTRYCODE, szCurCountry);
  SetDlgItemText(hwnd, IDC_AREACODE, szCurArea);
  return TRUE;
}
return FALSE;
}
```

(continued)

```c
/**********************************************************************
 * C function to convert letters into dialable digits
 **********************************************************************/
void MakeLettersIntoDigits (LPSTR dialstring)
{
    int sz = strlen(dialstring);
    char c;
    int i;

    for (i = 0;i<sz;i++) {
        c = dialstring[i];              //get next character
                                        //in dial string
        switch (c) {
            case 'A':
            case 'B':
            case 'C':
            case 'a':
            case 'b':
            case 'c':
                c = '2';
                break;
            case 'D':
            case 'E':
            case 'F':
            case 'd':
            case 'e':
            case 'f':
                c = '3';
                break;
            case 'G':
            case 'H':
            case 'I':
            case 'g':
            case 'h':
            case 'i':
                c = '4';
                break;
            case 'J':
            case 'K':
            case 'L':
            case 'j':
            case 'k':
            case 'l':
                c = '5';
                break;
            case 'M':
            case 'N':
            case 'O':
```

```
        case 'm':
        case 'n':
        case 'o':
            c = '6';
            break;
        case 'P':
        case 'R':
        case 'S':
        case 'p':
        case 'r':
        case 's':
            c = '7';
            break;
        case 'T':
        case 'U':
        case 'V':
        case 't':
        case 'u':
        case 'v':
            c = '8';
            break;
        case 'W':
        case 'X':
        case 'Y':
        case 'w':
        case 'x':
        case 'y':
            c = '9';
            break;
        case 'Z':
        case 'Q':
        case 'z':
        case 'q':
            c = '1';
            break;
        default:
            break;
        }

    dialstring[i] = c;
    }


} /* end function MakeLettersIntoDigits */
```

(continued)

```c
DWORD ReadThread (LPDWORD lpdwParam1)
{
    BYTE inbuff[100];
    DWORD nBytesRead;
    COMMTIMEOUTS to;
    LONG lrc;

    /* The next two lines check to make sure that interval
    timeouts are supported by the port */
    if (!(mytapi.pCommprop->dwProvCapabilities & PCF_INTTIMEOUTS)) {
        return 1L; /* error; can't set interval timeouts */
    }

    // get the modem handle for the call
    lrc = mylineGetCallID ();
    if (lrc) {
        MessageBox (NULL,
            "Error getting modem handle for data transfer", "", MB_OK);
        return 1L;
    }

    /* the next three lines tell the read function to return
    immediately even when there are no bytes waiting in the
    port's receive queue */
    memset (&to, 0, sizeof(to));
    to.ReadIntervalTimeout = MAXDWORD;
    SetCommTimeouts (mytapi.hComm, &to);

    /* this loop polls the port reading bytes until the control
    variable bReading is set to FALSE
    by the controlling process */
    while (mytapi.bReading) {
        /* poll the port and read bytes if available */
        if (!ReadFile(mytapi.hComm, inbuff, 100, &nBytesRead, NULL)) {
            /* handle error */
            locProcessCommError(GetLastError ());
        } /* end if (error reading bytes) */
        else {
            /* if there were bytes waiting, display them in TTY
            window */
            if (nBytesRead)
                locProcessBytes(inbuff, nBytesRead);
        }
    } /* end while (thread active) */

    /* clean out any pending bytes in the receive buffer */
    PurgeComm(mytapi.hComm, PURGE_RXCLEAR);
```

```
    // close the use of the modem for data transfer
    CloseHandle (mytapi.hComm);
    mytapi.bGotcommhandle = FALSE;

    return 0L;
} /* end function (ReadThread) */

// local function to process COM errors - fill in your own error
// handler
void locProcessCommError (DWORD dwError)
{
DWORD lrc;
COMSTAT cs;

    /* clear error */
    ClearCommError (mytapi.hComm, &lrc, &cs);
} /* end function (locProcessCommError) */

// local function to process bytes read from the COM port - just
// displays them in the terminal window;
// put your own handler code here
void locProcessBytes (LPBYTE buf, DWORD dwBytes)
{
    WriteTTYBlock(hTTYWnd, buf, dwBytes);
} /* end function (locProcessBytes) */
//-----------------------------------------------------------------
//  End of File: comdial.c
//-----------------------------------------------------------------
```

Making Phone Calls

What you've learned so far about Windows telephony is not much use without some way to make and answer phone calls. After all, getting connected is what telephony is all about. This section takes a look at what it takes to make a phone call in Windows.

When the Telephony API was first defined, it included a function for dialing data calls named *tapiRequestMediaCall*. It's still prototyped in the TAPI header file, TAPI.H, but it is not implemented in Windows 95, with good reason. The function was difficult to implement and even more difficult to use. It was supposed to save developers from confusion, but it only created more. The good news, then, is that a bad function has fallen by the wayside. The bad news is that now we need to find another way to dial.

In Chapter 2, we discussed the function *tapiRequestMakeCall,* which dials a phone number. But the function has a serious limitation: It doesn't tell an application when the call is connected. It puts the burden on the user to listen on the phone for a connection at the other end. This is fine for phone calls to humans, but for calls to other computers an application needs to know when the connection is made so that it can start sending data. We need another way to make phone calls.

Two TAPI functions are available for making calls, *lineMakeCall* and *lineDial*. The reason there are two functions instead of one is that sometimes a phone number is dialed in stages. *lineDial* is for dialing a phone number in stages. It can also be used in some environments to make what is known as a *consultation call,* a temporary call that is being conferenced or transferred. In general, *lineMakeCall* is called at least once when making a call, and *lineDial* might be called multiple times after *lineMakeCall* is called. The precise interaction of the two functions will become clear in the following sections. Both functions are *asynchronous,* which means that they return immediately but don't complete until a later time.

Asynchronous Functions

We first encountered asynchronous functions in Chapter 3, when we discussed the I/O functions *ReadFile* and *WriteFile*. These functions have dual modes of operation; they can be used synchronously or asynchronously. Early versions of TAPI had functions with this dual personality, but an application could not control whether they acted in a synchronous or asynchronous manner. A function would simply act the way that best suited it under the circumstances. This made coding applications difficult, to say the least. With Windows 95, all of the telephony functions that used to have a split personality are now either synchronous or asynchronous. All of the functions we have discussed so far are synchronous. In this section you'll learn about some of the asynchronous ones.

Asynchronous telephony functions use *request IDs*—small integers that identify the instance of an asynchronous function. Asynchronous functions return either a positive request ID or a negative error value. Just because an asynchronous function returns a request ID and not an error does not mean that the function succeeded. Its success or failure is determined later, when it completes asynchronously. And just because a function successfully completes asynchronously does not mean that it has succeeded in a literal sense. An asynchronous function usually returns an immediate error code only for immediately apparent errors, such as invalid parameters. Other errors are returned later, when the function completes asynchronously.

The following example shows how asynchronous TAPI functions work.

1. Call the function, as shown on the facing page, and check the return value. If the return value is positive, it is the request ID, which you should save. If the return value is negative, an error has occurred.

```
lResult = asyncTAPIFunction();
if (lResult > 0)
    lRequestID = lResult;
else
    /* handle error */
```

2. Check the asynchronous return code of the function. If it is 0, the function was successful. If the return code is negative, an error has occured. The asynchronous return code is passed to the application's line callback function (the one defined in the call to *lineInitialize*). The following code is an example of a line callback function.

```
/* callback function */
VOID FAR PASCAL LineCallbackFunc(DWORD dwDevice,
          DWORD dwMessage, DWORD dwInstance, DWORD dwParam1,
          DWORD dwParam2, DWORD dwParam3)
{

    switch (dwMessage) {

            case LINE_REPLY:
                /* the request ID returned by the function is
                    in dwParam1 */
                /* dwparam2 contains the return code, which is 0
                    if the function succeeds or a negative
                    error code
                    otherwise */
                switch (dwParam2) {
                        case LINEERR_ADDRESSBLOCKED:
                                break;
                        case LINEERR_ALLOCATED:
                                break;
                        case LINEERR_BADDEVICEID:
                                break;
                        case LINEERR_BEARERMODEUNAVAIL:
                                break;
                        case LINEERR_CALLUNAVAIL:
                                break;
                        case LINEERR_COMPLETIONOVERRUN:
                                break;
                        case LINEERR_CONFERENCEFULL:
                                break;
                        case LINEERR_DIALBILLING:
                                break;
                        case LINEERR_DIALDIALTONE:
                                break;
```

(continued)

```
                            case LINEERR_DIALPROMPT:
                                    break;
                            case LINEERR_DIALQUIET:
                                    break;
                            case LINEERR_INCOMPATIBLEAPIVERSION:
                                    break;
                            case LINEERR_INCOMPATIBLEEXTVERSION:
                                    break;
                            case LINEERR_INIFILECORRUPT:
                                    break;
                            case LINEERR_INUSE:
                                    break;
                            case LINEERR_INVALADDRESS:
                                    break;
                            case LINEERR_INVALADDRESSID:
                                    break;
                            case LINEERR_INVALADDRESSMODE:
                                    break;
                            case LINEERR_INVALADDRESSSTATE:
                                    break;
                            case LINEERR_INVALAPPHANDLE:
                                    break;
                            case LINEERR_INVALAPPNAME:
                                    break;
                            case LINEERR_INVALBEARERMODE:
                                    break;
                            case LINEERR_INVALCALLCOMPLMODE:
                                    break;
                            case LINEERR_INVALCALLHANDLE:
                                    break;
                            case LINEERR_INVALCALLPARAMS:
                                    break;
                            case LINEERR_INVALCALLPRIVILEGE:
                                    break;
                            case LINEERR_INVALCALLSELECT:
                                    break;
                            case LINEERR_INVALCALLSTATE:
                                    break;
                            case LINEERR_INVALCALLSTATELIST:
                                    break;
                            case LINEERR_INVALCARD:
                                    break;
                            case LINEERR_INVALCOMPLETIONID:
                                    break;
                            case LINEERR_INVALCONFCALLHANDLE:
                                    break;
                            case LINEERR_INVALCONSULTCALLHANDLE:
                                    break;
```

```
case LINEERR_INVALCOUNTRYCODE:
        break;
case LINEERR_INVALDEVICECLASS:
        break;
case LINEERR_INVALDIGITLIST:
        break;
case LINEERR_INVALDIGITMODE:
        break;
case LINEERR_INVALDIGITS:
        break;
case LINEERR_INVALEXTVERSION:
        break;
case LINEERR_INVALFEATURE:
        break;
case LINEERR_INVALGROUPID:
        break;
case LINEERR_INVALLINEHANDLE:
        break;
case LINEERR_INVALLINESTATE:
        break;
case LINEERR_INVALLOCATION:
        break;
case LINEERR_INVALMEDIALIST:
        break;
case LINEERR_INVALMEDIAMODE:
        break;
case LINEERR_INVALMESSAGEID:
        break;
case LINEERR_INVALPARAM:
        break;
case LINEERR_INVALPARKMODE:
        break;
case LINEERR_INVALPOINTER:
        break;
case LINEERR_INVALPRIVSELECT:
        break;
case LINEERR_INVALRATE:
        break;
case LINEERR_INVALREQUESTMODE:
        break;
case LINEERR_INVALTERMINALID:
        break;
case LINEERR_INVALTERMINALMODE:
        break;
case LINEERR_INVALTIMEOUT:
        break;
```

(continued)

```
                                case LINEERR_INVALTONE:
                                        break;
                                case LINEERR_INVALTONELIST:
                                        break;
                                case LINEERR_INVALTONEMODE:
                                        break;
                                case LINEERR_INVALTRANSFERMODE:
                                        break;
                                case LINEERR_LINEMAPPERFAILED:
                                        break;
                                case LINEERR_NOCONFERENCE:
                                        break;
                                case LINEERR_NODEVICE:
                                        break;
                                case LINEERR_NODRIVER:
                                        break;
                                case LINEERR_NOMEM:
                                        break;
                                case LINEERR_NOMULTIPLEINSTANCE:
                                        break;
                                case LINEERR_NOREQUEST:
                                        break;
                                case LINEERR_NOTOWNER:
                                        break;
                                case LINEERR_NOTREGISTERED:
                                        break;
                                case LINEERR_OPERATIONFAILED:
                                        break;
                                case LINEERR_OPERATIONUNAVAIL:
                                        break;
                                case LINEERR_RATEUNAVAIL:
                                        break;
                                case LINEERR_REINIT:
                                        break;
                                case LINEERR_RESOURCEUNAVAIL:
                                        break;
                                case LINEERR_STRUCTURETOOSMALL:
                                        break;
                                case LINEERR_TARGETNOTFOUND:
                                        break;
                                case LINEERR_TARGETSELF:
                                        break;
                                case LINEERR_UNINITIALIZED:
                                        break;
                                case LINEERR_USERUSERINFOTOOBIG:
                                        break;
```

```
                    case LINEERR_BILLINGREJECTED:
                            break;
                    default:
                            break;
            } //end switch
        break;

    }


}
```

Notice that for the asynchronous completion of a function, the *dwMessage* parameter to the callback function is set to the value LINE_REPLY. The *dwParam1* parameter is set to the request ID of the function. The *dwParam2* parameter is set to the return code, which, as we mentioned, is either 0 if the function succeeds or a negative error code otherwise. The code above lists all possible errors, so you can fill in your own error handling code where appropriate.

Creating a Call

You create a call using *lineMakeCall*. Like lines, calls are referenced by a handle, which is returned by *lineMakeCall*. The syntax for *lineMakeCall* is as follows:

```
LONG lineMakeCall   (HLINE hLine, LPHCALL lphCall,
                     LPCSTR lpszDestAddress, DWORD dwCountryCode,
                     LPLINECALLPARAMS const lpCallParams)
```

The first parameter, *hLine,* is a handle to the open line device. The second parameter, *lphCall,* is a pointer to a call handle. If *lineMakeCall* is successful, a new call is created and the handle is placed in *lphCall*. All TAPI functions that operate on calls use call handles. Call handles are similar to line handles in this regard. They differ from line handles in that they do not represent fixed, physical devices as line handles usually do. Calls come and go, but during the lifetime of a call, the call is always referenced by its handle.

The *lpszDestAddress* parameter is a pointer to the phone number to dial. The number must be in the dialable format, which means that canonical phone numbers must first be translated, either by the calling application directly or through a call to *lineTranslateAddress*. The *dwCountryCode* parameter tells the function which country the called party resides in. You might wonder why this parameter is included, since the dialable phone number often contains country information. The country code is included as a separate parameter because the country is not always ascertainable from the phone number, and some telephony drivers can dial more efficiently if they know the country the call is being placed to. The country code is not present in the dial string, for example, for calls made within a single country. If you go to France and make a local call using *lineMakeCall,* a smart telephony driver could use special dialing rules unique to France. Not many telephony drivers are this smart, but the country code parameter is included in *lineMakeCall* for the ones that are.

The last parameter, *lpCallParams,* points to a LINECALLPARAMS structure. We first encountered this structure when calling *lineOpen* to open the line and retrieve a line handle. In the call to *lineOpen,* the structure was used to specify parameters of the line to open. In *lineMakeCall,* the structure identifies characteristics of the call to make, such as the bearer mode and media mode of the call.

One of the most important things to know about *lineMakeCall* is that the returned call handle is not valid immediately upon return. An application must be very careful not to use the returned call handle until *lineMakeCall* completes asynchronously. Otherwise, any function that attempts to use the not-yet-valid call handle will return LINEERR_INVALCALLHANDLE. Also, the destination address can be NULL. When the destination address is NULL, *lineMakeCall* creates a new call but does not attempt to do any dialing (since no address is specified). In this case, *lineMakeCall* usually takes the phone off the hook and the new call enters the DIALTONE state. With Unimodem, the call enters the DIALING state and remains there until actual dialing is performed (using *lineDial,* as you'll see shortly). A common mistake is to attempt to call *lineDial* immediately after taking the phone off the hook by calling *lineMakeCall,* as in the following example:

```
lineMakeCall (hLine, &hCall, NULL, 0, NULL);
lineDial (hCall, "555 2345", 0);
```

This won't work because the call handle is not valid until the asynchronous completion of *lineMakeCall,* which occurs in the line callback function. Notice in the above example that the country code is set to 0. This tells Windows to assume either the country specified in the phone number, or the default country (the country configured on the Control Panel as the current country). Notice also that the pointer to the LINECALLPARAMS structure is NULL, indicating that it is not used. When LINECALLPARAMS is not used, *lineMakeCall* automatically places an interactive voice call (not a data modem call). It doesn't matter what media mode or privileges were specified when opening the line; an interactive voice call is still placed. If this occurs when Unimodem is installed, a dialog box like the one in Figure 4-12 appears.

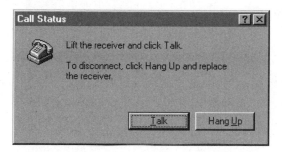

Figure 4-12. *The Call Status dialog box for interactive voice calls.*

The dialog box contains two buttons, Talk and Hang Up. The buttons do pretty much what you expect. Clicking Hang Up disconnects the call, and the call typically transitions to the IDLE state. You can click Hang Up while the call is in the DIALTONE state or is dialing, but once you click Talk the dialog box disappears. With Unimodem, you can also click Talk while the call is in the DIALTONE or DIALING state. Clicking Talk does not connect the call; that is up to the party at the other end. It simply tells the modem to connect the phone line with the handset (or headset) so that you can begin talking to the remote party. Clicking Talk also results in Unimodem sending a CONNECTED state indication to the application, no matter what state the call is actually in. The bottom line is that Unimodem cannot determine when an interactive voice call is actually connected, so it relies on the user to inform it by clicking Talk. If an impatient user clicks Talk while the call is still dialing, the calling application gets a CONNECTED indication from Windows and thinks the call is connected. The possible call states were described in the discussion of the LINEADDRESSCAPS structure earlier in this chapter, in the section titled "Exploring Addresses."

You must use the LINECALLPARAMS structure to place a modem call. Only the *dwBearerMode* and *dwMediaMode* members of LINECALLPARAMS need to be set, as shown below; you can safely ignore the other members.

```
LINECALLPARAMS lcp;
lcp.dwBearerMode = LINEBEARERMODE_VOICE;
lcp.dwMediaMode = LINEMEDIAMODE_DATAMODEM;
lcp.dwTotalSize = sizeof(LINECALLPARAMS);
lineMakeCall (hLine, &hCall, "555 2222", 0, &lcp);
```

A modem call is connected differently from an interactive voice call. The Call Status dialog box is not displayed because the connection is established through the negotiation of the two modems. However, the CONNECTED state is not sent by Windows when the other modem picks up the phone. Rather, it is sent after the two modems complete negotiation, which can take several seconds. This delay has some rather important repercussions for applications that perform call logging and billing. Applications that log the duration of a call for billing purposes use the time period between the CONNECTED and IDLE states to determine the length of the call. Since there is a delay between the time the phone is answered and the time the CONNECTED state is received, the log will always be short several seconds for modem calls. This is because billing (from the phone company) begins immediately when the other modem picks up the phone, not after negotiation. There is probably no good way around this problem.

Once a modem call is complete, a modem icon appears next to the clock on the taskbar (the tray area). With Unimodem, the modem icon appears only if the LAUNCH_LIGHTS flag is set in the *fwOptions* member of the DEVCFG structure. Otherwise, the modem icon is not displayed.

The LINECALLPARAMS structure contains a member called *DialParams* that is typed as a LINEDIALPARAMS structure. *DialParams* can be used to specify timing characteristics of the call to make, such as the time between successive digits of the phone number, the duration of a digit, and the amount of delay that the comma (,) and wait-for-dial-tone *(W)* characters will cause when placed in a phone number.

```
typedef struct linedialparams_tag {
    DWORD dwDialPause;        // delay in milliseconds of a comma
    DWORD dwDialSpeed;        // interdigit time period, milliseconds
    DWORD dwDigitDuration;    // digit duration, milliseconds
    DWORD dwWaitForDialtone;  // time to wait for dialtone, millisec-
                              // onds
} LINEDIALPARAMS;
```

You might want to set these parameters to default values before calling *lineMakeCall*. (Especially useful is setting the delay of a comma, since users love to use the comma). At worst, the telephony driver will simply ignore the LINEDIALPARAM settings and use its own defaults.

lineMakeCall can fail for many reasons. With Unimodem, when the phone line is disconnected from the modem, *lineMakeCall* might fail asynchronously, with the error message LINEERR_CALLUNAVAIL. Also, Unimodem lets you make only one call at a time. If you try to make a second call while another call is in progress (for example, while the first call is in the DIALTONE or PROCEEDING state), *lineMakeCall* fails asynchronously with the error LINEERR_CALLUNAVAIL. Obviously, an application should check both the return code of *lineMakeCall* and the results of the asynchronous completion of the function.

Dropping a Call

All good things must end, including phone calls. A call ends when it is dropped. A call does not have to be connected in order to be dropped. Calls in the DIALTONE, DIALING, and other states can all be dropped. The most straightforward way to drop a call is to call *lineDrop,* which has the following syntax:

```
LONG lineDrop (HCALL hCall, LPCSTR lpsDropInfo, DWORD dwSize)
```

The first parameter is the call handle from *lineMakeCall.* The second and third parameters specify a text message that can be sent to the remote party as the call is dropped. Unimodem does not support the sending of messages on call drop, and nondigital phone systems generally do not support this feature either. A typical call to *lineDrop,* on an analog phone system with Unimodem installed, is as follows:

```
lineDrop(hCall, NULL, 0);
```

Of course, calling *lineDrop* changes the state of the call. Typically, an interactive voice call transitions from connected (LINECALLSTATE_CONNECTED) to disconnected (LINECALLSTATE_DISCONNECTED) and then to idle (LINECALLSTATE_IDLE). *lineDrop* is an asynchronous function, and the DISCONNECT and IDLE states are reported to the application callback function before *lineDrop* completes. The call handle is still valid after *lineDrop* completes. The application can still pass the call handle to other TAPI functions to retrieve information about the call, even after the call becomes idle. TAPI does not deallocate the resources associated with the call merely because the call becomes idle. To clean up after a call that has become idle, an application should call *lineDeallocateCall,* as shown below. An application should not attempt to deallocate the call unless the call is idle.

```
lineDeallocateCall(hCall);
```

With Unimodem, when *lineDrop* is called on a data modem call, the call transitions directly to the IDLE state. No LINECALLSTATE_DISCONNECTED state is sent to the calling application. Unimodem associates the DISCONNECT state with interactive voice calls only. An application should always look for the IDLE state, not the DISCONNECT state, to determine when a call is no longer connected. Also, if the phone is still off the hook, dropping the call using TAPI might not actually disconnect the phone from the remote party. Dropping the call might cause the modem to connect the line directly to the phone, and if the phone is off the hook, the call remains connected.

If you drop a call while the Call Status dialog box is displayed, the dialog box disappears and the call becomes idle. An application can drop a call in the middle of the negotiation phase between two modems. Dropping a connected modem call causes the modem icon to disappear from the desktop.

Another way to drop a call, besides calling *lineDrop,* is to close the line on which the call is made using *lineClose* or shut down TAPI altogether using *lineShutdown.* Calling either of these functions to drop a call has some disadvantages. First, the call will not be dropped unless the LINEDEVCAPFLAGS-_CLOSEDROP flag is set in the *dwDevCapFlags* member of LINEDEVCAPS. Second, TAPI might not send an IDLE state indication to the line callback function when *lineClose* is used to drop a call. This is the case when Unimodem is installed. The application might therefore receive no indication that the call is no longer connected. An advantage to using *lineClose* or *lineShutdown* instead of *lineDrop* is that TAPI automatically frees the resources associated with any calls on the line when *lineClose* or *lineShutdown* is called, so it is not necessary to call *lineDeallocateCall* as it is with *lineDrop.*

A word about busy signals. A telephony driver that can detect a busy signal will send a LINE_LINECALLSTATE/LINECALLSTATE_BUSY message to the calling application. However, many analog modems automatically disconnect upon detecting a busy tone. In this case, the telephony driver will send the application a LINE_LINECALLSTATE/LINECALLSTATE_DISCONNECTED message with the disconnect mode (*dwParam2*) set to LINEDISCONNECTMODE_BUSY. Unimodem exhibits this behavior.

Dialing on an Existing Call

An application might not want to do all of its dialing with a single function call. For example, to navigate a voicemail system, it might need to dial several series of digits at different times, as in the following example:

1. Dial phone number of voicemail system: 555 2345

2. Enter mailbox number: 123

3. Enter password: 44551

There are a couple of ways to do this in Windows, as shown on the facing page. In both cases, *lineMakeCall* is first called to get a call handle. In the first case, *lineMakeCall* is called with a NULL phone number, just to place the call in the DIALTONE state but not to do any actual dialing. In the second case, *lineMakeCall* actually dials the phone number. Keep in mind that this is just an example of filling in the parameters required for these actions to take place. As we discussed earlier in this chapter, attempting to call *lineDial* immediately after *lineMakeCall* will fail because the asynchronous processing of *lineMakeCall* will not be completed yet.

Case 1

```
// place an interactive voice call in the DIALTONE state
lineMakeCall (hLine, &hCall, NULL, 0, NULL);
// wait for asynchronous completion of prior function, then
// dial the voicemail system
lineDial (hCall, "555 2345;", 0);
// wait for asynchronous completion of prior function, then
// dial the mail box number
lineDial (hCall, "123;", 0);
// wait for asynchronous completion of prior function, then
// dial the password
lineDial (hCall, "44551", 0);
```

Case 2

```
// place an interactive voice call to the voicemail system
lineMakeCall (hLine, &hCall, "555 2345;", 0, NULL);
// dial the mailbox number
lineDial (hCall, "123;", 0);
// dial the password
lineDial (hCall, "44551", 0);
```

In the first case, Windows takes the phone off the hook. A new call object is allocated and returned to the calling application. The call is typically in the DIALTONE or DIALING state. With Unimodem, the application typically receives a DIALTONE state followed by one or two DIALING states, even though no actual dialing occurs as a result of the call to *lineMakeCall*. After *lineMakeCall* completes asynchronously, *lineDial* is called to actually place the call to the voicemail system. A call to *lineDial* is as follows:

```
lineDial (hCall, lpszDestAddress, dwCountryCode);
```

The first parameter is the call handle returned by *lineMakeCall*. The second parameter is the number to dial, and the third parameter is the country code. The country code can be set to 0 in the same situations as for *lineMakeCall*. Notice that in Case 1 above the phone number in the first call to *lineDial* is terminated by a semicolon. This is very important; it tells *lineDial* that there is more dialing to be done before the call can be connected. For interactive voice calls, such as the call to the voicemail system, the result is that the Call Status dialog box is not displayed. This first call to *lineDial* dials the voicemail system; the second call dials the mailbox number; the third and final call enters the password. Notice that the number in the last call to *lineDial* is not terminated by a semicolon. Windows displays the Call Status dialog box after this last call to *lineDial*.

Case 2 is similar to Case 1, except that *lineMakeCall* dials the number of the voicemail system. A semicolon terminates the number in *lineMakeCall*, indicating that more dialing will be done on the call using *lineDial*. In both cases, the voicemail system can also be navigated using *lineGenerateDigits,* a function not implemented in the initial version of Unimodem.

When a NULL address is used with *lineMakeCall,* or when a semicolon is used to terminate the dial string in *lineMakeCall* or *lineDial,* the modem might not make dialing audible on the phone's handset or headset; it depends on the model of the modem. Also, some modems require that there be a dial tone on the line before they will dial any digits. You can forget about trying to navigate voicemail systems with these modems, because obviously there won't be any dial tone on the line when the application tries to dial the mailbox number and password. When calling *lineMakeCall,* you can try setting the LINECALLPARAM-FLAGS_IDLE flag in the *dwCallParamFlags* member of LINECALLPARAMS to suppress dial-tone detection. However, even this will not make partial dialing work on all modems. Depending on who you ask, this is either a bug in the modems or a bug in Unimodem.

The following are examples of different ways to place calls using *lineMakeCall.*

```
// create a new call object but don't actually dial any digits. the
// new call will be in either the DIALTONE or the DIALING state.
// the actual phone number must be dialed with a subsequent call to
// lineDial.
LPCSTR lpszDestAddress=NULL;
DWORD dwCountryCode=0;
LPLINECALLPARAMS const lpCallParams=NULL;
lResult =  lineMakeCall(hLine, &hCall, lpszDestAddress,
                        dwCountryCode, lpCallParams);


// place an interactive voice call
LPCSTR lpszDestAddress="555 2345";
DWORD dwCountryCode=0;
LPLINECALLPARAMS const lpCallParams=NULL;
lResult =  lineMakeCall(hLine, &hCall, lpszDestAddress,
                        dwCountryCode,lpCallParams);


// another way to dial an interactive voice call
LPCSTR lpszDestAddress="555 2345";
DWORD dwCountryCode=0;
LINECALLPARAMS callparams;
LPLINECALLPARAMS const lpCallParams=&callparams;
memset (&callparams, 0, sizeof(LINECALLPARAMS));
callparams.dwTotalSize = sizeof(LINECALLPARAMS);
callparams.dwBearerMode=LINEBEARERMODE_VOICE;
callparams.dwMediaMode=LINEMEDIAMODE_INTERACTIVEVOICE;
lResult =  lineMakeCall(hLine, &hCall, lpszDestAddress,
                        dwCountryCode, lpCallParams);
```

```
// dial a data modem call
LPCSTR lpszDestAddress="555 2345";
DWORD dwCountryCode=0;
LINECALLPARAMS callparams;
LPLINECALLPARAMS const lpCallParams=&callparams;
memset (&callparams, 0, sizeof(LINECALLPARAMS));
callparams.dwTotalSize = sizeof(LINECALLPARAMS);
callparams.dwBearerMode=LINEBEARERMODE_VOICE;
callparams.dwMediaMode=LINEMEDIAMODE_DATAMODEM;
lResult =  lineMakeCall(hLine, &hCall, lpszDestAddress,
                        dwCountryCode, lpCallParams);
```

Answering a Call

To answer incoming calls of any type, you call *lineAnswer,* as shown here.

```
lineAnswer(hCall, lpsUserUserInfo, dwSize)
```

The first parameter, *hCall,* is a handle to the call to answer. How, you might ask, can the application have a handle to a call it has not yet answered? When an incoming call arrives, Windows sends a LINE_CALLSTATE message to the line callback function, with *dwParam1* set to LINECALLSTATE_OFFERING. The first parameter to the callback function, *dwDevice,* is set to the call handle that Windows has assigned to the incoming call. The application should check *dwParam3* of the callback function to ensure that it has owner privileges for the call. The value of *dwParam3* is LINECALLPRIVILEGE_OWNER if the application has owner privileges. Windows will not present offering calls to an application that does not open the line with owner privileges, but it is good practice to check for owner privileges before attempting to answer a call. If the application is an owner of the call, Windows will let the application answer the call. The application can then save the call handle and call *lineAnswer.* If an application tries to answer a call it does not own (for example, if it opens the line with monitor privileges only), *lineAnswer* returns LINEERR_NOTOWNER.

The second and third parameters to *lineAnswer* are useful only in digital telephony environments. They should be set to NULL and 0, respectively, when using Unimodem.

lineAnswer is an asynchronous function, which means that the return value is a small positive number (the request ID) if there is no immediate error, or a negative error code otherwise. As you know, just because *lineAnswer* does not return an immediate error does not mean that the call has been successfully answered. The application must wait for the asynchronous completion (as it did for *lineMakeCall* and *lineDrop*) and check the return code at that time to be sure the call was successfully answered. An example of an error is that an incoming call might arrive on a line on which another call is already connected.

This can happen when the line has call waiting or in a digital office environment in which a single line has multiple extensions. Answering the new call will affect the existing call in different ways depending on the particular telephony hardware and drivers installed. Typically, the act of answering the new call will either place the existing call on hold or drop the existing call. After all, you can't talk to two people at once (unless you make a conference call, which is beyond the scope of this chapter).

With Unimodem, calling *lineAnswer* causes the call to transition to the ACCEPTED state after *lineAnswer* returns asynchronously. (We'll discuss the ACCEPTED state in greater detail shortly). *lineAnswer* can be called when a call is either in the OFFERING state or in the ACCEPTED state.

Instead of calling *lineAnswer,* the application can call *lineAccept* to tell Windows (and other applications that might want to answer the call) that the application has accepted responsibility for answering the call. The main difference between answering a call and accepting a call is this: Answering a call typically causes the modem to take the phone off the hook and begin negotiating with tones for a data connection. Accepting a call merely tells other applications that you are taking ownership of the call, and that they therefore should not call *lineAnswer.* (The accepting application should call *lineAnswer* soon after *lineAccept* completes asynchronously.) In digital environments, accepting a call has other implications that are beyond the scope of this chapter. Actually, an application does not have to answer a call merely because it has accepted the call. But at the very least, the application should indicate that an incoming call has arrived, so that the person using the application can decide whether to answer the call. (This is known as call screening.)

The call to *lineAccept* is as follows:

```
lineAccept(hCall, lpsUserUserInfo, dwSize)
```

The parameters to *lineAccept* are the same as the parameters to *lineAnswer.* Only the call handle is used by Unimodem; the other two parameters should be set to NULL and 0, respectively. *lineAccept,* like *lineAnswer,* is asynchronous. With Unimodem, the call transitions to the ACCEPTED state before *lineAccept* completes. *lineAccept* can be called when the call is in the OFFERING state, and the application must have owner privileges to accept the call. If an application does not want to accept the call, it can either do a handoff (as we shall see in a moment), or it can drop the call. Dropping the call without first attempting to do a handoff is considered rude, and there is really no good reason for it (except perhaps if you have caller ID and the caller is someone you don't want to talk to). Unimodem does not allow an application to call *lineAccept* more than once on the same call.

A call in both the OFFERING and ACCEPTED states can be dropped using *lineDrop*. Calling *lineClose* or *lineShutdown* also drops the call, but the application does not receive the IDLE state or any other message indicating that the call was dropped. What happens when a human caller dials into a computer that has the line open to answer modem calls? The caller usually hangs up right away when the modem begins sending tones. With Unimodem, when the caller hangs up the modem keeps trying to negotiate a connection for a short period of time, and then gives up. Windows sends the application a LINECALLSTATE-_DISCONNECTED message, with *dwParam2* set to LINEDISCONNECTMODE-_NOANSWER. The call then transitions to the IDLE state.

When an application with owner privileges to a call decides, for whatever reason, that it does not want to answer the call, it can hand off the call instead. This is done by passing the call handle to *lineHandoff,* as shown below.

```
lineHandoff(hCall, lpszFileName, dwMediaMode)
```

The first parameter is the call handle. An application can hand off a call at any time, not just when the call is in the OFFERING state, but it must have owner privileges for the call. The second parameter, *lpszFileName,* specifies the name of the application that should receive the call. This is either the executable filename of the target process (the filename only, not the full path of the executable) or the "friendly" name of the application used in the call to *lineInitialize*. If the filename is NULL, Windows selects the application with the next-highest priority to receive the call. The last parameter, *dwMediaMode,* specifies the media mode of the call. Remember, when an application opens the line to answer calls (opens the line with owner privileges), it must specify the type of calls it wants to answer. With Unimodem installed, the only type of calls that an application can request to answer are data modem calls—that is, calls with the LINEMEDIAMODE_DATAMODEM type. The *dwMediaMode* parameter of *lineHandoff* tells Windows to pass the call handle to the next-highest privileged application that has owner privileges for calls with that media mode. This parameter is valid only when the calling application does not specify a target application by name in the *lpszFileName* parameter.

It is possible for an application to do its own media mode determination when the telephony driver won't or can't do it, and then to change the media mode of the call with a call to *lineSetMediaMode,* as shown below.

```
lineSetMediaMode (hCall, dwMediaMode)
```

This function tells Windows to change the media mode of the call to the media mode specified in the second parameter. Determining the media mode of a call is not a trivial task; it usually involves tone detection and other digital signal processing techniques. Media modes can also be detected by distinctive ringing patterns if the telephone service and drivers support it. (Unimodem for voice modems has this capability.) If an application isn't ready to do all the work, it has no business telling Windows to change the call's media mode. Most telephony applications will never call this function.

Unlike *lineAnswer* and *lineAccept, lineHandoff* is synchronous. The function either succeeds (returns 0) immediately or returns a negative error code. When you call *lineHandoff* from your application, you should be especially careful to check for the LINEERR_TARGETNOTFOUND error code. If this error is returned, it means that a target application with the specified name, or with the specified media mode, was not found. If this error is returned, your application is still the owner of the call and can do several things. If the call is in the OFFERING state, your application can answer the call. Or in any state your application can call *lineDrop* to hang up the call, since presumably you don't want the call and no other application does either. Or your application can simply let the call continue in the state that it is in without doing anything. Usually, an application will call *lineDrop* to hang up the call. If your application has borrowed a modem handle from Windows (using *lineGetID*), after successfully handing off the call it should remember to call *CloseHandle* on the modem handle. This way, other applications that receive the call handle from the handoff will be able to transfer data over the phone line.

The application that receives the call receives the call handle as part of a LINE_CALLSTATE message. The call state is whatever state the call was in when it was handed off. This presents a sticky problem for applications that answer calls. Because of *lineHandoff,* a new call handle can appear at any time, not just with the LINE_CALLSTATE/LINECALLSTATE_OFFERING message. Every time a call state message is received, an application should check the call handle in the *dwDevice* parameter that was passed with the message. If the call handle is not familiar to the application, the application should treat it like a new call.

Almost everything an application could want to know about a call is stored in a structure called LINECALLINFO. An application can retrieve this structure from Windows using a call to *lineGetCallInfo,* as shown below.

```
lineGetCallInfo(hCall, lpCallInfo)
```

Like all TAPI informational functions, *lineGetCallInfo* is synchronous. The first parameter is the handle of the call to retrieve information for. The second parameter points to a LINECALLINFO structure. The information in LINECALLINFO is read-only; there is no corresponding *lineSetCallInfo* function to change the member values of LINECALLINFO. To change the member values, an application must use more indirect means, such as calling *lineSetMediaMode* to change the *dwMediaMode* member of LINECALLINFO. LINECALLINFO has the following format:

```
typedef struct linecallinfo_tag {
DWORD      dwTotalSize;
DWORD      dwNeededSize;
DWORD      dwUsedSize;

HLINE      hLine;
DWORD      dwLineDeviceID;
DWORD      dwAddressID;

DWORD      dwBearerMode;
DWORD      dwRate;
DWORD      dwMediaMode;

DWORD      dwAppSpecific;
DWORD      dwCallID;
DWORD      dwRelatedCallID;
DWORD      dwCallParamFlags;
DWORD      dwCallStates;

DWORD      dwMonitorDigitModes;
DWORD      dwMonitorMediaModes;
LINEDIALPARAMS    DialParams;
DWORD      dwOrigin;
DWORD      dwReason;
DWORD      dwCompletionID;
DWORD      dwNumOwners;
DWORD      dwNumMonitors;

DWORD      dwCountryCode;
DWORD      dwTrunk;

DWORD      dwCallerIDFlags;
DWORD      dwCallerIDSize;
DWORD      dwCallerIDOffset;
DWORD      dwCallerIDNameSize;
DWORD      dwCallerIDNameOffset;

DWORD      dwCalledIDFlags;
DWORD      dwCalledIDSize;
DWORD      dwCalledIDOffset;
DWORD      dwCalledIDNameSize;
DWORD      dwCalledIDNameOffset;
```

(continued)

```
DWORD       dwConnectedIDFlags;
DWORD       dwConnectedIDSize;
DWORD       dwConnectedIDOffset;
DWORD       dwConnectedIDNameSize;
DWORD       dwConnectedIDNameOffset;

DWORD       dwRedirectionIDFlags;
DWORD       dwRedirectionIDSize;
DWORD       dwRedirectionIDOffset;
DWORD       dwRedirectionIDNameSize;
DWORD       dwRedirectionIDNameOffset;

DWORD       dwRedirectingIDFlags;
DWORD       dwRedirectingIDSize;
DWORD       dwRedirectingIDOffset;
DWORD       dwRedirectingIDNameSize;
DWORD       dwRedirectingIDNameOffset;

DWORD       dwAppNameSize;
DWORD       dwAppNameOffset;
DWORD       dwDisplayableAddressSize;

DWORD       dwDisplayableAddressOffset;

DWORD       dwCalledPartySize;
DWORD       dwCalledPartyOffset;

DWORD       dwCommentSize;
DWORD       dwCommentOffset;

DWORD       dwDisplaySize;
DWORD       dwDisplayOffset;

DWORD       dwUserUserInfoSize;
DWORD       dwUserUserInfoOffset;

DWORD       dwHighLevelCompSize;
DWORD       dwHighLevelCompOffset;

DWORD       dwLowLevelCompSize;
DWORD       dwLowLevelCompOffset;

DWORD       dwChargingInfoSize;
DWORD       dwChargingInfoOffset;

DWORD       dwTerminalModesSize;
DWORD       dwTerminalModesOffset;
```

```
DWORD      dwDevSpecificSize;
DWORD      dwDevSpecificOffset;
} LINECALLINFO, FAR *LPLINECALLINFO;
```

We'll discuss only the members of LINECALLINFO that are relevant to basic analog telephone lines. Most of the members of LINECALLINFO are related to digital telephony environments or telephony environments that support caller identifications (such as caller ID). *lineGetCallInfo* should be called whenever an application receives a LINE_CALLSTATE message or a LINE_CALLINFO message. The LINE_CALLINFO message is sent to an application whenever a member of LINECALLINFO changes. The member that has changed is identified by the *dwParam1* parameter to the callback function. It can have the following values:

LINECALLINFOSTATE_OTHER	Information items other than those listed below have changed. The application should check the current call information to determine which items have changed.
LINECALLINFOSTATE_DEVSPECIFIC	The device-specific member of the call-information record (LINCALLINFO) has changed.
LINECALLINFOSTATE_BEARERMODE	The bearer mode member of the call-information record has changed.
LINECALLINFOSTATE_RATE	The rate member of the call-information record has changed.
LINECALLINFOSTATE_MEDIAMODE	The media mode member of the call-information record has changed.
LINECALLINFOSTATE_APPSPECIFIC	The application-specific member of the call-information record has changed.
LINECALLINFOSTATE_CALLID	The call ID member of the call-information record has changed.
LINECALLINFOSTATE_RELATEDCALLID	The related call ID member of the call-information record has changed.
LINECALLINFOSTATE_ORIGIN	The origin member of the call-information record has changed.
LINECALLINFOSTATE_REASON	The reason member of the call-information record has changed.

LINECALLINFOSTATE_COMPLETIONID	The completion ID member of the call-information record has changed.
LINECALLINFOSTATE_NUMOWNERINCR	The number of owners member in the call-information record was increased.
LINECALLINFOSTATE_NUMOWNERDECR	The number of owners member in the call-information record was decreased.
LINECALLINFOSTATE_NUMMONITORS	The number of monitors member in the call-information record has changed.
LINECALLINFOSTATE_TRUNK	The trunk member of the call-information record has changed.
LINECALLINFOSTATE_CALLERID	One of the caller-ID-related members of the call-information record has changed.
LINECALLINFOSTATE_CALLEDID	One of the called-ID-related members of the call-information record has changed.
LINECALLINFOSTATE_CONNECTEDID	One of the connected-ID-related members of the call-information record has changed.
LINECALLINFOSTATE_REDIRECTIONID	One of the redirection-ID-related members of the call-information record has changed.
LINECALLINFOSTATE_REDIRECTINGID	One of the redirecting-ID-related members of the call-information record has changed.
LINECALLINFOSTATE_DISPLAY	The display member of the call-information record has changed.
LINECALLINFOSTATE_USERUSERINFO	The user-to-user information of the call-information record has changed.
LINECALLINFOSTATE_HIGHLEVELCOMP	The high-level compatibility member of the call-information record has changed.
LINECALLINFOSTATE_LOWLEVELCOMP	The low-level compatibility member of the call-information record has changed.

LINECALLINFOSTATE_CHARGINGINFO	The charging information of the call-information record has changed.
LINECALLINFOSTATE_TERMINAL	The terminal mode information of the call-information record has changed.
LINECALLINFOSTATE_DIALPARAMS	The dial parameters of the call-information record has changed.
LINECALLINFOSTATE_MONITORMODES	One or more of the digit, tone, or media monitoring members in the call-information record has changed.

The LINECALLINFO structure contains the handle of the line on which the call exists (member *hLine*), the line ID (*dwLineDeviceID*), and the ID of the address the call is on (*dwAddressID*). The *dwBearerMode* member contains the bearer mode of the call. Calls on analog lines almost always have the bearer mode set to LINEBEARERMODE_VOICE. Remember, the LINEBEARERMODE_VOICE bearer mode supports analog voice, modem, and fax calls. The specific type of data being sent over the call is specified by the *dwMediaMode* member. As we stated earlier, typical media mode values for analog lines are LINEMEDIA-MODE_INTERACTIVEVOICE (human caller), LINEMEDIAMODE_DATAMODEM (analog modem), and LINEMEDIAMODE_G3FAX (analog fax). An application should examine the *dwMediaMode* member for the LINEMEDIAMODE-_UNKNOWN flag. This flag can be set along with one or more of the other media mode flags. If it is set, it means that the media mode of the call is unknown but that it will probably turn out to be one of the other media modes specified in *dwMediaModes,* once media mode determination is complete. If the LINEMEDIAMODE_UNKNOWN flag is not set, only one other flag will be set—the flag that specifies the media mode of the call. Here is an example of how an application can check for the media mode of a call.

```
if (!(callinfo.dwMediaMode & LINEMEDIAMODE_UNKNOWN))
    dwMediaMode = callinfo.dwMediaMode;
else
    /* media mode is still unknown */
```

If the media mode is unknown and the application knows how to determine whether the call is one of the media modes specified in *dwMediaModes,* the application should try to determine the media mode. If the application determines the media mode, it should set the media mode flags to that specific media mode using *lineSetMediaMode.*

With Unimodem, when the line is opened for data modem calls, the *dwMediaMode* member of offering calls is set to LINEMEDIAMODE_UN-KNOWN and LINEMEDIAMODE_DATAMODEM. When the call is answered, Unimodem attempts to determine if the call is truly a data modem call by negotiating tones with the caller. If negotiation between the modems is successful, the call transitions to the CONNECTED state and the LINEMEDIAMODE-_UNKNOWN flag is cleared.

If the application does its own media mode determination and determines that the call is not one of the media modes specified in *dwMediaModes,* it should eliminate that particular media mode bit, as follows:

```
/* application has determined that the call is not a data modem
call */
dwMediaMode = callinfo.dwMediaMode;
dwMediaMode &=~ LINEMEDIAMODE_DATAMODEM;
lineSetMediaMode(hCall, dwMediaMode);
```

Next, the application should hand off the call because another running application might be able to determine the media mode. As shown below, the application should specify LINEMEDIAMODE_UNKNOWN in the call to *lineHandoff* because the media mode of the call is still unknown at that time. After the handoff, the application should give up control of the call by calling *lineDeallocateCall.* With Unimodem, an application does not have to worry about determining whether a call is from an analog modem; Unimodem does the work required.

```
lineHandoff(hCall, NULL, LINEMEDIAMODE_UNKNOWN);
lineDeallocateCall(hCall);
```

If the application wants to continue monitoring the call after handoff, it can simply change its privileges from owner to monitor privileges after handing off the call, as shown below.

```
lineSetCallPrivilege (hCall, LINECALLPRIVILEGE_MONITOR);
```

If only one application has owner privileges for the call, that application cannot change its privileges to LINECALLPRIVILEGE_MONITOR. Someone has to own the call, so the function returns LINEERR_INVALCALLSTATE if the last owner of a call tries to become a monitor. The only exception is for idle calls; Windows allows idle calls to have no owners.

The *dwCallStates* member of LINECALLINFO lists the call states for which the application will be notified for this call. Discovering at run time which call states will appear on a call is not very useful to most telephony processes because the applications must be coded ahead of time to handle the states that might occur at run time. For incoming modem calls, Unimodem reports the OFFERING, ACCEPTED, CONNECTED, DISCONNECTED, DIALTONE, DIALING, RINGBACK, BUSY, PROCEEDING, IDLE, and UNKNOWN call states. For incoming calls, an application can discover which media modes the telephony drivers will test for by checking the *dwMonitorMediaModes* member. Knowing that the drivers have tested or will test for these modes can save the application the trouble of checking for these media modes itself. The application can focus on testing for media modes that the drivers do not know how to detect. Unimodem does not set this member, although other telephony drivers might.

An application can check the *dwOrigin* member to determine whether the call is inbound or outbound. For outbound calls, the LINECALLORIGIN_OUTBOUND flag is set. For inbound calls, the LINECALLORIGIN_EXTERNAL flag is set, indicating an inbound call originating externally to any internal phone equipment (such as an office PBX). For calls originating internally, *dwOrigin* has the LINECALLORIGIN_INTERNAL flag set.

A value in *dwOrigin* of LINECALLORIGIN_UNKNOWN means the origin of the call is currently unknown. LINECALLORIGIN_UNAVAIL indicates that the origin of the call is unknown and will never be known. LINECALLORIGIN-_CONFERENCE indicates the call handle is for a conference call. And finally, LINECALLORIGIN_INBOUND indicates that the call is inbound, but it is unknown whether it is an internal or an external call. Unimodem supports LINECALLORIGIN_OUTBOUND and LINECALLORIGIN_INBOUND.

An application can learn how many other applications have owner or monitor privileges for the call by examining the *dwNumOwners* and *dwNumMonitors* members. For outbound calls, *dwCountryCode* specifies the country code of the destination party. An application can learn the name of the application that first dialed or answered a call by examining the (variable-length) string specified by the members *dwAppNameSize* and *dwAppNameOffset*. This is either the same name that the originating application passes to the call to *lineInitialize* or, if no name is specified in the call to *lineInitialize,* it is the filename of that application.

You might have noticed that some important information about the call is missing from the LINECALLINFO structure. For example, nowhere in the structure is the call state specified. This is because LINECALLINFO is used to store static information about the call; more volatile information about the call, such as the current call state, is stored in a structure called LINECALLSTATUS. This structure is retrieved using the function *lineGetCallStatus,* as shown below.

```
lineGetCallStatus(hCall, lpCallStatus)
```

The first parameter is the call handle and the second parameter is a pointer to a LINECALLSTATUS structure, with the following format:

```
typedef struct linecallstatus_tag {
    DWORD       dwTotalSize;
    DWORD       dwNeededSize;
    DWORD       dwUsedSize;

    DWORD       dwCallState;
    DWORD       dwCallStateMode;
    DWORD       dwCallPrivilege;
    DWORD       dwCallFeatures;

    DWORD       dwDevSpecificSize;
    DWORD       dwDevSpecificOffset;
} LINECALLSTATUS, FAR *LPLINECALLSTATUS;
```

The current state of the call is specified by the member *dwCallState*. Details about the call state are specified in the *dwCallStateMode* member. For example, a call that is in the LINECALLSTATE_DISCONNECT state might also specify the reason for the disconnect using the LINEDISCONNECTMODE_NORMAL flag when the remote party has hung up the call (a normal disconnect) or the LINEDISCONNECTMODE_UNKNOWN flag when the reason for the disconnect is not known. The current privilege for the call is specified in the *dwCallPrivilege* member. Probably the most interesting member, from the point of view of the application that owns the call, is *dwCallFeatures*. This member indicates which TAPI functions are available for the call in its current state. With Unimodem, the possible values are as follows:

LINECALLFEATURE_ACCEPT	*lineAccept*
LINECALLFEATURE_ANSWER	*lineAnswer*
LINECALLFEATURE_DIAL	*lineDial*
LINECALLFEATURE_DROP	*lineDrop*
LINECALLFEATURE_GENERATEDIGITS	*lineGenerateDigits* (Unimodem only)
LINECALLFEATURE_MONITORDIGITS	*lineMonitorDigits* (Unimodem only)
LINECALLFEATURE_MONITORMEDIA	*lineMonitorMedia*
LINECALLFEATURE_SETCALLPARAMS	*lineSetCallParams*

Not all of the TAPI functions listed above will be available for the call in every state. For example, *lineDial* is not enabled for inbound calls. An application should typically call *lineGetCallStatus* whenever it receives a LINE_CALLSTATE message, to get the latest list of available functions. This list can be used to disable or enable menu items.

Two functions are available to help an application count rings before answering inbound calls: *lineSetNumRings* and *lineGetNumRings*. A call to *lineSetNumRings* is shown here.

```
lineSetNumRings(hLine, dwAddressID, dwNumRings)
```

Notice that the first parameter is a line handle, not a call handle, because typically no call will exist when *lineSetNumRings* is called. After all, an application needs to know the number of rings it will have to wait to answer the phone—before any calls actually come in. *lineSetNumRings* allows the application to specify a line and address using the first two parameters. The last parameter is the number of rings. Multiple applications with the line open can call *lineSetNumRings,* and Windows will extract the minimum number of rings specified by any application that calls *lineSetNumRings* and return that minimum value when *lineGetNumRings* is called, as shown below.

```
lineGetNumRings(hLine, dwAddressID, lpdwNumRings)
```

The last parameter specifies a pointer to a DWORD where the number of rings that an application should wait before answering a call is returned. If no application has called *lineSetNumRings,* Windows returns 0xffffffff for the number of rings. When an inbound call arrives, Windows sends the callback function a LINE_LINEDEVSTATE message with *dwParam1* set to LINEDEVSTATE_RINGING. The call handle is offered immediately upon the occurrence of the first ring; it is up to the application to wait the specified number of rings before answering. The application does not need to count LINEDEVSTATE_RINGING messages; instead, it can check the ring count in *dwParam3* for a match with the number of rings returned by *lineGetNumRings*. A separate message is sent for each ring on the line, with *dwParam2* set to the ring mode and *dwParam3* set to the ring count. The application should answer the call only after a number of messages equal to the number returned by *lineGetNumRings* has occurred.

What this all adds up to is a toll saver feature. Toll saver works like this: Say you have an answering machine at home, and you call home regularly to check your messages. If the toll saver option is turned on, when there are no messages the answering machine lets the phone ring four times before picking up and recording the caller's message. When there are messages waiting, the answering machine picks up after two rings. Result: when you call home to check your messages, and there are none, you know it after three rings and you can hang up before the fourth ring, which saves the cost of a wasted call. Telephony applications, including software answering machines, can use this same methodology to save callers the expense of a call when there are no messages waiting.

Finally, an application that wants to transfer data other than voice data can secure the call against unwanted intrusions by calling *lineSecureCall,* as shown below.

```
lineSecureCall(hCall)
```

It is a good idea for an application to check the currently available call features in LINECALLSTATUS before attempting to secure a call. *lineSecureCall* is asynchronous. Once a call is secure, it typically cannot be unsecured. An outbound call can be secured at call setup time using *lineMakeCall* with the LINECALLPARAMFLAGS_SECURE flag set in the LINECALLPARAMS structure.

Completing the Skeleton Telephony Application

With this new knowledge of how to make and answer calls, we can now round out the telephony skeleton application. First, we can add a menu option called Make Call, for making outbound calls. When this menu option is called, the application first checks whether the line is open; if it isn't open, the application opens it. The application opens the line just prior to dialing to avoid resource conflicts with other applications that also want to use the line. If the address supports the making of outbound calls, the application prompts you for a telephone number by displaying a Phone Number dialog box. The dialog procedure and the application will convert the number to canonical format and add the leading + to the phone number if you don't add it. Next, the application calls *lineTranslateDialog* on the phone number to let you select dialing options (such as local and long-distance prefix codes, whether to use tone or pulse dialing, and whether to use a calling card) and see the effects of those options on the dialable number.

The following code is the IDM_MAKECALL case in COMDIAL.C.

```
case IDM_MAKECALL:
    char szTemp[60];
    ⋮
    if (!mytapi.bLineopen) {
        if (telephonyOpen(hWnd, ghInst)) {
            MessageBox(hWnd, "Error", "Error opening line", MB_OK);
            break;
        }
    }

    if (!(mytapi.pLineaddressstatus->dwAddressFeatures &
        LINEADDRFEATURE_MAKECALL)) {
        MessageBox(hWnd, "Error",
                    "Line/address does not support \
                    lineMakeCall", MB_OK);
        break;
    }
```

```
if (!DialogBox (GetModuleHandle(NULL),
    MAKEINTRESOURCE(IDD_DIAL),
    hWnd, (DLGPROC)DialDialogProc))
    break;

if (mytapi.szDialNumber[0] != '+') {
    szTemp[0] = '+';
    lstrcpy(&szTemp[1], mytapi.szDialNumber);
    lstrcpy(mytapi.szDialNumber, szTemp);
}
lResult =  lineTranslateDialog(mytapi.hTAPI,
    mytapi.dwLine, mytapi.dwVersionToUse,
    hWnd, mytapi.szDialNumber);
if (!(lResult==0)) {
    /* Process error */
    ProcessTAPIError(lResult);
    MessageBox(hWnd, "ERROR",
            "Error translating address", MB_OK);
    break;
}
    ⋮
```

Next, the application calls *lineTranslateAddress* on the phone number. The call is made using the "lazy" method of allocating far more memory for the data structures than TAPI could possibly need. *lineTranslateAddress* applies the dialing options you selected during the call to *lineTranslateDialog* to form a dialable address that can be used by *lineMakeCall*. If *lineTranslateAddress* returns successfully, the application copies the dialable number from the variable-length string in the LINETRANSLATEOUTPUT structure. The size and offset of the dialable number in the structure are specified by the members *dwDialableStringOffset* and *dwDialableStringSize*. Finally, the number is dialed with a call to *lineMakeCall*. To make a data modem call, the LINECALLPARAMS parameter must be used with the bearer mode set to LINEBEARERMODE_VOICE and the media mode set to LINEMEDIAMODE_DATAMODEM. Notice that the LINECALLPARAMS parameter must be allocated either from global memory or from the local heap; *lineMakeCall* returns LINEER_INVALPOINTER if the structure is a stack variable. If *lineMakeCall* succeeds, the Disconnect menu option is enabled. Technically, this is bad practice since *lineMakeCall* is asynchronous and the menu option should be enabled only in the callback procedure once the call enters a state from which it can be dropped. This code also can be found in COMDIAL.C and follows the code from the previous example.

```
LPLINETRANSLATEOUTPUT lto;
static LINECALLPARAMS callparams;
⋮
// call lineTranslateAddress on the phone number.
// lineTranslateAddress will apply the dialing options
// selected by the user during the call to lineTranslateDialog
// to the phone number to form a dialable address.
lto = (LINETRANSLATEOUTPUT)
        calloc(sizeof(LINETRANSLATEOUTPUT)+5000,1);
lto->dwTotalSize = sizeof(LINETRANSLATEOUTPUT)+5000;
lResult =  lineTranslateAddress(mytapi.hTAPI,
    mytapi.dwLine, mytapi.dwVersionToUse,
    mytapi.szDialNumber, 0,
    0,lto);
if (!(lResult==0)) {
    /* Process error */
    ProcessTAPIError(lResult);
    MessageBox(hWnd, "ERROR", "Error translating \
              address", MB_OK);
    free (lto);
    break;
}
else {
    // copy the dialable number from the variable-length
    // string in LINETRANSLATEOUTPUT specified by
    // dwDialableStringOffset and dwDialableStringSize
    memcpy (mytapi.szDialNumber,
            (LPSTR)((DWORD)lto+lto->dwDialableStringOffset),
            lto->dwDialableStringSize);
    mytapi.szDialNumber[lto->dwDialableStringSize] = 0;
}
free (lto);


// make an outbound call
// call params must be static or allocated dynamically;
// cannot be a stack variable or else LINEERR_INVALPOINTER
// is returned by lineMakeCall
pCallParams = (LINECALLPARAMS *)
              calloc(sizeof(LINECALLPARAMS),1);
pCallParams->dwTotalSize = sizeof(LINECALLPARAMS);
pCallParams->dwBearerMode = LINEBEARERMODE_VOICE;
pCallParams->dwMediaMode = LINEMEDIAMODE_DATAMODEM;
```

```
    pCallParams->dwCallParamFlags = LINECALLPARAMFLAGS_IDLE;
    pCallParams->dwAddressMode = LINEADDRESSMODE_ADDRESSID;

    lResult =  lineMakeCall(mytapi.hLine, &mytapi.hCall,
                            mytapi.szDialNumber, 0,
                            pCallParams);
    if (!(lResult>0)) {
        ProcessTAPIError(lResult);
        MessageBox(hWnd, "ERROR", "Error making call",
                   MB_OK);
        free (pCallParams);
        break;
    }
    free (pCallParams);
    hMenu = GetMenu(hWnd);
    EnableMenuItem( hMenu, IDM_DISCONNECT, MF_ENABLED |
                    MF_BYCOMMAND ) ;

    break;
    ⋮
```

Once *lineMakeCall* is called, the application begins receiving LINE_CALLSTATE messages to its line callback function. (In this example, the line callback function is *LineCallBackProc* in MYTAPI_.C.) These messages are trapped, and the call handle is extracted from the *dwDevice* parameter. The application checks *dwParam3* in the LINE_CALLSTATE case to see if it has owner privileges for the call, and if it does, it saves the call handle in the MYTAPI structure in the *hCall* member. Applications that can handle more than one phone call simultaneously will want to create a linked list of call handles instead of working with only the most recent call, as the skeleton does. After saving the call handle, the application calls *mylineGetCallStatus,* a wrapper function for *lineGetCallStatus.* This function, shown below, retrieves the LINECALLSTATUS structure, which contains status information about the call. This function is included in the MYTAPI_.C sample application.

```
///////////////////////////////////////////////////////////////////
//  mylineGetCallStatus - get LINECALLSTATUS structure
///////////////////////////////////////////////////////////////////
LONG mylineGetCallStatus()
{
    LONG lrc;
    DWORD dwsize;
```

(continued)

```
    // if space already allocated for structure, free it up
    if (mytapi.bLinecallstatusalloced) {
        free (mytapi.pLinecallstatus);
        mytapi.bLinecallstatusalloced = FALSE;
    }

    // allocate memory for structure
    mytapi.pLinecallstatus =
        (LINECALLSTATUS *) calloc(1, sizeof(LINECALLSTATUS));
    if (!mytapi.pLinecallstatus)
        return LINEERR_NOMEM;
    mytapi.bLinecallstatusalloced = TRUE;
    // set structure size
    mytapi.pLinecallstatus->dwTotalSize = sizeof(LINECALLSTATUS);

    do {
        // get information into structure
        lrc = lineGetCallStatus(mytapi.hCall,
                                mytapi.pLinecallstatus);
        // bomb out if error
        if (lrc) {
            free (mytapi.pLinecallstatus);
            mytapi.bLinecallstatusalloced = FALSE;
            return lrc;
        }

        // reallocate and try again
        dwsize = mytapi.pLinecallstatus->dwNeededSize;
        if (mytapi.pLinecallstatus->dwTotalSize < dwsize) {
            free (mytapi.pLinecallstatus);
            mytapi.bLinecallstatusalloced = FALSE;
            mytapi.pLinecallstatus = (LINECALLSTATUS *)
                                      calloc(1, dwsize);
            if (!mytapi.pLlinecallstatus)
                return LINEERR_NOMEM;
            mytapi.bLinecallstatusalloced = TRUE;
            mytapi.pLinecallstatus->dwTotalSize = dwsize;
            continue;
        }
        break;
    } while (TRUE);

    return lrc;
}
```

After *mylineGetCallStatus* completes, the wrapper function *mylineGetCallInfo* is called to retrieve the LINECALLINFO structure for the call. These two wrapper functions are similar, so the listing for *mylineGetCallInfo* is omitted.

mylineGetCallInfo is also called when the application receives a LINE-_CALLINFO message. This message indicates that one or more members of LINECALLINFO have changed.

The application is particularly interested in the *dwCallFeatures* member of the LINECALLSTATUS structure that was retrieved in the call to *mylineGetCall-Status*. This member has flags that indicate which functions are available for the call. The application first checks for the LINECALLFEATURE_DROP flag. If this flag is set, the Disconnect menu option is enabled, which means you can drop the call. The application next checks for the LINECALLFEATURE-_ANSWER flag. If this flag is set, the Answer Call menu item is enabled, which means you can answer the call. With Unimodem, LINECALLFEATURE-_ANSWER is set only for calls in the OFFERING or ACCEPTED call states. The application uses the Answer Call menu item merely to set a flag indicating that inbound calls should be automatically answered; therefore this menu item can be enabled even when there are no calls on the line. When the IDLE state is received, the resources for the call are freed by calling *lineDeallocateCall*. Here is some of the code for the LINE_CALLSTATE state. This code can be found in MYTAPI_.C in the *LineCallBackProc* callback function.

```
case LINE_CALLSTATE:

    switch (dwParam3) {
        case LINECALLPRIVILEGE_MONITOR:
            break;
        case LINECALLPRIVILEGE_OWNER:
            // save call handle
            mytapi.hCall = (HCALL)dwDevice;
            // update local call information
            mylineGetCallStatus();
            mylineGetCallInfo();

            // update menus
            hMenu = GetMenu(hTTYWnd);
            // enable drop call?
            if (mytapi.pLinecallstatus->dwCallFeatures &
                LINECALLFEATURE_DROP)
                    EnableMenuItem( hMenu, IDM_DISCONNECT,
                                    MF_ENABLED |
                                    MF_BYCOMMAND ) ;
        else
                    EnableMenuItem( hMenu, IDM_DISCONNECT,
                                    MF_GRAYED |
                                    MF_DISABLED |
                                    MF_BYCOMMAND ) ;
```

(continued)

```
                    // enable answer call?
                    if (mytapi.pLinecallstatus->dwCallFeatures &
                        LINECALLFEATURE_ANSWER)
                            EnableMenuItem( hMenu, IDM_ANSWER,
                                           MF_ENABLED |
                                           MF_BYCOMMAND );
                    else
                            EnableMenuItem( hMenu, IDM_ANSWER,
                                           MF_GRAYED |
                                           MF_DISABLED |
                                           MF_BYCOMMAND );

                    break;
                default:
                    break;
            } //end switch

            switch (dwParam1) {
                case LINECALLSTATE_IDLE:

                    // deallocate call resources
                    lineDeallocateCall (mytapi.hCall);
                    ⋮
                default:
                    break;
            } //end switch
                    break;
```

Now let's discuss a few more of the call states that are of interest in this application. When the OFFERING call state is received, the application checks to see if you selected the automatic answering of calls. If so, *lineAnswer* is called to answer the call. When the CONNECTED call state is received, it means that the two modems have negotiated a connection over which data may be exchanged. The application creates and runs a thread for reading incoming bytes. (The thread uses the polling method.) When the DISCONNECTED call state is received, the application kills the thread that reads bytes and allows it to die gracefully. This code is also in the *LineCallBackProc* function under the LINE_CALLSTATE case.

```
case LINE_CALLSTATE:
    ⋮
    switch (dwParam1)
    ⋮
    case LINECALLSTATE_OFFERING:
        if (mytapi.bWaitForCall){
            // answer incoming calls
            lrc =  lineAnswer(mytapi.hCall,NULL,0);
```

```
        if (!(lrc>0)) {
            ProcessTAPIError(lrc);
            myMessageBox("Error answering call");
        }
    }
    break;
⋮
case LINECALLSTATE_CONNECTED:

    /* create the thread for reading bytes */
    mytapi.bReading = TRUE;
    if ((mytapi.hThread=CreateThread
                    (NULL /*def security */
                    0,    /* def stack size */,
                    (LPTHREAD_START_ROUTINE)ReadThread,
                    NULL, /* param to pass to thread */
                    0, &id)) == INVALID_HANDLE_VALUE) {
        /* handle error */
        MessageBox (NULL, "Error creating READ thread",
                    "",MB_OK);
        break;
    } /* end if (error creating read thread) */

    break;
⋮
case LINECALLSTATE_DISCONNECTED:

    /* kill the read thread */
    if (mytapi.bReading) {
        mytapi.bReading = FALSE;
        /* wait for thread to die... */
        while (GetExitCodeThread(mytapi.hThread, &id)) {
            if (id == STILL_ACTIVE)
                continue;
            else
                break;
        } /* end while (no error reading thread exit code) */
        CloseHandle (mytapi.hThread);
    }
⋮
```

Sending Data over the Phone Line

Once a call is connected, data can be transmitted over the phone line using the modem. Because modems connect to the serial port of the computer, data transfer through modems is accomplished in the same manner that it is for serial ports. (See Chapter 3.) Once the LINECALLSTATE_CONNECTED state is received, the modems have concluded their handshaking protocol and the line is ready for data transfer. Data transfer is accomplished using *ReadFile* and *WriteFile,* just as it is for serial ports. The only difference is that instead of passing the serial port handle to *ReadFile* and *WriteFile,* the modem handle returned by *lineGetID* is passed. The modem handle is retrieved for the active call using the local function *mylineGetCallID*. This avoids resource conflicts with other applications that might result from retrieving the modem handle for the line device (as opposed to the particular call). In general, it is a good idea to retrieve the modem handle at the last moment before using it to transfer data, to avoid resource conflicts. Any one of the data transfer methods described in Chapter 3 can be used with modems, including polling, event-driven data transfer, and overlapped data transfer. The example on the companion disk uses the polling method for reading bytes from the modem and performs synchronous writes to the modem, as shown in the *ReadThread* function below.

```
DWORD ReadThread (LPDWORD lpdwParam1)
{
    BYTE inbuff[100];
    DWORD nBytesRead;
    COMMTIMEOUTS to;
    LONG lrc;

    /* The next two lines check to make sure that interval
    timeouts are supported by the port */
    if (!(mytapi.pCommprop->dwProvCapabilities & PCF_INTTIMEOUTS)) {
        return 1L;  /* error;  can't set interval timeouts */
    }

    // get the modem handle for the call
    lrc = mylineGetCallID ();
    if (lrc) {
        MessageBox (NULL,
            "Error getting modem handle for data transfer",
            "", MB_OK);
        return 1L;
    }

    /* the next three lines tell the read function to return
    immediately even when there are no bytes waiting in the
    port's receive queue */
    memset (&to, 0, sizeof(to));
    to.ReadIntervalTimeout = MAXDWORD;
    SetCommTimeouts (mytapi.hComm, &to);

    /* this loop polls the port reading bytes until the control
    variable bReading is set FALSE
    by the controlling process */
```

```
    while (mytapi.bReading) {
        /* poll the port and read bytes if available */
        if (!ReadFile(mytapi.hComm, inbuff, 100, &nBytesRead, NULL))
        {
            /* handle error */
            locProcessCommError(GetLastError ());
        } /* end if (error reading bytes) */
        else {
            /* if there were bytes waiting, display them in TTY
            window */
            if (nBytesRead)
                locProcessBytes(inbuff, nBytesRead);
        }
    } /* end while (thread active) */

    /* clean out any pending bytes in the receive buffer */
    PurgeComm(mytapi.hComm, PURGE_RXCLEAR);
    // close the use of the modem for data transfer
    CloseHandle (mytapi.hComm);
    mytapi.bGotcommhandle = FALSE;

    return 0L;
} /* end function (ReadThread) */
```

5

The Simple Messaging API

The MAPI Architecture

To be well rounded in communications programming, it is important to understand both interactive and messaging methods. The distinction between interactive communications and message-based communications is not always clear. Most people would consider online services interactive, and yet most types of online communications involve messages—collections of data that are composed ahead of time and then sent as a unit.

Architecturally, the Messaging API (MAPI) is divided into four components: three *service providers* (the message store, the address book, and the message transport) and the *MAPI DLL* (also known as the plumbing code). Service providers are drivers that MAPI uses to implement many of its features. Message store drivers implement message storage, organization, and retrieval. Address book drivers implement message address lookup and maintenance. Transport drivers move messages across the network. A fourth kind of driver, called a profile driver, stores configuration information. MAPI DLLs connect the service providers with applications and with each other.

Windows 95 ships with sets of all four drivers. Third parties can write their own drivers to replace the ones supplied by Microsoft. The drivers that MAPI uses to send a particular class of messages can be configured from the Windows Control Panel, using the Mail and Fax applet. This applet by default brings up the MS Exchange Settings Properties dialog box with a list of available information services. Selecting a service from the list and clicking the Properties button allows you to configure the service.

MAPI also includes a message spooler. This spooler does for messages what a print spooler does for print jobs; it lines them up to be serviced one at a time.

The message spooler acts as a valve between the message store and the message transport, ensuring that messages flow smoothly in and out of the system. An application does not need to deal with the functioning of the spooler; the spooler is a background process that runs as part of MAPI.

The MAPI DLL is known as the plumbing code because MAPI supplies the plumbing that lets the other components work together. MAPI coordinates the activities of multiple messaging applications. It provides common user interfaces for sending, saving, and receiving messages. MAPI is responsible for managing address books and message stores, providing security for messages, spooling messages, and managing the message transport components.

Consider what happens when three different message transports are installed on the same PC. One transport is for fax messages, another is for CompuServe messages, and the third is for Novell MHS messages. When an application submits a message to be sent, MAPI determines which network the message is being sent to and gives the message to the appropriate message transport. MAPI ensures that the message uses the correct address book and message store for the network it belongs to. If the message is sent to multiple users on different networks, MAPI routes the message through multiple address books, stores, and transports to get the message to all destinations. MAPI ensures that inbound messages find the right message store for the network they arrived on. Sometimes, when an outbound message can't be delivered because the message transport for the network is missing or is out of commission, the message is sidetracked to the message store. Later, when the transport is available, the message is automatically taken out of storage and sent on its way.

MAPI is responsible for pooling the resources of multiple drivers, managing the messaging session, and opening resources. But despite all this, most advanced MAPI function calls pass straight through the MAPI DLL to the underlying drivers.

The Message Structure

Regardless of the platform, computer messages tend to have a common structure. They usually have a list of recipients, which are divided into direct, copy, and blind copy recipients. A direct recipient is someone for whom the message is specifically created. A copy recipient gets a copy of the message but is not a primary recipient. A copy recipient might be a boss, a secretary, or someone else whose interest is primarily in knowing that the message was sent, and to whom and when. A blind copy recipient is a recipient that the sender does not want the direct recipients or the copy recipients to know about.

Usually, the message identifies the sender (also known as the originator or owner) of the message. The message contains the text of the message (the message body) and perhaps some file attachments. In Microsoft Windows, a message is a data structure with members for the originator and recipients, among others. The structure of a Windows MAPI message is shown below.

```
typedef struct
{
    ULONG ulReserved;              // Reserved for future use
    LPSTR lpszSubject;             // Message Subject
    LPSTR lpszNoteText;            // Message Text
    LPSTR lpszMessageType;         // Message Class
    LPSTR lpszDateReceived;        // in YYYY/MM/DD HH:MM
                                   // format
    LPSTR lpszConversationID;      // conversation thread ID
    FLAGS flFlags;                 // unread, receipt
                                   // requested, sent
    lpMapiRecipDesc lpOriginator;  // Originator descriptor
    ULONG nRecipCount;             // Number of recipients
    lpMapiRecipDesc lpRecips;      // Recipient descriptors
    ULONG nFileCount;              // # of file attachments
    lpMapiFileDesc lpFiles;        // Attachment descriptors
}   MapiMessage, FAR * lpMapiMessage;
```

The first member is reserved and should be set to 0. The next member, *lpszSubject,* points to a z-string containing the subject of the message. An example of a message subject is *Agenda for the 4:30 pm Meeting.* Notice that the *lpszSubject* member does not allocate any memory for the string; it points to a string you must allocate elsewhere in your application. This is generally true of all the members of the Windows message structure.

The *lpszNoteText* member points to the text of the message. The *lpszMessageType* member describes the type of the message. It is interpreted by the MAPI drivers and is limited to one of a set of predefined values. The most common message type, supported by the standard Microsoft implementation, is interpersonal messaging, or IPM.Note. Depending on the drivers that are installed, the IPM.Note message type can be used for e-mail or fax. When a message is received, MAPI places a timestamp on it. The timestamp appears in the MapiMessage member *lpszDateReceived.* The format of the timestamp is *YYYY/MM/DD HH:MM.* On systems that support conversation threads, the *lpszConversationID* member specifies the conversation thread to which the message belongs. The conversation thread is typically duplicated when a reply is generated for a message, and can be useful, for example, for compiling message streams into FAQ (Frequently Asked Question) files about a particular topic.

The *flFlags* member is a bitmask of flags that identify certain characteristics of the message. The possible values of the member are as follows:

MAPI_UNREAD	Indicates that a message in the Inbox has not been read. (This is sort of like a dirty flag that is cleared once a received message is read.)
MAPI_RECEIPT_REQUESTED	Indicates that a read receipt is requested for outbound messages.
MAPI_SENT	Indicates that an outbound message has been sent.

The *lpOriginator* member points to a structure that describes the message originator (also known as the owner or the "FROM" party). This member takes the form of a MapiRecipDesc structure, which, like the other members, is allocated externally to the message structure. The format of the MapiRecipDesc structure is as follows:

```
typedef struct
{
    ULONG ulReserved;          // Reserved for future use
    ULONG ulRecipClass;        // Recipient class
                               // MAPI_TO, MAPI_CC, MAPI_BCC,
                               // MAPI_ORIG
    LPSTR lpszName;            // Recipient or sender name
    LPSTR lpszAddress;        // Recipient or sender address
                               // (optional)
    ULONG ulEIDSize;          // Count in bytes of size of
                               // pEntryID
    LPVOID lpEntryID;         // System-specific recipient
                               // reference
} MapiRecipDesc, FAR * lpMapiRecipDesc;
```

The first member of MapiRecipDesc is reserved and should be set to 0. The recipient class member, *ulRecipClass,* must be one of the following types:

MAPI_ORIG	Identifies the message originator. There should be only one originator.
MAPI_TO	Identifies the direct recipient(s) of the message.
MAPI_CC	Identifies the copy recipient(s).
MAPI_BCC	Identifies the blind copy recipient(s).

In the message structure, the member *lpOriginator->ulRecipClass* must be set to MAPI_ORIG to identify the message originator. The name of the owner or recipient(s) is specified in the *lpszName* member. The owner or recipient's address (phone number or Internet address) can be specified in the *lpszAddress* member, but usually MAPI uses an address extracted from a Windows address book. MAPI uses the *ulEIDSize* and *lpEntryID* members to uniquely identify the recipient in subsequent calls to MAPI.

Getting back to the MapiMessage structure, the *nRecipCount* member specifies the number of recipients in the *lpRecips* member. No such count is required for the *lpOriginator* member because a message can have only one originator. But there can be many recipients, so the count must be specified. The member *lpRecips* points to the list of recipients, which is an array of MapiRecipDesc structures you must allocate in your application. Recipients are identified in a manner similar to that used to specify the originator, except that the recipient class is set to MAPI_TO (direct recipient), MAPI_CC (copy recipient), or MAPI_BCC (blind copy recipient).

The specified recipient information is usually extracted from a Windows address book, so the application does not have to fill the *lpszAddress, ulEIDSize,* or *lpEntryID* members. (The address book does this.)

Two members of the MapiMessage structure specify the file attachments. The member *nFileCount* specifies the number of file attachments. File attachments are specified by the member *lpFiles,* which is an array of size *nFileCount* of MapiFileDesc structures. The MapiFileDesc structure has the following format:

```
typedef struct
{
    ULONG ulReserved;     // Reserved for future use (must be 0)
    ULONG flFlags;        // Flags
    ULONG nPosition;      // character in text to replace with
                          // attachment
    LPSTR lpszPathName;   // Full pathname of attachment file
    LPSTR lpszFileName;   // Original filename (optional)
    LPVOID lpFileType;    // Attachment file type (optional)
}   MapiFileDesc, FAR * lpMapiFileDesc;
```

Like all simple MAPI structures, the first member is reserved. The *flFlags* member can be 0 or one or both of the following values:

MAPI_OLE	The attached "file" is an OLE object that can be activated and edited.
MAPI_OLE_STATIC	The attachment is a static OLE object that cannot be edited, only viewed.

The *nPosition* member of MapiFileDesc is useful for embedding objects, particularly OLE objects, in the body of the message. For example, an *nPosition* value of 1000 embeds an attachment after 1000 bytes of the message text. A value of −1 in this member indicates that the attachment is a separate file and should not be embedded. Be careful not to embed two objects in the same location, and don't embed them in a position beyond the end of the message text.

The *lpszPathName* member specifies the full pathname of the attached file, including the drive specifier and all directories. It is often the case that the file is a temporary file created for the express purpose of being sent as part of a message. (For example, it might be a small piece of a larger file.) If this is the case, you can ask MAPI to rename the file by specifying the new filename in the *lpszFileName* member. The *lpFileType* member identifies the file type of the attachment. (You rarely need to specify a value for this member, because the filename extension usually identifies the type of data in the file.)

Now you have the background you need to program Windows messaging applications. The following sections cover specific messaging topics. One word of warning: Never, ever specify undefined flags in the calls to the MAPI functions. Some of the functions will change behavior if certain flags, beyond the scope of this chapter, are set. So stick to documented MAPI flags, at least for now.

Logging On and Logging Off

To send and receive messages, an application must log onto the Windows messaging system. Part of the process of logging on is selecting a profile. A profile is configured using the Mail and Fax applet on the Windows Control Panel. Among other things, a profile specifies the collection of MAPI drivers to use with a particular class of messages. Profiles are not backed up, so you cannot recover from a damaged profile. Also, you can't reliably copy profiles from one machine to another and expect them to work. But this is not a problem in general, because profiles can be easily reconstructed using the Mail and Fax applet.

A *messaging session* consists of everything that happens from the time an application logs onto the messaging system until it logs off. Upon successful logon, MAPI returns a session handle for use in subsequent calls to the MAPI functions. The session handle becomes invalid once the application logs off.

To log on, an application calls *MAPILogon,* as shown below.

```
MAPILogon(ulUIParam, lpszProfileName, lpszPassword, flFlags,
          ulReserved, lplhSession);
```

The first parameter, *ulUIParam,* is a handle to the window that will serve as the parent of the dialog box(es) that *MAPILogon* displays. If this parameter is set to 0, the dialog boxes are application modal. In the second parameter, *lpszProfile-Name,* you can enter the name of the profile you want as the default. If the specified profile name does not exist, MAPI returns MAPI_E_LOGIN_FAILURE.

lpszProfileName can be NULL. If a password is required for the given profile, it can be programmatically set in the *lpszPassword* parameter. Note that this is not the same password that you specify to access stored messages; MAPI requests the latter password when you try to read or send messages.

In the *flFlags* parameter you can set a flag to specify whether or not the logon will allow a user interface. If you set *lpszProfileName* to NULL, setting the flag MAPI_LOGON_UI displays the Choose Profile dialog box, in which you interactively select a profile. This flag is ignored if you did specify a profile. If you did not specify a password in *lpszPassword* and the profile requires one, you are asked to enter a password.

If you don't set a profile in *lpszProfileName* and you also don't set the MAPI_LOGON_UI flag, MAPI chooses the default profile that you configured from the Control Panel. If you do set the MAPI_LOGON_UI flag, you can make the selected profile for logon the default profile by clicking the Options button in the Choose Profile dialog box. (See Figure 5-1.) The Options section of the dialog box includes a check box that you can select to make the profile you selected the default profile for future logons.

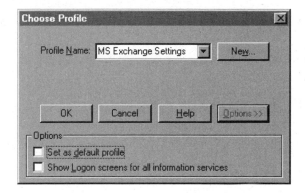

Figure 5-1. *The Choose Profile dialog box with the Options section displayed.*

The Options section of the Choose Profile dialog box also includes a check box called "Show Logon screens for all information services." Do not select this check box unless you enjoy being bombarded with a lot of dialog boxes asking a lot of questions every time you log on. Selecting this check box causes MAPI to present the configuration dialog boxes for the various MAPI components, such as the address book, transport, and message store.

You can create new profiles by clicking the New button in the Choose Profile dialog box. This launches the Inbox Setup Wizard for selecting a new set of services (drivers) for a new profile.

If messages are stored on a remote computer, you can access them by specifying the flag MAPI_FORCE_DOWNLOAD. This flag causes MAPI to download all of the remote messages before *MAPILogon* returns. Setting this flag can considerably slow down the performance of *MAPILogon*.

The *ulReserved* parameter is, not surprisingly, reserved for future use. The last parameter, *lplhSession,* points to a variable in which *MAPILogon* returns a session handle if logon succeeds. The session handle has the type HANDLE and is used in all subsequent calls to MAPI functions. Later we'll explore a special shortcut for calling MAPI functions without a session handle. To create a new messaging session, set the MAPI_NEW_SESSION flag in *flFlags*.

If other MAPI applications (such as Microsoft Exchange) are running, your messaging application can save resources by "sharing" the session of the other application. When a second application shares a session, it shares the same profile as the first application. However, MAPI returns a different session handle than it does for the first application. To share in the existing session, simply omit the MAPI_NEW_SESSION flag. If you omit the flag and no other session is available, MAPI creates a new session for the application anyway.

To end a session, you call *MAPILogoff,* as shown below. *MAPILogoff* deallocates any resources associated with the session unless another application is sharing the session. The session handle is no longer valid once *MAPILogoff* returns.

```
MAPILogoff(lhSession, ulUIParam, flFlags, ulReserved);
```

The first parameter is the session handle returned by *MAPILogon*. The *ulUIParam* parameter is the parent window handle for any dialog boxes that the function displays. Usually, logging off does not require the display of any dialog boxes. The last two parameters, *flFlags* and *ulReserved,* are not used and should be set to 0.

Reading Messages

Messages are read from the message store, which is like a filing cabinet for messages. The message store can have various folders. For example, by default Exchange uses four folders. One folder is for received messages (the Inbox), one is for outbound messages (the Outbox), one is for outbound messages that have already been sent (Sent Items), and one is for deleted messages that have not been discarded (Deleted Items, also known as the wastebasket).

The function for reading messages is called *MAPIReadMail*. However, before *MAPIReadMail* can be called, the message to read must be located in the message store using the function *MAPIFindNext,* whose syntax is shown on the facing page.

```
ULONG FAR PASCAL MAPIFindNext(LHANDLE lhSession, ULONG ulUIParam,
                              LPSTR lpszMessageType,
                              LPSTR lpszSeedMessageID,
                              FLAGS flFlags, ULONG ulReserved,
                              LPSTR lpszMessageID);
```

MAPIFindNext locates a message of a particular type within the message store and returns a unique identifier for the message. The first parameter, *lhSession,* is the session handle returned by *MAPILogon.* The second parameter, *ulUIParam,* is a handle to the window that will serve as parent to any dialog boxes that the function displays. Because calling *MAPIFindNext* involves accessing the message store (the Inbox folder in particular), the function displays a dialog box requesting the password for accessing the message store (if the message store requires a password). The fourth parameter, *lpszMessageType,* is a string that identifies the type of message the application is looking for. Usually, this string is IPM.Note to indicate a search of the interpersonal messages folder. In fact, when *lpszMessageType* is NULL, MAPI assumes a default type of IPM.Note.

If *MAPIFindNext* locates a message of the specified type, it returns a unique identifier for the message in the *lpszMessageID* parameter. This parameter must point to at least 64 bytes of space for the message ID, although to ensure compatibility with longer IDS the parameter should point to 512 bytes of space. Don't try to print this string or display it; it is a meaningless sequence, except to MAPI. The returned message ID can be passed in the *lpszSeedMessageID* parameter in subsequent calls to *MAPIFindNext* to specify a starting point for locating a next message of the same type. *lpszSeedMessageID* should be NULL when searching for the first message of a given type. When there are no more messages of the specified type to be found, *MAPIFindNext* returns MAPI_E_NO_MESSAGES.

The *ulReserved* parameter is reserved for future use. It should be set to 0.

The *flFlags* parameter is a bitmask of flags that control the behavior of *MAPIFindNext.* The MAPI_UNREAD_ONLY flag tells the function to locate only messages that have not been read. When a message is read, MAPI marks the message as read. When MAPI_UNREAD_ONLY is set, *MAPIFindNext* checks each message of the specified type for this read mark, and returns only messages that do not have the mark. Another flag that can be specified is MAPI_GUARANTEE_FIFO, which forces *MAPIFindNext* to search for the messages and return them in the order in which they were received. Setting the flag MAPI_LONG_MSGID indicates that the value in the *lpszMessageID* parameter can be up to 512 bytes long. If this flag is not set, message IDs can only be up to 64 bytes.

When the fax transport drivers are installed, calling *MAPIFindNext* activates the Windows fax server. You can tell when the fax server is active because a fax server icon appears on the taskbar next to the time. The fax server remains active until the session is terminated by logging off, and even then you might see the fax server icon displayed on the taskbar for a few seconds while Windows resets the modem.

Activating the fax server has several implications, depending on how the fax server is configured. To configure the fax server, click the fax server icon on the taskbar. This displays the Microsoft Fax Status dialog box, shown in Figure 5-2.

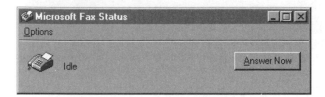

Figure 5-2. *The Microsoft Fax Status dialog box.*

The Microsoft Fax Status dialog box includes an icon of a fax machine and a status indication next to the icon, such as *Idle*. The dialog box also includes a button called Answer Now. If the phone is ringing and you know that the call is an incoming fax, you can click this button to cause Windows to answer the phone and send a fax tone to the caller. The caller will then respond with fax tone, and once the two modems have negotiated a connection, the fax is received.

In the Microsoft Fax Status dialog box, you can select Modem Properties from the Options menu to display the Fax Modem Properties dialog box, shown in Figure 5-3.

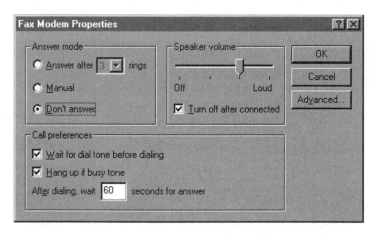

Figure 5-3. *The Fax Modem Properties dialog box.*

This is a very useful dialog box. Some of the options in it should be familiar to you by now. In the Call Preferences section you can specify that, for outbound fax calls, the modem should wait for a dial tone before dialing. This corresponds to the functionality of the *W* in dial strings that we learned about in Chapter 4. You'll also find an option to hang up the call if a busy tone is received; but selecting this option does not always have the desired effect because some modems (especially in foreign countries) cannot detect a busy tone. The dialog box also lets you enter the number of seconds that the modem should wait for an answer after dialing. Specifying the number of seconds to wait is preferable to specifying the number of rings because many modems cannot detect a remote ring and therefore have no means of counting the number of rings.

The Speaker Volume section includes a slide control for the modem speaker volume and a check box to turn off the modem speaker after a connection is made. This is usually desirable because the sounds of fax transmission are not exactly music to the ears. Finally, in the Answer Mode section you'll find option buttons for specifying how Windows treats incoming calls. Select the Don't Answer option if you don't want Windows to answer incoming calls. Select the Manual option if you want Windows to prompt you when an incoming call arrives. This option is most useful when the line is shared between voice and fax calls (a typical situation in a home office). When an incoming call arrives, Windows asks if you want to answer the call as a fax call. If you indicate yes, Windows answers the call with a fax tone.

The remaining option in the Answer Mode section is the auto-answer option, called "Answer after [ ] rings." Select this option to have Windows automatically answer incoming calls as fax calls after a certain number of rings. (Modems typically can detect incoming rings on the phone line; unlike the ringing of a remote phone on outgoing calls, incoming rings create an electrical pulse on the line that is easily detected.) Selecting the auto-answer option is most useful when you have a dedicated fax line, or when you are away from home and you want your line to function as a fax while you are gone. Neither the auto-answer option nor the manual answer option will function unless the fax server is active.

The Fax Modem Properties dialog box also contains a button called Advanced, which displays the Advanced dialog box with options for tweaking the performance of faxes. The options include enabling compression, suppressing high-speed fax transmission, and suppressing error correction. These options are useful for increasing the performance of faxes when the line is highly reliable and free of noise.

Once the message ID is retrieved using *MAPIFindNext,* the message corresponding to that ID can be retrieved using *MAPIReadMail,* whose syntax is shown below.

```
ULONG FAR PASCAL MAPIReadMail(LHANDLE lhSession, ULONG ulUIParam,
                             LPSTR lpszMessageID, FLAGS flFlags,
                             ULONG ulReserved,
                             lpMapiMessage FAR *lppMessage);
```

The first parameter, *lhSession,* is the session handle. The parameter *ulUIParam* is the parent window handle for any dialog boxes that the function displays. The default implementation provided by Microsoft currently does not display any dialog boxes, although other implementations might. The *lpszMessageID* parameter is the message ID returned by *MAPIFindNext.* There is a reserved parameter, *ulReserved,* which must be set to 0, and a pointer to a MapiMessage structure pointer to where the message is returned.

You can specify flags to control the behavior of the function. The flags specified in the *flFlags* parameter primarily affect the information returned in the message structure and the manner in which it is returned. Setting the MAPI_ENVELOPE_ONLY flag tells *MAPIReadMail* not to return the message text or any file attachments. This flag is most useful for quickly browsing through message headers without reading the contents. Setting the MAPI_BODY_AS_FILE flag causes *MAPIReadMail* to package the message text into a file that is then added as an attachment. This can be useful if you find it more convenient to manipulate the message text through the use of the file system. To suppress the return of any attached files, specify the MAPI_SUPPRESS_ATTACH flag. The MAPI_BODY_AS_FILE flag and MAPI_SUPPRESS_ATTACH flag are mutually exclusive, as you might imagine. Finally, reading a message with *MAPIReadMail* causes MAPI to mark the message as read. To prevent MAPI from marking the message as read, set the MAPI_PEEK flag. With this flag set, you can read the message as many times as you like, and it will not be marked as read.

Notice that *MAPIReadMail* does not take a pointer to a MapiMessage structure. (See the section titled "The Message Structure" toward the beginning of this chapter for a description of this structure.) Instead, the function takes a *pointer to a pointer* to the structure. In other words, *MAPIReadMail* allocates the MapiMessage structure memory, fills in the message information, and returns a pointer to the allocated structure. It is more convenient for MAPI to allocate the memory for the structure because only MAPI knows how much memory is required by the message body, recipient list, header, and attachments. Of course, Microsoft could have used an allocation scheme like the one for TAPI (see

Chapter 4), in which the function is called twice by the application—the first time to learn how much memory to allocate and the second time after allocating the memory. However, Microsoft chose not to take this road with MAPI. Instead, *MAPIReadMail* allocates all of the memory required for the message in a contiguous block, and then it returns a pointer to that memory to the application. Once the application has completed processing the message, it can free the associated memory by calling *MAPIFreeBuffer,* with the syntax shown below.

```
ULONG MAPIFreeBuffer( LPVOID lpBuffer);
```

The single parameter to *MAPIFreeBuffer* is a pointer to a memory block allocated by MAPI. Passing the message pointer returned by *MAPIReadMail* to *MAPIFreeBuffer* frees up the memory associated with the message.

Saving and Deleting Messages

The message ID returned by *MAPIFindNext* is useful for more than just reading messages. You can use it to delete messages from the message store and to change the contents of messages in the message store.

To delete a message, pass the message ID to the function *MAPIDeleteMail,* whose syntax is shown below:

```
ULONG FAR PASCAL MAPIDeleteMail(LHANDLE lhSession, ULONG ulUIParam,
                                LPSTR lpszMessageID, FLAGS flFlags,
                                ULONG ulReserved);
```

The first parameter, *lhSession,* is the session handle returned by *MAPILogon.* The second parameter, *ulUIParam,* is a handle to the parent window for any dialog boxes that the function displays. The parameter *lpszMessageID* contains the ID of the message to delete. The *flFlags* and *ulReserved* parameters are not currently used and must each be set to 0. Once *MAPIDeleteMail* deletes a message, the message ID is no longer valid and should not be used by the application.

One of the most versatile functions for managing messages is *MAPISave-Mail,* whose syntax is shown below. You can use *MAPISaveMail* to create new messages or change the contents of existing messages.

```
ULONG FAR PASCAL MAPISaveMail(LHANDLE lhSession, ULONG ulUIParam,
                              lpMapiMessage lpMessage,
                              FLAGS flFlags, ULONG ulReserved,
                              LPSTR lpszMessageID);
```

The first and second parameters are the session handle and the window handle, respectively. The *lpMessage* parameter points to a MapiMessage structure with the message information to save. You can use *MAPISaveMail* to create a new message by specifying an empty (not NULL) message ID. (An empty message ID is a string with a first character set to 0.) MAPI treats newly created messages as if they were newly received messages; it places them in the appropriate Inbox folder in the message store.

Calling *MAPISaveMail* with an empty message ID and a NULL session ID causes *MAPISaveMail* to prompt you to choose a profile and enter a password for the message store. This is known as an *implicit logon*. Implicit logon is useful when *MAPISaveMail* is called in isolation—in other words, when it is unnecessary to establish a messaging session because the only function to call is *MAPISaveMail*. A common situation in which this might occur is when the application wants to create a new message and save it in the message store but does not want to send the message right away. You can use *MAPISaveMail* in your application to implicitly log on and save a new message by specifying a NULL session handle and an empty message ID string. For implicit logon, you can set the MAPI_LOGON_UI and MAPI_NEW_SESSION flags, which have the same effect as they do in the call to *MAPILogon*. If MAPI_LOGON_UI is not set but the session handle is NULL and the message ID is empty, you will be logged on with the default profile (which you can configure from the Mail and Fax applet). A NULL session handle and nonempty message ID will result in an error code of MAPI_E_INVALID_SESSION. Implicit logon can be used with several MAPI functions, not just *MAPISaveMail*. In every case where an implicit logon is performed, the function logs the user off again before returning, and the application is never presented with a session handle.

Addressing Messages

MAPI uses address books to store information about the parties with whom you exchange messages. Each address book entry contains the name of the party, the address (a phone number or a network address string), and the message transport for reaching the party (for example, by fax).

Like message stores, address books are organized into a hierarchy. Within an address book are distribution lists and individual addresses. A distribution list is a collection of addresses with some common characteristic—for example, everyone in a particular department. A distribution list can be the recipient of a message; everyone on the list will receive a copy of the message.

There are two types of address books, the *Postoffice address book* and the *personal address book*. The Postoffice address book contains the addresses of all of the users of a particular computer system who can receive messages on that computer system. For example, the Postoffice address book might contain one entry for each member of a family that receives messages on a particular computer. Each user also typically has a personal address book containing lists of his or her own message recipients. MAPI normally provides a Postoffice address book, which lists the parties who can originate messages from the computer, and one or more personal address books, each of which lists the parties who can receive messages from users of the computer.

MAPI provides two functions for addressing messages: *MAPIResolveName* and *MAPIAddress.*

The *MAPIResolveName* function, whose syntax is shown below, is useful for searching the address book by recipient name. This function takes the name (or, often, the partial name) of a message recipient as input, locates the nearest unambiguous match in the address book, and returns a pointer to a MapiRecip-Desc structure describing the recipient to the application. The application can use the returned recipient structure to address an outbound message.

```
ULONG FAR PASCAL MAPIResolveName(LHANDLE lhSession, ULONG ulUIParam,
                      LPSTR lpszName, FLAGS flFlags,
                      ULONG ulReserved,
                      lpMapiRecipDesc FAR *lppRecip);
```

The first and second parameters of *MAPIResolveName* are the session handle and the window handle. The third parameter, *lpszName,* is a string containing the name of the recipient that the function should resolve. If the name can be resolved unambiguously, a MapiRecipDesc structure is allocated by the function and returned in the *lppRecip* parameter. Like *MAPIReadMail, MAPIResolveName* allocates the memory for the structure it returns, so memory for the returned MapiRecipDesc structure must be freed using *MAPIFreeBuffer.* The *ulReserved* parameter is reserved and must be set to 0.

MAPIResolveName accepts several flags that control its behavior. The first two of these flags, MAPI_NEW_SESSION and MAPI_LOGON_UI, should be familiar by now. These parameters are useful when the function is to perform an implicit logon, retrieve a recipient, and log off again before returning. The flag MAPI_DIALOG tells the function to display the Check Names dialog box when there are several potential matches for the supplied name in the address book. For example, suppose the name *charl* is passed to *MAPIResolveName,* and that two parties in the personal address book could potentially resolve this name: *charles* and *charlotte.* If MAPI_DIALOG is set, a dialog box appears displaying both *charles* and *charlotte,* and the user is prompted to select one. If MAPI_DIALOG is not set and the name is ambiguous, the function returns MAPI_E_AMBIGUOUS_RECIPIENT. If you don't want the user to modify details about the parties (such as names or addresses) listed in the dialog box, set the MAPI_AB_NOMODIFY flag. When this flag is set, the entries in the dialog box displayed by *MAPIResolveName* are read-only. This flag is ignored if the MAPI-_DIALOG flag isn't set.

If MAPI_DIALOG is set and MAPI cannot find a likely candidate to resolve the name, the dialog box will indicate that it has no suggestions, as shown in Figure 5-4. You can select the "Create a new address for" option in the dialog box to create a new entry in the address book; click OK and you will be prompted for the full name, address, and other details about the party to add. There is also a button in the dialog box called Show More Names. Clicking this button brings up the Select Name dialog box with a list of all the names in the selected address book. The dialog box is capable of displaying parties from only one address book at a time; you can select a different address book from the drop-down list. You can tell MAPI which address book to search first when resolving recipient names by using the Mail and Fax applet on the Control Panel.

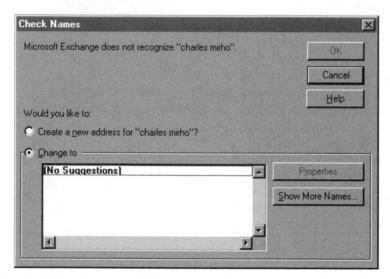

Figure 5-4. *The Check Names dialog box with an unresolved name.*

MAPIResolveName considers both the first and last name of the party when attempting to resolve a name. Therefore, if the address book contains an entry for someone named *peter doe* and another for *peter roe,* the name *peter* is ambiguous. If *peter doe* is the only *peter* in the address book, *peter* resolves to *peter doe* unambiguously. Likewise, the name *peter d* would resolve unamiguously to *peter doe* even if the address book also contained a party named *peter roe.*

MAPIResolveName is useful for searching the address book by name. However, for addressing messages, you should use *MAPIAddress,* whose syntax is shown below.

```
ULONG FAR PASCAL MAPIAddress(LHANDLE lhSession, ULONG ulUIParam,
                    LPSTR lpszCaption, ULONG nEditFields,
                    LPSTR lpszLabels, ULONG nRecips,
                    lpMapiRecipDesc lpRecips,
                    FLAGS flFlags, ULONG ulReserved,
                    LPULONG lpnNewRecips,
                    lpMapiRecipDesc FAR *lppNewRecips);
```

MAPIAddress is the most complicated of all the MAPI functions. It builds a list of message recipients, consisting of the originator and the direct, copy, and blind copy recipients. It can build the list either from scratch or from a list of "seed" recipients supplied to the function.

First, the familiar parameters. The first two parameters are the session handle and parent window handle for dialog boxes. There is also a reserved member, *ulReserved,* which must be set to 0. The parameter *flFlags* specifies MAPI-_LOGON_UI and MAPI_NEW_SESSION for implied logon.

To understand the other parameters, you must understand the dialog box that *MAPIAddress* displays. The dialog box will look different depending on the way the function is called. Figure 5-5 shows a fairly representative sample.

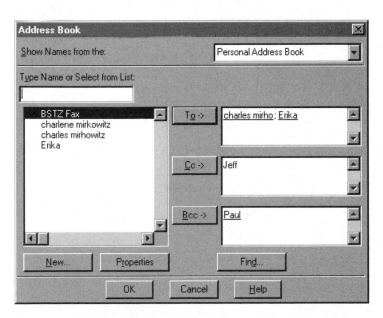

Figure 5-5. *A MAPIAddress Address Book dialog box with direct, copy, and blind copy recipient fields.*

The figure shows the Address Book dialog box. On the right side of the dialog box is a list box of recipient names to select from, representing the contents of the address book named in the upper-right corner of the dialog box. You can select a different address book from the drop-down list in the upper-right corner. In the center of the dialog box are three buttons, To->, Cc->, and Bcc->. Each button controls the selections in the three list boxes on the right side of the dialog box. The To button controls the selection of direct recipients. The Cc button controls the selection of copy recipients. The Bcc button controls the selection of blind copy recipients. All three list boxes are scrollable; you can specify a large number of recipients.

You can alter the appearance of the Address Book dialog box. For starters, you can change the caption name from *Address Book,* the default, by specifying a different caption in the *lpszCaption* parameter, which points to a string containing the new name. A value of NULL or an empty string indicates that the default name should be used. The number of list boxes on the right side of the dialog box is controlled by the *nEditFields* parameter. If *nEditFields* is set to 1, only the To list box is displayed, and only direct recipients can be selected for the message. (You can override this behavior, as you will see in a moment.) If *nEditFields* is set to 2, both the To and Cc list boxes appear, and you can select direct and copy recipients for the message. If *nEditFields* is set to 3, the To, Cc, and Bcc list boxes appear, and you can select direct, copy, and blind copy recipients for the message. A value of 4 tells MAPI to display as many list boxes for different recipient types as the underlying drivers support. Usually, specifying 4 has the same effect as specifying 3—it displays a list box for the direct, copy, and blind copy recipients. A value greater than 4 is invalid.

The parameter *lpRecips* points to a list of "seed" recipients for the dialog box to display. The number of recipients in the list is specified by the parameter *nRecips*. You need not specify any seed recipients; *nRecips* can be 0 and *lpRecips* will be ignored. If you do specify seed recipients, they must be of one of the classes supported by the underlying drivers. For most drivers, supported recipient classes are MAPI_TO (direct), MAPI_CC (copy), and MAPI_BCC (blind copy); MAPI_ORIG (originator) is generally not supported. You can override the *nEditFields* parameter by specifying a greater number of classes of recipients in the seed list than the value in *nEditFields*. For example, suppose that *nEditFields* is 1, indicating that the dialog box should display list boxes for direct recipients only. Suppose also that *lpRecips* specifies two types of recipients; one each of a direct and a copy recipient. The dialog box will then display list boxes for direct and copy recipients; the value of *nEditFields* is overridden. The exception to this behavior is when blind copy recipients are specified in the seed list but *nEditFields* is less than 3. In this case, the blind copy recipient list box is not displayed. In other words, *nEditFields* must be 3 or greater in order to display the list box for blind copy recipients.

When specifying recipients in the seed list, you must specify the recipient name and class. You have the option to specify the recipient address member; the recipient name will then appear underlined in the appropriate list box. Double-clicking the underlined recipient will "hot link" to a dialog box containing recipient properties. The address that you specified for the recipient is displayed here. The address string has the format *TYPE: ADDRESS*. For example, the address for a recipient can be specified in the form *FAX: +1 (908) 555 8331*. When the recipient properties are displayed, the "E-Mail type" field will indicate *FAX* and the "E-Mail address" field will indicate the number *+1 (908) 555 8331*. As you can see from this example, it is best to express phone numbers in canonical format.

When there are only direct recipients, you can use the *lpszLabels* parameter of the *MAPIAddress* function to change the default To button label to something more descriptive. If *nEditFields* is greater than one, or if there are more than only direct recipients in the seed list, *lpszLabels* is ignored.

The last two parameters, *lpnNewRecips* and *lppNewRecips,* specify the list of recipients returned by *MAPIAddress*. The parameter *lpnNewRecips* is a pointer to a long value where *MAPIAddress* returns the number of recipients in the return list. The parameter *lppNewRecips* is a pointer to a pointer to a list of Mapi-RecipDesc structures. *MAPIAddress* fills the list with the recipients specified in the list boxes in the dialog box. MAPI allocates the memory for the list and returns a pointer to the allocated memory, which you must later free with a call to *MAPIFreeBuffer.*

You can call the function *MAPIDetails* (whose syntax is shown below) to display the same Properties dialog box that is displayed when you double-click on an underlined recipient in the Address Book dialog box.

```
ULONG FAR PASCAL MAPIDetails(LHANDLE lhSession, ULONG ulUIParam,
                    lpMapiRecipDesc lpRecip, FLAGS flFlags,
                    ULONG ulReserved);
```

The first two parameters are the session handle and parent window handle for the dialog box. The *lpRecip* parameter is a pointer to a MapiRecipDesc structure returned from the *MAPIAddress, MAPIResolveName,* or *MAPIReadMail* function. The *flFlags* parameter can be MAPI_LOGON_UI and MAPI_NEW_SESSION (for implicit logon, when the session handle is NULL), and can also take the value MAPI_AB_NOMODIFY. Setting this last flag causes the displayed Properties dialog box to be read-only. The *ulReserved* parameter is reserved for future use.

Sending Messages

Two functions are available for sending messages: *MAPISendMail* (whose syntax is shown below) and *MAPISendDocuments*.

```
ULONG FAR PASCAL MAPISendMail(LHANDLE lhSession, ULONG ulUIParam,
                             lpMapiMessage lpMessage,
                             FLAGS flFlags, ULONG ulReserved);
```

The first two parameters of *MAPISendMail* are the session handle and the parent window handle for the dialog boxes that the function displays. Actually, the function displays more than a mere dialog box; it launches a full-blown message authoring window, complete with menu, toolbars, and integrated word processor for the message text. *MAPISendMail* has a reserved parameter, *ulReserved,* and flags, *flFlags*. The flag can have the values MAPI_LOGON_UI and MAPI_NEW_SESSION for implicit logon when the session handle is NULL. The flag can also have the value MAPI_DIALOG, in which case the message authoring window is displayed.

The *lpMessage* parameter points to the MAPIMessage structure with the message to send. Only one message can be sent at a time. If the MAPI_DIALOG flag is not set, *MAPISendMail* does not display the message authoring window, and the message is sent with whatever information is contained in the message structure parameter. The subject member can be NULL or empty, as can the originator descriptor. The datestamp member is ignored, and so is the conversation thread ID. There does not have to be any note text, and even the message class need not be specified. (MAPI will substitute the system default, which is typically IPM.Note.) No attachments need be specified. However, at least one recipient must be specified.

When the MAPI_DIALOG flag is set, you should set all unused pointers in the message structure to NULL. Otherwise, MAPI will try to access the pointers to fill in default values in the message authoring window. For example, if MAPI_DIALOG is set, MAPI will try to use whatever text is referenced by the *lpszSubject* member of MAPIMessage to initialize the Subject edit box in the window. This is true for the message text and message type as well. If recipients are specified in the *lpRecips* member of the message structure, *MAPISendMail* will attempt to read the recipient names and use them to initialize the direct, copy, and blind copy edit fields in the message authoring window. Therefore, these members within the *lpRecips* member should be set to NULL if not used.

If recipients for the message are specified, the address for the recipients can also be specified (in the *lpszAddress* member of each MapiRecipDesc structure). If the address is specified, *MAPISendMail* will use the supplied address to deliver the message. Otherwise *MAPISendMail* will attempt to resolve the specified name of the recipient into an address book entry, much like *MAPIResolveName* does. If the name can be unambiguously resolved, the address specified in the address book entry is used. Otherwise, you are prompted to resolve the ambiguity (if the MAPI_DIALOG flag is set). If attachments are specified, the files they reference must be closed so that MAPI can make a copy and send it along. When the fax transport drivers are installed, calling *MAPISendMail* launches the fax server, causing the fax server icon to appear on the taskbar. Like the call to *MAPIReadMail*, the call to *MAPISendMail* causes the fax server to remain active until the user logs off.

The *MAPISendDocuments* function, whose syntax is shown below, was designed for use in environments where specifying structures (especially nested structures) is difficult. Such environments include WordBasic and Visual Basic for Applications.

```
ULONG FAR PASCAL MAPISendDocuments(ULONG ulUIParam,
                                   LPSTR lpszDelimChar,
                                   LPSTR lpszFilePaths,
                                   LPSTR lpszFileNames,
                                   ULONG ulReserved);
```

The use of this function was described in Chapter 2 and won't be repeated here.

Linking MAPI Functions

The MAPI functions described in this chapter cannot be linked with the MAPI32.LIB library file that ships with the latest SDK. In order to link with MAPI32.LIB you must use the extended versions of these functions, such as *MapiLogonEx*. Some of the extended versions have slightly different parameters, so you should look them up before trying to use them.

To use the simple MAPI functions described in this chapter, you must dynamically link the MAPI DLL file, either MAPI.DLL or MAPI32.DLL. To do this, you must first call the *LoadLibrary* function, as shown below. This function loads the specified DLL into the running instance of the application.

```
LoadLibrary(lpLoadFileName)
```

The return value from *LoadLibrary* is then used as the first parameter in a call to *GetProcAddress,* shown below. The return value of *GetProcAddress* is the address of the function specified in *lpProcName,* the second parameter in the call. This second parameter is where you enter the name of the MAPI function you want to call, such as *MapiLogon.*

```
GetProcAddress(hModule, lpProcName)
```

Now, rather than making a direct call to a simple MAPI function, you use the address to the function returned by *GetProcAddress* to make the call, as shown in the following example.

```
hlibMAPI = LoadLibrary(szMAPIdll);
lpfnMAPILogon = (LPMAPILOGON) GetProcAddress(hlibMAPI, "MapiLogon");
lResult = *lpfnMAPILogon((ULONG) hWnd, NULL, NULL, MAPI_LOGON_UI, 0,
                         &lhSession);
```

INDEX

X

Charles Mirho has a master's degree in computer engineering from Rutgers University. He has worked as a software consultant for various high-tech companies, including IBM, AT&T, Intel, and Microsoft. His articles have appeared over the years in *Microsoft Systems Journal, Dr. Dobb's Journal,* and several other computer trade magazines. His areas of expertise include multimedia, graphics, and communications. Charles lives in Silicon Valley with his wife, Erika, and is currently studying intellectual property under scholarship at a law school there. He can be reached on CompuServe at 70563,2671 and on the Internet at cmirho@mcimail.com.

Andre Terrisse has been involved with telecommunications at Intel. He coauthored an article with Charles Mirho on the communications APIs for *Microsoft Systems Journal.* He lives in Oregon.

The manuscript for this book was prepared using Microsoft Word 6.0 for Windows and submitted to Microsoft Press in electronic form. Galleys were prepared using Word 6.0 for Windows. Pages were composed by VersaTech Associates using Aldus PageMaker 5.0 for Windows, with text type in Garamond and display type in Futura Medium Bold. Composed pages were delivered to the printer as electronic prepress files.

Cover Graphic Designer
Glen Mitsui, Studio MD

Interior Graphic Designer
Kim Eggleston

Principal Artist
Travis Beaven

Principal Compositor
Sybil Ihrig, VersaTech Associates

Principal Proofreader
Lorraine Maloney

Indexer
Irv Hershman

IMPORTANT—READ CAREFULLY BEFORE OPENING SOFTWARE PACKET(S). By opening the sealed packet(s) containing the software, you indicate your acceptance of the following Microsoft License Agreement.

MICROSOFT LICENSE AGREEMENT

(Book Companion Disk)

This is a legal agreement between you (either an individual or an entity) and Microsoft Corporation. By opening the sealed software packet(s) you are agreeing to be bound by the terms of this agreement. If you do not agree to the terms of this agreement, promptly return the un-opened software packet(s) and any accompanying written materials to the place you obtained them for a full refund.

MICROSOFT SOFTWARE LICENSE

1. GRANT OF LICENSE. Microsoft grants to you the right to use one copy of the Microsoft software program included with this book (the "SOFTWARE") on a single terminal connected to a single computer. The SOFTWARE is in "use" on a computer when it is loaded into the temporary memory (i.e., RAM) or installed into the permanent memory (e.g., hard disk, CD-ROM, or other storage device) of that computer. You may not network the SOFTWARE or otherwise use it on more than one computer or computer terminal at the same time.

2. COPYRIGHT. The SOFTWARE is owned by Microsoft or its suppliers and is protected by United States copyright laws and international treaty provisions. Therefore, you must treat the SOFTWARE like any other copyrighted material (e.g., a book or musical recording) except that you may either (a) make one copy of the SOFTWARE solely for backup or archival purposes, or (b) transfer the SOFTWARE to a single hard disk provided you keep the original solely for backup or archival purposes. You may not copy the written materials accompanying the SOFTWARE.

3. OTHER RESTRICTIONS. You may not rent or lease the SOFTWARE, but you may transfer the SOFTWARE and accompanying written materials on a permanent basis provided you retain no copies and the recipient agrees to the terms of this Agreement. You may not reverse engineer, decompile, or disassemble the SOFTWARE. If the SOFTWARE is an update or has been updated, any transfer must include the most recent update and all prior versions.

4. DUAL MEDIA SOFTWARE. If the SOFTWARE package contains both 3.5" and 5.25" disks, then you may use only the disks appropriate for your single-user computer. You may not use the other disks on another computer or loan, rent, lease, or transfer them to another user except as part of the permanent transfer (as provided above) of all SOFTWARE and written materials.

5. SAMPLE CODE. If the SOFTWARE includes Sample Code, then Microsoft grants you a royalty-free right to reproduce and distribute the sample code of the SOFTWARE provided that you: (a) distribute the sample code only in conjunction with and as a part of your software product; (b) do not use Microsoft's or its authors' names, logos, or trademarks to market your software product; (c) include the copyright notice that appears on the SOFTWARE on your product label and as a part of the sign-on message for your software product; and (d) agree to indemnify, hold harmless, and defend Microsoft and its authors from and against any claims or lawsuits, including attorneys' fees, that arise or result from the use or distribution of your software product.

DISCLAIMER OF WARRANTY

The SOFTWARE (including instructions for its use) is provided "AS IS" WITHOUT WARRANTY OF ANY KIND. MICROSOFT FURTHER DISCLAIMS ALL IMPLIED WARRANTIES INCLUDING WITHOUT LIMITATION ANY IMPLIED WARRANTIES OF MERCHANTABILITY OR OF FITNESS FOR A PARTICULAR PURPOSE. THE ENTIRE RISK ARISING OUT OF THE USE OR PERFORMANCE OF THE SOFTWARE AND DOCUMENTATION REMAINS WITH YOU.

IN NO EVENT SHALL MICROSOFT, ITS AUTHORS, OR ANYONE ELSE INVOLVED IN THE CREATION, PRODUCTION, OR DELIVERY OF THE SOFTWARE BE LIABLE FOR ANY DAMAGES WHATSOEVER (INCLUDING, WITHOUT LIMITATION, DAMAGES FOR LOSS OF BUSINESS PROFITS, BUSINESS INTERRUPTION, LOSS OF BUSINESS INFORMATION, OR OTHER PECUNIARY LOSS) ARISING OUT OF THE USE OF OR INABILITY TO USE THE SOFTWARE OR DOCUMENTATION, EVEN IF MICROSOFT HAS BEEN ADVISED OF THE POSSIBILITY OF SUCH DAMAGES. BECAUSE SOME STATES/COUNTRIES DO NOT ALLOW THE EXCLUSION OR LIMITATION OF LIABILITY FOR CONSEQUENTIAL OR INCIDENTAL DAMAGES, THE ABOVE LIMITATION MAY NOT APPLY TO YOU.

U.S. GOVERNMENT RESTRICTED RIGHTS

The SOFTWARE and documentation are provided with RESTRICTED RIGHTS. Use, duplication, or disclosure by the Government is subject to restrictions as set forth in subparagraph (c)(1)(ii) of The Rights in Technical Data and Computer Software clause at DFARS 252.227-7013 or subparagraphs (c)(1) and (2) of the Commercial Computer Software — Restricted Rights 48 CFR 52.227-19, as applicable. Manufacturer is Microsoft Corporation, One Microsoft Way, Redmond, WA 98052-6399.

If you acquired this product in the United States, this Agreement is governed by the laws of the State of Washington.

Should you have any questions concerning this Agreement, or if you desire to contact Microsoft Press for any reason, please write: Microsoft Press, One Microsoft Way, Redmond, WA 98052-6399.